W9-BPQ-597

MS-13

Also by Steven Dudley

Walking Ghosts: Murder and Guerrilla Politics in Colombia

MS-13

THE MAKING OF AMERICA'S MOST NOTORIOUS GANG

STEVEN DUDLEY

Recycling programs for this product may not exist in your area.

ISBN-13: 978-1-335-00554-0

MS-13: The Making of America's Most Notorious Gang

This edition published by arrangement with Harlequin Books S.A.

Library of Congress Cataloging-in-Publication Data has been applied for.

Hanover Square Press
22 Adelaide St. West, 40th Floor
Toronto, Ontario M5H 4E3, Canada
HanoverSqPress.com
BookClubbish.com

Printed in U.S.A.

To my mother, the pillar of the family; my father, my inspiration;
and Juli, for everything since.

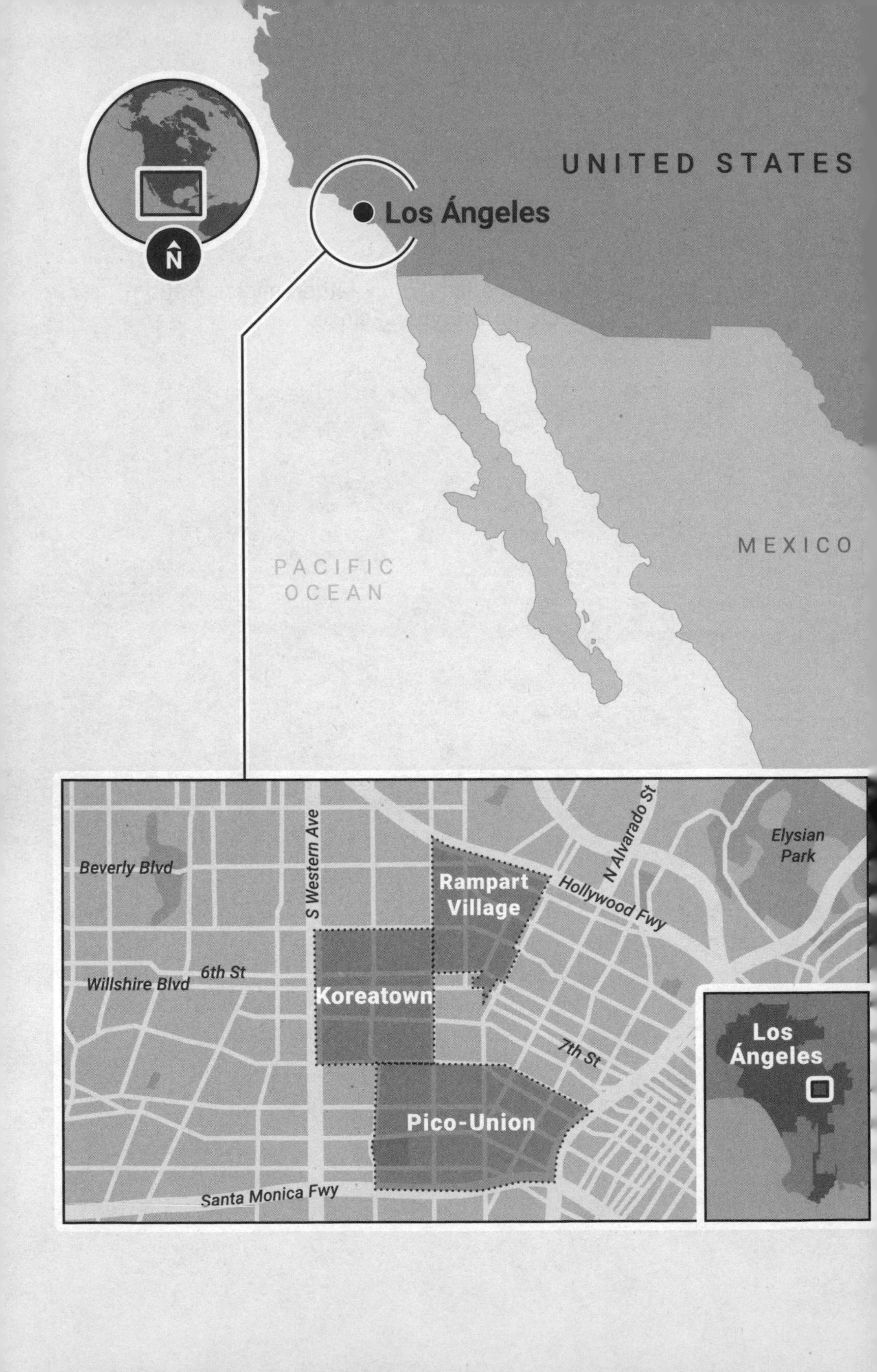
UNITED STATES
Los Ángeles
N
PACIFIC
OCEAN
MEXICO
S Western Ave
N Alvarado St
Elysian
Park
Beverly Blvd
Rampart
Village
Hollywood Fwy
Willshire Blvd
6th St
Koreatown
7th St
Los
Ángeles
Pico-Union
Santa Monica Fwy

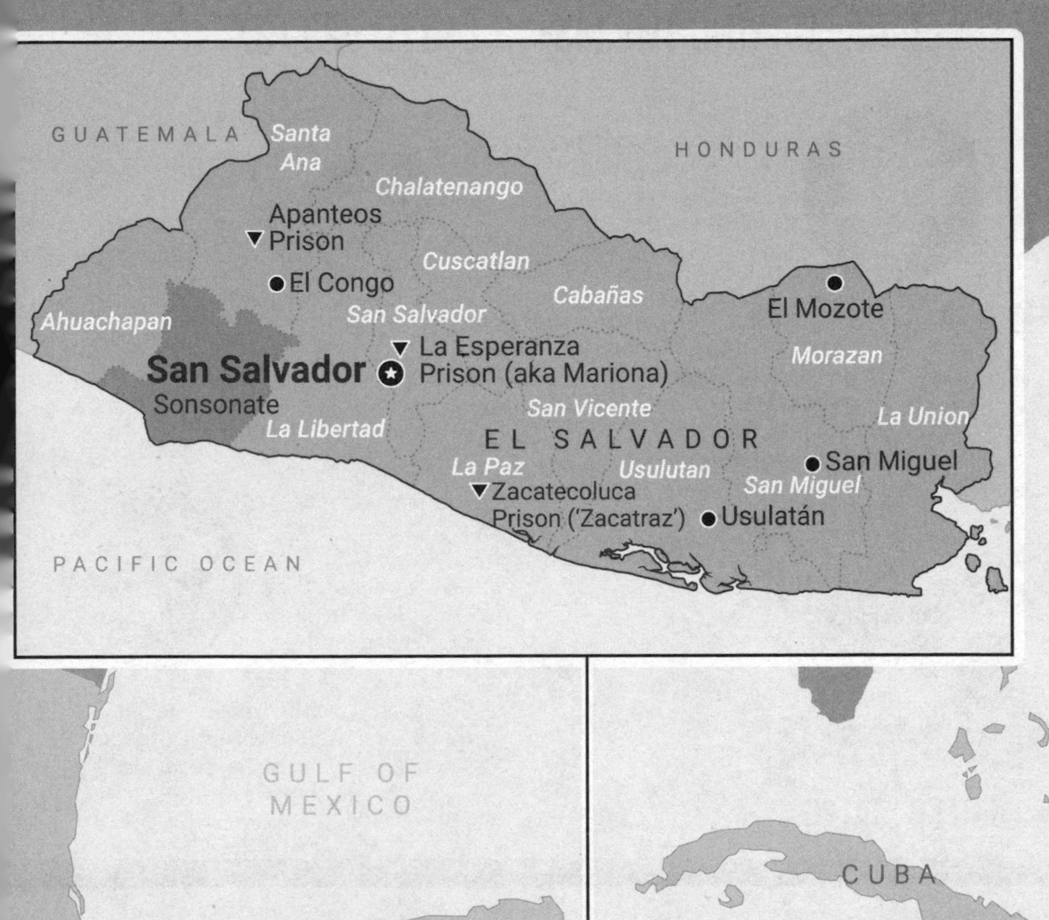
GUATEMALA
Santa Ana
HONDURAS
Chalatenango
Apanteos Prison
Cuscatlan
El Congo
Cabañas
El Mozote
Ahuachapan
San Salvador
La Esperanza Prison (aka Mariona)
Morazan
San Salvador
Sonsonate
San Vicente
La Union
La Libertad
EL SALVADOR
La Paz
Usulutan
San Miguel
San Miguel
Zacatecoluca Prison ('Zacatraz')
Usulatán
PACIFIC OCEAN

GULF OF MEXICO
CUBA
BELIZE
GUATEMALA
HONDURAS
EL SALVADOR
PACIFIC OCEAN

TIMELINE: MAKING THE MS-13 (1979–2019)

UNITED STATES

1979
As civil conflict in El Salvador ramps up, Salvadorans begin to arrive in Los Angeles en masse

1983
A gang made up of mostly Salvadoran refugees calling themselves the Mara Salvatrucha Stoners appears in Central Los Angeles

1985
First Mara Salvatrucha member gets shot and killed; MS begins to better arm itself

1987
LA issues first gang injunction; stricter laws follow as well as gang databases to try to quell violence

1989
LAPD's CRASH units and immigration authorities begin deporting gang members to Central America; Mara Salvatrucha and 18th Street begin long-running feud

1993
Mara Salvatrucha become part of Sureños umbrella organization under Mexican Mafia, begin to call themselves MS-13

1996
Deportations rise exponentially after Clinton administration increases number of crimes for which ex-convicts can be deported

EL SALVADOR

1980
Archbishop Óscar Romero assassinated; civil war breaks out in El Salvador

1981
US-trained Atlacatl Battalion kills more than 900 civilians in El Mozote massacre; Carter and Reagan administrations ramp up US military assistance

1986
El Salvador is the largest recipient of US aid in the hemisphere in spite of the government's continued human rights abuses

1989
Alfredo Cristiani elected president of El Salvador, initiates neoliberal economic reforms; guerrillas' "final offensive" gives more urgency to peace talks

1992
Guerrillas and government sign peace deal, rebels become political party; gang members arrive from the US in ever larger numbers

1998
Violence rises as MS-13 and 18th Street's battles spread in El Salvador and other parts of Central America

2000
LAPD's CRASH is
disbanded following
candal in the Rampart
division CRASH unit

2004
Bush administration
starts first federal MS-13
task force, declaring the
gang has between 8,000
and 10,000 members in
the US

2004
ron Fist anti-gang law mirroring
alifornia anti-gang laws passes
Congress in El Salvador;
ncarceration rates skyrocket as
does violence in prisons

2005
Gangs begin to
systematically extort the
public transportation system
in El Salvador; government
separates gangs inside
prisons

2012
Government and
nongovernmental mediators
broker a truce between major
gangs in El Salvador;
homicides drop by half

2013
Obama administration
deports over 400,000
undocumented migrants
in one year, the most
in US history

2014
Tens of thousands
of unaccompanied alien
children (UAC) arrive in the
United States, thousands
of whom settle in places like
Long Island, New York

2014
Political parties in El Salvador
pay gangs for support
during presidential elections;
the victor, ex-guerrilla
Salvador Sánchez Cerén, wins
by just over 6,000 votes

2015
Not long after the unceremonious
end of the gang truce, violence in
El Salvador reaches levels not
seen since the civil war

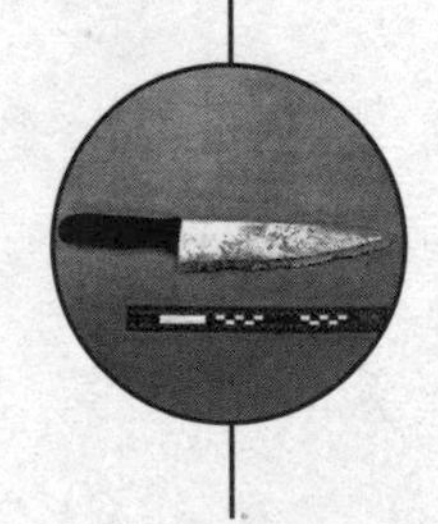

2017
Amidst a surge in
MS-13–related violence
in numerous places
around the country, the
Trump administration
makes the gang a law
enforcement priority

2019
El Salvador elects new
president, Nayib Bukele,
who promises to crack
down on street gangs

CONTENTS

AUTHOR'S NOTE

THIS BOOK IS ABOUT THE MARA SALVATRUCHA, or MS-13, the ruthless forty-year-old street gang that has spread across a half-dozen countries and two continents. It follows a number of characters—most notably a gang leader, whom I call Norman, and his family. These stories allow us to trace the history of the gang from its beginnings in Los Angeles to its export to El Salvador and other Central American nations, and back again.

The book is divided into three parts. The first part recounts the gang's origins; the second, its process of maturation; the third, the various efforts by those involved to leave the gang or mitigate its influence. Broadly speaking, the three parts mirror most gang members' experiences as well: you are enveloped, become serious, then try to leave.

The gang has been compared by Donald Trump to Al-Qaeda and is considered the US government's number one target as it continues its nationwide effort to rid the US of "criminal aliens."

Indeed, the MS-13 is a threat that trades on its reputation for brutal murders, which has helped make Central America one of the most violent regions in the world and has devastated many US communities.

But the MS-13 is also greatly misunderstood. Its capacity is erroneously likened to much more sophisticated groups such as the Zetas in Mexico and the Yakuza in Japan. While the MS-13 does have an international presence, it is a hand-to-mouth organization whose criminal economy is based mostly on small-time extortion schemes and petty drug dealing, not international drug trafficking or sophisticated corruption.

In fact, the gang is perhaps better described as a loosely knit social and criminal community that reinforces its bonds via extreme versions of individual and collective violence. And it is as much the result of bad individual decisions as it is the result of flawed US and Central American policy, and the exploitative and unequal economic systems they foster.

Norman's family, for example, was devastated by the US-backed war in El Salvador, which included widespread human rights abuses that led directly to the massive migration that Norman's family experienced. Politics and war followed these refugees to the US, where they were treated differently depending on their nationality, then deported back to their countries of origin in disproportionate numbers, especially as it relates to criminal deportations. These deportations of ex-convicts are what led to the surge of gangs in Central America. Now, ironically, this surge in gang activity in Central America has led to another flood of refugees and, with the advent of the Donald Trump administration, the hyper-politicization of immigration as a catchall for every US problem.

At the ground level—Norman's level—the reality obliterates any moral clarity and political platitudes. He is the first to admit that he is no angel and neither are his fellow gang members. He and several brothers and half brothers entered the gang, pledging allegiance to something they call *la bestia*, the beast. But the gang is also a surrogate family, one that replaced his real family, which, by the time he was a teenager, was spread across a thousand miles. This surrogate family is what the MS-13 calls *el barrio*, roughly translated in this context as *community*. This is the gang's central paradox: the MS-13 is a surrogate family and a vicious criminal organization.

My experience with gangs has been through a journalistic, policy-oriented and academic lens. After spending the previous fifteen years in Latin America working for major news outlets, I cofounded InSight Crime in 2010, a think tank focused on organized crime in the Americas. Part of my job is to cover the gangs in Central America, specifically those operating in El Salvador, Honduras and Guatemala. I am also a senior fellow at the Center for Latin American and Latino Studies at American University, where I recently codirected a three-year study funded by the US Justice Department on the MS-13 in El Salvador, the Greater Washington, DC, and Los Angeles areas.

I mention these projects only because they have led to numerous and regular interactions with gang members, communities and families hit hard by gang violence, law enforcement corralling the gangs and policymakers trying to deal with them. This book is a distillation of these interactions, a history of the MS-13 as told through the human lives they've made and destroyed: the victims and victimizers; the undocumented migrants and those who deport them; the gangs and the police who fight them.

The story of the MS-13 is difficult to fit into one book. I believe the characters in this book are representative of the issues I wanted to cover, and they allowed me to tell the history of the gang. But there are gaps in research in this work that will be obvious to the specialist and general reader alike. Honduras and Guatemala, two vital hubs of MS-13 activity, are absent, for example. My treatment and understanding of the role of women as well as the role that notions of masculinity play in recruitment, cohesion and violence of the gang are also largely superficial. These are all potential books on their own, and I would encourage more work on this subject.

That is because the MS-13 is not just a gang problem. It is a manifestation of our collective failures across a huge geographic expanse. Gang members need to take personal responsibility for what they do, but we are playing an active role in perpetuating this violent, antisocial community. As a very smart person once said to me about marginalized criminal groups: they will stop biting us when we stop treating them like dogs.

December 2019

INTRODUCTION

JUDGING NORMAN

1.

"SIR, PLEASE STATE YOUR…NAME FOR THE RECORD."

"Norman…"[1]

"Where were you born?"

"En… El Salvador."

It was July 2017. Norman was dressed in an orange jumpsuit, sitting at a table in a dimly lit US immigration court. He was forty-two, but he spoke with the tired cadence of an elderly man. A judge, flanked by an interpreter, scrutinized him from the podium. Norman's legal representative continued his questions.

"Tell me, sir, why are you afraid of returning to El Salvador?"

"Este, me quieren quitar la vida, me quieren matar."

---

1 For security reasons, his name and those of all of his relatives have been changed, as well as the names of his gang clique, names of colleagues and other information that could potentially compromise his identity.

"They want to take my life, they want to kill me," the interpreter said.

The *este* was a tic. It doesn't translate. The interpreter rightfully ignored it, but the rhythm it gave Norman's speech betrayed his gang origins. Most gang members talk to outsiders in a low voice, almost a mumble with frequent pauses that are punctuated with words like *este*, an equivalent to "um." The effect is that of an unhurried person, someone who does not need to overstate his case or yell to get his point across. This way of speech reflects the narrative gang members perpetuate—that they are not in a hurry to live, or to die. In reality they're running toward both at full speed.

"And who is it that wants to kill you?" his legal representative—a tall, thin man dressed in a dark suit and tie—asked.

"Este, la policía y la pandilla."

"The police and gangs."

"And when you say the gangs, what gangs are you referring to?"

"A la MS y a la 18."

The MS was the Mara Salvatrucha 13, or MS-13, as it is more popularly known. They had been Norman's gang—until they weren't, and he had to flee to save himself from them. The 18th Street was the gang's eternal rival.

The MS-13 was, by then, the most notorious street gang in the Americas. What began in Los Angeles as a casual group of Salvadoran émigrés some forty years earlier had expanded coast to coast, down to El Salvador, Guatemala, Honduras, Mexico, and beyond.

The gang was more of a loose social and criminal network than a top-down mafia, but one that inspired fierce loyalty and offered few ways of escape. Tattoos marked them. Violence bonded them. They had grown by coming at their enemies in waves, like a *marabunta*, or army of ants, as the street gangs were baptized so many years before in El Salvador. Using machetes, they'd hacked their victims into butcher-sized chunks of flesh, often passing the long-bladed tool from member to member so each could take their turn. It had become their signature kill and, perversely, their most formidable recruiting tool.

Sitting shyly in front of the judge, Norman did not betray his violent tendencies. He was five foot four, but sturdy and noticeably strong for his size. He kept his arms to his sides, careful to cover as much of his body art as he could. Beneath his jumpsuit lurked numerous tattoos, including one of a hand folded like horns—a nod to the devil, and a classic sign of the gang.

"Tell me, why are you afraid the police will kill you?" his legal representative asked.

"Temo porque, este, me andaban buscando."

"I'm afraid because they were looking for me, to kill me."

Norman did not use the phrase "to kill me." The translator added it. Norman, he'd surmised, was pleading for his life.

2.

Norman was both victim and victimizer, a product of a family that embodied all the complexity and contradictions that make up the story of the MS-13.

He grew up in El Salvador, the youngest of seven. When he was a boy, the army came to his house, took two of his brothers to their barracks, and forced his mother to choose which one to leave in the army and which one to take home.

Norman and his family had lived through gun battles. Death squads interrupted dinner. People in his neighborhood disappeared, and rebels executed a soldier on leave right in front of him.

His home life was equally turbulent. His father left his mother for one of Norman's maternal cousins when Norman was just a toddler, creating a parallel family that competed with his. Norman's mother plunged into depression, attempting suicide on at least one occasion.

The tumult led to a family exodus. By the time Norman

was sixteen, the civil war in El Salvador was over, but all of his brothers and sisters had fled to the United States.

Norman and his family sought stability within the gang. Its brash leaders—most of whom had been deported from the US—became his stand-in guardians. Two of his brothers joined the MS-13 in Los Angeles; two of his half brothers would later become members in El Salvador. Norman joined in El Salvador after his most beloved brother—who'd long acted as a surrogate father—had been murdered in the US.

The MS-13, he decided, would be his family, his community. Together they partied, break dancing and drinking in the streets. They robbed, extorted and murdered together. As the gang evolved from a public nuisance to a national menace in his home country, Norman rose through the ranks. By the early 2000s, law enforcement took action, rounding up gang members in dramatic crackdowns. Norman was convicted for two murders and spent more than a decade in prison, where he had a front row seat to the continued evolution of the gang amidst an upheaval in the prison system. Norman survived this period—which included earthquakes, rape, abuse and bloody riots—with a combination of cunning, gall and luck.

His release from prison in 2012 preceded yet another crackdown on gangs in El Salvador. By then, Norman had five kids and a wife who'd stayed by his side through his transgressions. Out of prison, he says he steered clear of gang life. Salvadoran authorities tell a different story. They say Norman was involved in several more murders. In one case, they said he ordered a hit from jail. In another, he allegedly oversaw a killing on the street. In a third, he purportedly ran into a rival at a repair shop and called in a hit.

During the immigration process, Norman admitted he was a gang leader but denied these accusations. He said he'd been slowly trying to leave the MS-13. He claimed he was trying to work honestly, selling farm-fresh vegetables and fruit at the market with his wife and living near his mother and other family members in El Salvador. In court, he said that when MS-13 leaders asked him to join the leadership council and he refused, they'd issued an order to assassinate him. He described how he'd fled to the US after evading the hit, which was organized by his half brother. His wife and three of his children followed him to the states.

"Because in the gang, there was only one way to enter, and I already knew how the departure was," he said through the interpreter.

"What do you mean when you say that you already knew how the departure was?" his legal representative asked.

"That there is no departure, but rather they assassinate you."

3.

It was an inauspicious moment to appear in a US immigration court. President Donald Trump and an adjacent apparatus of political action committees, think tanks and media had by then closed ranks on the issue of immigration. The goal was to conflate migrants with crime, and the MS-13 seemed to be the perfect illustration. Many members of the gang were foreign-born, hailing from countries with some of the highest homicide rates in the world. The gang was widespread, operational in over a dozen US states. And they were terrifying, massacring rivals in a bloody, almost ritualistic fashion. In 2017, the MS-13 killed some forty people in the US, a record number for the gang nationally.

But the MS-13 was not a drug cartel or a terrorist organization, as Trump and his allies alleged. They had not "invaded" by the thousands, and they had not "occupied" towns. Other countries were not marshaling the MS-13 to the United States (though the US had been deporting them for years), and immigrant caravans making their way through Mexico were not full of gang members—the caravans were mostly women and children. To be sure, of the 527,000 people US border agents detained in 2017, only 228 were believed to be MS-13.

The MS-13 was not even the biggest domestic gang. As the Trump administration entered office, the 18th Street, as well as the Latin Kings, the Crips, and the Bloods, were all between three and five times larger by the US government's own count. A Virginia Commonwealth University study counted 178 MS-13 murders between 2009 and 2018; during the same time period, the Anti-Defamation League claimed there were 427 "domestic extremist-related murders."

Still, by the time Norman's case was in front of the judge, the facts mattered little. The vast majority of MS-13 victims were not White supporters of Trump, but Latinos. Yet by 2018, 85 percent of Trump voters categorized the gang as a "very serious" or a "somewhat serious" threat to national security, and a majority feared they or someone in their family would "become a victim of violence from MS-13."

"They kidnap, they extort, they rape, and they rob. They prey on children," Trump told a group of law enforcement officers during a speech a few weeks after Norman appeared in court. "They shouldn't be here. They stomp on their victims, they beat them with clubs, they slash them with machetes and they stab them with knives. They have transformed peaceful parks and beautiful quiet neighborhoods into blood-stained killing fields. They're animals."

4.

Norman ignored Trump, telling me at one point in between court appearances that he didn't think the president's outbursts mattered since, "I no longer feel like I'm part of the gang."

But the political atmosphere bent Norman's trial toward the surreal. Outside, Trump was warning about an MS-13 "invasion" via migrant caravans, leveraging the trope to separate families and send children to detention centers. Meanwhile, Norman was pleading for mercy, asking a judge to allow him to make the US his home, at least temporarily.

In this, Norman had three options: asylum; "withholding" of removal; or deferral based on the Convention Against Torture (CAT), an international treaty the US signed years before Trump had become president. For Norman, asylum and withholding were not options because of his gang ties and criminal past. They also would have required he establish that he was persecuted on "account of race, religion, nationality, membership in a particular social group, or political opinion."

Instead, Norman's legal representative was applying for deferral from deportation using CAT. For a CAT deferral to succeed, the "alien" must show that it is "more likely than not" they will face torture or death in the country to which they will be deported. The judge is especially considerate of state violence, which Norman also described to the court in detail that day: how he'd been stopped after his release from prison by the Salvadoran police and thrown into the bed of their truck; how they'd taken him to the edge of a sugarcane field where one officer told Norman he was "trash," that "he wasn't worth anything," and started to beat him; how that same policeman reached toward his pocket and pulled out a revolver and told him, "You know what, you're going to die right now."

Norman always had good luck in situations like this. By my count, he dodged death at least five times. On this occasion, a man—and potential witness—drove by in a tractor trailer, at just the right time. The police told Norman to go hide in a ditch. To save himself, he fled into the sugarcane field.

The police gave chase and began to shoot. A river ran along the edge of the field, and Norman told the court he jumped in and let the current take him. After a few blocks, he emerged from the water and walked to his aunt's house, where he found refuge. It was the beginning of an odyssey that would eventually land him in front of the judge.

5.

People enter the US without authorization to escape violence, threats, civil war, natural catastrophes and economic peril, as well as to reunite with family. But these migration patterns are also the result of a long-established colonial relationship between the United States and Latin America.

Few countries exemplify this history better than El Salvador. From cacao to coffee to cotton to textiles, the Salvadoran economy has long served foreign interests—first Spain and later the US—with devastating domestic consequences: near constant economic turmoil matched with massacres, war and gang violence. The US has had a strong hand in these events: supporting military dictatorships and unscrupulous politicians; training repressive army battalions and covering up for their atrocities; deporting gang members en masse to El Salvador and then washing its hands of the problems this creates.

Despite, or perhaps because of this dynamic, many Salvadorans revere the United States. They adorn themselves with US status symbols—tennis shoes, name-brand clothes, baseball hats. They adopt US sports. They integrate English into their everyday vernacular. They eat American food and purchase large, US-made vehicles. In 2001, the country even adopted the US dollar as its national currency. As the Salvadoran poet Roque Dalton once wrote: "The president of the United States is more president of my country than the president of my country."

Life as a neo-colony means watching US sitcoms because they are the only ones on TV, driving US cars because they are the only ones on the lot and wearing US clothes because they are the only ones on the racks. Salvadorans pay for it on both ends: accepting cheap wages to make US clothes, harvest US crops, and fight US wars. El Salvador did not so much adopt the US dollar as accept it as the best way to attract foreign investment from the same country that walks all over them.

Still, at this point, the bond is unbreakable. No other country has resettled in the US at the same rate relative to its population than El Salvador. In the late 1970s and throughout the 1980s during the country's civil war, around a quarter of El Salvador's population moved to the United States. Over 1.4 million first-generation Salvadorans still live in the US—or about 1 in every 5 Salvadoran-born people—a population nearly as large as the Chinese immigrant community in the US.

Salvadorans have settled in Los Angeles, Houston, Washington, DC, and other major Latino urban hubs. Half of all Salvadorans in the US live in California or Texas, and Los Angeles is the second largest "Salvadoran" city in the world behind the country's capital, San Salvador. But they've also moved to smaller towns like Annapolis, Maryland, and parts of Suffolk County, Long Island.

Most come for the reasons stated above, and many have become US citizens or are US residents. A good portion work menial jobs with little security or benefits—the type of jobs US citizens shun. Some set up restaurants or construction businesses, and support their children through college. Salvadoran immigrants benefit from government services—the schools, the health care system, the police and social welfare agencies—but they also pay taxes, and still send what they can back home. Nearly 17 percent of El Salvador's GDP comes from remittances.

Many Salvadorans I have spoken to think of their country constantly, often longing to return in spite of its troubles. To them, it's not a "shithole," as Trump once famously described El Salvador and numerous other developing nations, it's a postcard. This strong sense of national identity helps sustain families through adversity. There is no easy way to fix the relationship between a mother and a son who have been separated for a decade, no magic renovation when five families are piled into a two-bedroom apartment. There's no extra money for tutors or babysitters while guardians go to their second or third job of the day.

Those that are left behind in El Salvador are sometimes saddled with worse problems. Endemic corruption and grinding poverty. Impunity and rampant violence. Broken schools and filthy hospitals. But while it is clear that a major part of their problem is the neo-colonial system the US helped to establish and maintain, many still dream of America, long for it, want to experience it themselves. The US is at once repressor and liberator.

6.

It is from this tumultuous love-hate relationship that the MS-13 was born. The gang is the bastard child that no one wants to acknowledge from an affair that most choose to ignore. Lost in this unhealthy relationship are the children, many of whom are victims of circumstance, caught in a system that marginalizes, vilifies and tries to destroy them.

The MS-13 began in Los Angeles in the early 1980s, in part because the Reagan administration's proxy wars in Central America led to mass displacement. As violence spiked domestically, California passed special laws to arrest suspected members en masse, ensuring convictions and lengthening sentences. In response the gangs got more sophisticated, learning how to operate from within the prison system.

Eventually, violence and crime abated, but by then cities and states across the US were beginning to replicate LA's anti-crime model. What's more, Clinton, in his 1997 state of the union, declared his own "war on gangs," implementing draconian measures that increased incarceration rates.

The administration also doubled down on laws to accelerate deportations of ex-convicts, which in turn precipitated the spread of US-style gangs in Central America like the one Norman would join. In response, the George W. Bush administration eventually set up a special antigang task force in El Salvador where they repeated the process: Los Angeles–type policies that led to mass incarceration, which in turn consolidated gang power from within the prisons.

Frustrated, police in El Salvador began to target gang members in the way Norman was describing that day in court. El Salvador began to look like it did during the 1980s, at the height of its civil war.

The violence forced Central American families to flee to the US as refugees, which culminated in a surge of unaccompanied minors during the Obama administration. Obama reacted by increasing deportations yet again, this time to the highest levels in US history, thus starting the process all over again.

After nearly forty years, the MS-13 is more widespread than ever.

7.

It was this vicious cycle that had led Norman to the immigration court that July day, pleading for his life.

The judge—who acts as both judge and jury in immigration proceedings—was noticeably moved by the case. He intervened frequently, clarifying details about how Norman escaped from his half brother's grasp, and questioning Norman at length about prison guards and their penchant for torture, their ability to facilitate murders inside the prisons.

He winced as Norman described how guards forced them to strip to their boxers, cuffed them, doused them with excessive amounts of pepper spray, urinated on them and left them for hours to wallow in the smell and feel of another person's pee.

The judge probed for facts about how the police, wearing balaclavas, had gone looking for Norman several times at his mother's house, busting down the door in the middle of the night and pointing assault rifles at his wife and kids.

"What will happen to you if you are put in jail in El Salvador?" the judge asked.

"Me matarían señ…" His voice trailed off before he could finish his sentence.

"They would kill me, sir."

"Who would kill you?"

"Either the gang themselves or the government would kill me, sir."

By then, the gang had issued a *luz verde*, or "green light"—an order to kill on sight—for him and his family, Norman said.

The judge was troubled. He was in an impossible position: send Norman to El Salvador where he would almost certainly die, possibly at the hands of US allies in the police, or let a convicted killer who had been part of a brutal gang stay in the US, where the MS-13 had been declared public enemy number one.

As if part of a script, in the days prior roaches had invaded the courthouse, and court officers had been spraying insecticide to keep them at bay. The chemical scent was bothering the judge, so he called for a break in the hearing.

"This case is haunted," the judge said.

PART I

GETTING IN
(1979–1990)

1

THE BEGINNING

1.

FOR A LONG TIME AFTER THEY ARRIVED IN LOS Angeles, Alex and Oscar Sanchez[2] thought their mother was not really their mother. It was a natural feeling, since their parents had left them in El Salvador and gone to the United States when Alex was three and Oscar was one. The boys had been passed to relatives, who sent them to live with close friends. The brothers stayed with those friends for the next four years. This was their normal.

Alex and Oscar still talk about those years in El Salvador with fondness. Alex had no shoes, but he had a grassy area to explore, trees to climb and mangoes that he could snatch from the branches. They were well cared for by their family friends' three daughters. For a while, Oscar thought he had three moms.

The area was picturesque. El Salvador is about the size of

2 Throughout this book, the use of Spanish names and surnames follows the use by the people interviewed or cited in other accounts, including whether or not they apply accents used in standard Spanish.

New Jersey but boasts twenty-three active volcanoes that seem to drag the hills toward the sky. In the back of the house, a steep cliff led to the edge of Lake Ilopango. Surrounded by lush, dark green mountains, the water often bubbles, a result of the Ilopango volcano's steady rumble. On the far side of the lake, they could see the San Vicente volcano, the country's second tallest, where it rose from the plains.

Their house in San Martín was just fifteen miles from San Salvador, the country's capital, but felt worlds away. The family used an outhouse and had to walk a few hundred yards to fetch water using large clay receptacles, which they balanced across their shoulders with a stick. All but one of the receptacles went with them inside the house. The other they left in the yard for the girls' father, who used the water heated by the sun to bathe when he returned from work.

Oscar and Alex's grandparents lived in the area. Their grandfather had purchased a long stretch of land after leaving the military. It wasn't a farm so much as a retirement home, and the grandchildren had free rein until the land was cut in half by the construction of the Pan-American Highway. Their grandparents eventually parceled it out to their kids.

Beyond the one black-and-white photo Alex kept of his mother, the boys had little connection to their parents. When Oscar asked the sisters about them, they'd point toward the San Vicente volcano, explaining they were on the other side. "Why can't we go?" Oscar would enquire. "Why can't we visit them?"

It was the mid-1970s. Unions, peasant cooperatives, student organizations and church groups were openly protesting the military regimes that had taken power in El Salvador. Occasionally gunshots could be heard in the distance. One day, on their way to school, the boys were crossing the train tracks that cut through the village when they found a dead man. Ants were crawling into the man's ears, an image that Alex had trouble shaking. They had never seen a lifeless body before.

Another time, they went to fetch water behind the house and discovered a body hanging from a tree. From then on, Oscar believed the tree was haunted, and he refused to go to the well after dark.

After several years, Alex and Oscar's parents sent for them. The boys did not know what this meant, but when the girls had them bathe in sun-baked water, don button-down shirts and travel to San Salvador to have their pictures taken for little individual booklets, they knew something special was happening.

When a man and a woman came to pick them up, they said goodbye to their surrogate mothers and headed north. As they drove through Guatemala and into Mexico, Alex clung to his confused little brother who shat his pants rather than use the gas station toilets, which he confused for sinks. The couple, meanwhile, kept repeating the same instructions: *if anyone asks, you are our children.*

They switched to a train, then to another car, then to a van. They slept at motels and at random homes. After a week or so, they found themselves in a long line of cars. As the van inched along, Oscar fell asleep, but Alex remembers the couple telling them again, *You need to say we are your mom and dad.*

Suddenly the doors opened. The brothers sat silently as the uniformed men looked them up and down and inspected the dark corners of the vehicle. The couple and the men exchanged a few words. The boys didn't understand, but it didn't matter. The door swung shut, and they were through, bouncing along the highway again.

The road widened, and a cityscape flanked them on both sides. This was not San Salvador. They stopped, and the door opened again. They were in a parking lot in Skid Row, a ramshackle area of shady hotels and run-down low-income housing filled with homeless Vietnam veterans, street dwellers and junkies. Their mother, pregnant with their little sister, hugged them. Their father handed the couple a stack of cash, and the two boys never saw nor heard about them again.

The reunited Sanchez family piled into their father's Chevy Custom 10 and got on the highway again. Oscar spent most of the journey staring into the truck's seemingly huge rearview mirror. The lights from the other cars were blinding but mesmerizing. Alex watched the city stream past his window. *This is your family, your real family,* they were told. They were supposed to accept it, embrace it even. But they didn't. They couldn't, at least not at first.

You're not my mom, they both thought.

2.

The Sanchez family settled in a one-bedroom apartment in Koreatown, near downtown Los Angeles. They were one of thousands of Salvadoran families who moved there and to surrounding neighborhoods—Pico-Union, Rampart Village, and Wilshire—in the late 1970s and early 1980s. At first glance, it seemed a world of opportunity. Hollywood to the north, a bustling beach to the south; to the east, the Los Angeles skyline, the shiny buildings shimmering—a mirage of the American dream.

But by the time the Sanchez family had reunited, Central Los Angeles's sidewalks were littered with garbage—broken furniture, discarded appliances and fast-food wrappers. The pavement was stained with motor oil and beer. The stench of urine wafted through the air. The ocean was a distant bus ride.

The densely populated neighborhood, hemmed in by highways and byways, canals and buildings, sometimes felt like a prison. Even in MacArthur Park—where children could climb on the playground, and families could stroll around the glistening manmade lake—there were drug dealers lurking on the edges.

Central LA suffered from what the sociologist Frederic M. Thrasher, writing in the 1927 classic study aptly titled *The Gang*, would call "general disorganization." When Alex and Oscar Sanchez arrived, there were as many as 400 gangs in the city. A large number of these groups dated back to the 1920s, when cheap Mexican labor was in demand, and workers arrived in big numbers, settling in East Los Angeles and the San Fernando Valley. The gangs that formed around this migration included some legendary groups that remain in existence today: White Fence, Primera Flats, El Hoyo Maravilla and 38th Street, to name a few.

These gangs were a product of their environment: exclusion, lack of social mobility, few adequate and functioning public services, and fear. As it was in other parts of the country, migrant communities in Los Angeles entered a competitive urban landscape where they were preyed upon and underserved. Their working-class neighborhoods often lacked infrastructure, public transportation, hospitals and even potable water. Schools and social services were perennially under-resourced or nonexistent. James Diego Vigil, who wrote extensively on Chicano gangs in the city, called this "multiple marginality."

The fertile environment for gangs in Los Angeles was, in part, a legacy of US colonization of the Americas. In the 1830s, under the banner of Manifest Destiny, White colonists pressed west, bringing with them a slave trade that was illegal in Mexican-held territories like Texas. Their move to expand the slave trade precipitated the Mexican-American War and the eventual annexation of a tract of land that would nearly double the size of the United States. The area colonized by the Mexican-American War would come to resemble future colonial enclaves in Central America and elsewhere. In both instances, the government serviced the wealthy land-holding elite and destroyed organized labor.

"Ours is the government of the White Man," former Vice President John C. Calhoun famously said in 1848, as Congress debated whether to allow Mexicans living in the newly annexed territory to become US citizens.

Citizenship for those Mexicans conquered during the Mexican-American War did not come until the 1930s, after eighty years of exploitation, repression and violence that included thousands of lynchings.[3] For other Mexicans, citizenship never came at all. Instead many functioned as cheap labor, vital to keep the US economy growing in boom times but expendable during a downturn. Economic instability led to mass expulsions. During the Great Depression, Los Angeles–based civic organizations worked with immigration authorities to round up Mexicans in a process called "scare-heading." In the 1950s, the US government federalized this same policy under "Operation Wetback," expelling an estimated one million Mexicans. Cheap Mexican labor was fine, brown-skinned citizens were not.

Gangs were the result of this systemic marginalization. In the 1920s, groups dubbed "tomato gangs" would throw street vender food at their rivals. By today's standards, these gangs were relatively harmless—mostly restless youth engaging in fistfights and bravado, according to Joan Moore, who like Vigil chronicled the Chicano gangs in and around Los Angeles for decades.

These tomato gangs later became what were referred to as *pachucos*, which literally means "flashy" but would later become a euphemism for "gang member." The pachucos were mostly second-generation Mexican-Americans—Chicano youth who spoke an English-Spanish dialect called Caló, donned fedoras and wore pin-striped and brightly colored long-tailed coats and pants called zoot suits. They congregated in the cantinas and dance halls, eventually forming the foundation of today's Chicano gangs.

One of Los Angeles's most infamous gangs, the White Fence, formed in a church in the East Los Angeles neighborhood of Boyle Heights in the late 1920s. The church, La Purissima, was the center of life in the area, and through the 1930s, the so-called

3 In their book *Forgotten Dead: Mob Violence against Mexicans in the United States, 1848–1928*, historians William D. Carrigan and Clive Webb documented 547 cases but believe there were thousands more.

Purissima Crowd mostly played organized sports and helped with local festivals, Moore says.[4] In the 1940s, however, circumstances changed. During World War II, more parents worked, and violence rose. The Purissima became White Fence, a group at once protective of their own and predatory toward others.

The gang soon began to incorporate some of the rules and traditions that are still prevalent in Latino gangs today: establishing cliques, attending meetings, creating bloody initiation rituals and disciplining members who broke these rules. Moore, whose deep dive into the White Fence and El Hoyo Maravilla set the standard for gang studies in the area, says the introduction of heroin was also a "major turning point" for these gangs. Drug use and prison time would eventually become a central part of the gangs' ethos, setting the stage for the next evolution.

Chicano gang identity was linked to geographic location, but collectively they assumed the mantle of the neighborhood, or *el barrio.* Barrio, or *varrio* as it is often written, is not just where you live but a mythic notion of home—a safe place where you could be yourself without fear of rejection, long-term recrimination, prejudice or unwarranted repression, where you could speak your language, eat your food and wear your clothes without persecution.

Barrio soon became interchangeable with the word *gang.* To join el barrio was to join a team, a like-minded collective. In sports, physical rituals happened on the field; in gangs, they happened on the streets. Young people would see each other and ask: *¿Qué barrio?* Answering with pride could earn you a beating, a lifetime of respect or both.

3.

Alex's parents enrolled him in third grade at a school about three miles from their apartment. He was one of only a few Salvadorans. The bullies swarmed. His Mexican-American classmates

4 Today the church is referred to as La Purisima.

were particularly cruel. They made fun of his Salvadoran accent. They called him "wetback" and *"cerote,"* or "piece of shit."

At first, Alex hatched plans to get others to like him. One time, he stole one of his father's *Hustler* magazines and hid it amongst his books. At school, he showed it to some of his classmates in the hall. The other boys gathered around, but then one of them grabbed the magazine and ran. Alex gave chase. The two scurried down the hall until the other student tossed the magazine into an open classroom, and the teacher grabbed it. His classmates mocked him. His strategy to make friends had failed.

Transgressions in the Sanchez house often led to beatings. Alex's parents were managing several jobs and raising four rambunctious kids in the middle of Los Angeles. Alex and Oscar's sister, Melivea Rosabel, was born in December 1979, just a few months after their dramatic arrival in Skid Row; their brother, Alvin Juan, was already three. Their father worked two jobs—delivering newspapers and blowing glass at a small factory. Their mother worked long hours at a hospital, washing linens, smocks and uniforms.

They crowded into their tiny, one-room apartment, in a two-story building just off Olympic Avenue on the edge of Koreatown. The three brothers slept in the bedroom, their parents and sister in the living room. The apartment was about five-hundred square feet with five windows that overlooked a driveway where homeless people often slept. That patch of concrete and dead grass, smelling of urine and garbage, soon became the Sanchez brothers' de facto backyard. Alex and Oscar would climb on the garbage cans next to the barbed-wire fence on the edge of a factory that made venetian blinds. Alex once cut himself (and got a beating for it).

Alex and his brother eventually got to know some of the homeless by name. A woman who worked at the factory used to give the boys fresh fruit juice. During their first year in Los

Angeles, they spent Halloween, Thanksgiving and Christmas with their father's extended family—cousins, uncles and aunts.

In their second year in the city, their mother became a Jehovah's Witness. Her conversion seemed to happen on a whim, when a recently converted neighbor knocked on their door. It reflected her deeper need for a supportive community, but it split the family. Their father refused to join, and their mother's new religious community forced her to choose. She chose the Jehovah's Witnesses, and the two separated.

Soon afterward, the four Sanchez children went with their mother to an apartment just above the original Jehovah's Witness recruiter who'd knocked on their door. Their mother became fast friends with the recruiter, exchanging tips on how best to keep Oscar and Alex in line. The rules got stricter, the beatings worsened. Mess up your room—beating. Arrive late to Sunday School—beating. Fall asleep at church—beating. Fail to do the dishes—beating.

Oscar got it worse, often because he was more defiant. His mother used a belt for light beatings, and the thick black cord of the clothes iron when she really wanted to make her point, tearing open the flesh of his forearms that he raised to block the blows. "I'm doing this for your own good," she would say.

Oscar would never completely forgive her.

4.

On the night of August 1, 1942, a twenty-two-year-old Mexican-born son of migrant workers named José Díaz was killed during a melee at a birthday party near Sleepy Lagoon reservoir in a working-class neighborhood in Los Angeles. The murder shook the community, and the case became a bellwether for race relations in the city. At the time, the police were turning their attention away from busting up labor unions and cracking down on vice toward the growing phenomenon of gang violence.

During the sweeps that followed, police arrested twenty-two members of what they called the "38th Street gang." Lacking physical evidence, the police held these men for days and beat them into confessing. Later, during the trial of what became known as the Sleepy Lagoon case, prosecutors argued that the defendants had "malignant hearts" and a "lust for revenge." And in January 1943, a jury found twelve of the accused guilty of first- and second-degree murder; another five were found guilty of assault.

The trial sparked political outrage in Los Angeles. A newly formed Sleepy Lagoon Defense Committee appealed the verdict and regularly denounced repressive police tactics. The committee gained traction both inside and outside of the Chicano neighborhoods. Some prominent Hollywood stars even lent their names to the cause, attending five-dollar-a-head fundraising banquets across town and writing letters on the accused boys' behalf. "The case has importance aside from the boys incriminated," Orson Welles wrote in one such letter. "The whole community is undermined."

In June 1943, six months after the Sleepy Lagoon verdict, US servicemen and pachucos clashed in Los Angeles. Over the course of seven days, servicemen chased and beat anyone wearing baggy pants and loose-fitting jackets. The pachucos retaliated, which led to pitched battles and another police crackdown. Historian Edward Escobar says that as many as six hundred Mexican-Americans were arrested, and only a handful of servicemen. The Zoot Suit Riots, as they came to be called, inspired a Chicano awakening. "Identity politics began in 1943," Escobar wrote.

A little over a year later, in October 1944, a California appellate court overturned the Sleepy Lagoon verdict, noting the "complete lack of evidence," the illegal detention of the suspects and all the ways in which the judge "injured" the defense's case during the trial. But the legal victory did little to change the dynamic. A pattern was emerging, one with racial overtones. In this new paradigm, the barrios, with their Caló and zoot suits, were, as the newspapers noted during Sleepy Lagoon case, "Mexican Mobsters" and "Zoot Suit Gangsters." These nascent gangs were becoming, as Escobar noted, "the metaphor through which much of white society viewed Mexican Americans."

Ethnic street gangs had been a staple in US cities for more than a century, ranging from vigilante wannabes to predatory misfits. Some groups escaped the cycle of violence and poverty. A number of factors drove this evolution: strong ethnic networks, a steady decline of migration, racial integration, the industrial revolution and de facto political recognition. Martin Scorcese, in his film *Gangs of New York*, poignantly explores how politicians like Boss Tweed used the gangs in the Lower East Side's infamous Five Points neighborhood to maintain political control of Tammany Hall, and how the Irish moved from running gangs to running the police.

Chicano gangs, however, have had a different and more durable trajectory. White Fence and El Hoyo Maravilla, for instance, maintain a nearly century-long violent rivalry. Barrios throughout the city endure for decades.

Academics, policymakers and law enforcement have offered numerous explanations for this longevity. Proponents of the "cultural" or "ethnic" explanation argue that Mexican-Americans are predisposed toward creating and maintaining street gangs (the same would be said of Black gangs). This argument has persisted for decades, but its foundations are flawed with racist perceptions. A 2007 Justice Policy Institute analysis of police surveys about gangs, for instance, revealed that law enforcement consistently overestimates the number of gang members of color, in part because of an implicit bias—they assume gang members of color do not age out as often as White gang members.

The "systemic" explanation, like Vigil's multiple marginality theory, holds that the system is designed to relegate an underclass—mostly Latino and Black communities—to marginalized areas where discontent manifests through gangs. In this paradigm, gangs represent what Moore (and others) said could be called "resistance," an ad hoc, disorganized rebellion. Moore did not completely ascribe to this theory. In its most extreme form, it virtually absolves the gangs of all responsibility for their criminal acts and antisocial behavior.

In fact, no single theory can completely capture the complexity of gang life. Gangs are social structures, reinforced by ethnicity and a shared culture; they operate as a political group and rebel against a broken system; they can be motivated by shared economic needs; and they solidify their bonds via violence and predatory criminal acts. In other words, they are both products and shapers of their environment.

What made the Chicano story even more complicated, and their gangs more durable, was the continued influx of not just Mexican laborers but also workers from other Latin American countries. Over time intra-Latino stereotypes and prejudices emerged. Chicanos considered themselves a higher social status than recently arrived Mexicans, and both scoffed at Latinos from other countries. This derision is not surprising. Each population was competing for the same jobs, the same housing and the same scant social services. Ongoing migration created a permanent underclass. And it was this near constant flow of migrants that made Latino gangs more "institutionalized," as Moore described them.

5.

For fourth grade, Oscar and Alex's parents put them in school together. Oscar was adjusting. He was younger and picked up the language quicker. But Alex spent most of his time thinking about El Salvador. He struggled to make new friends. In

Los Angeles, there were no verdant hills, no volcanos rumbling in the distance, no fruit falling from the trees, no freedom to explore like he had on his grandfather's land. Everything was about the rules, the places he couldn't go, the things he had to avoid.

"I was isolated. I became antisocial," Alex said later. "I used to just try to figure out how to entertain myself."

One way was to go to his third-floor classroom during recess and throw paper airplanes out the window. As the planes spun toward the ground, young Alex would run down the stairs and outside to try and catch them. One time, Alex's paper plane landed by a group of schoolmates. One of them, who Alex said was the leader, picked it up.

"Dámelo." Give it to me, Alex pleaded. "It's mine."

The boy laughed, crumpled it up and threw it at him. The balled-up paper landed at Alex's feet. On another day, Alex might have walked away. But in that moment the isolation, the bullying, the frustration made him implode. Alex unleashed an awkward but forceful karate kick. Then came his fists. His next memory is of the boy beneath him, and him hitting the boy in his face with all his might. The boy's friends were stunned. Blood poured from the boy's mouth and nose as school officials dragged a kicking and crying Alex Sanchez off him.

"Why did you fuck with me!" he yelled.

As school officials hauled him into the principal's office, Alex felt different.

"I felt really good," he said. "I don't know. It really gave me a good feeling that I'd never felt before. I let it out."

The next time he was on the playground, the other kids approached him, some of whom had also been bullied. They wanted to be his friend. He wanted no part of them, and no one bothered him again.

"That was my first lesson in how to protect myself: you punch them in the mouth if they make you feel bad," he said. "That's how I lived for the next twenty years."

6.

In 1954, Paramount Pictures released *The Naked Jungle*, the film version of Carl Stephenson's short story "Leiningen Versus the Ants." In the story, the hero, Christopher Leiningen, is a stubborn plantation owner who, along with his mail-order bride, tries to fight off a legion of army ants that invade the farm. The ants are relentless, eating everything in their path.

In the film, Charlton Heston plays Leiningen. The movie was eventually translated and exported. Its title in Spanish was *Cuando ruge la marabunta*, "When the Ants Roar." In El Salvador, the term *mara* became a euphemism for a small, often rambunctious, group of friends. By the early 1980s, *mara* had also become a moniker for the relatively harmless facsimiles of today's gangs.

Migrants carried the term north to Los Angeles, where it took on a deeper meaning. There were hundreds of Latino gangs. There was only one mara.

The first time Alex saw them, he was on the balcony of an apartment in Pico-Union. It was around 1983. Alex was in sixth grade, attending his third school in three years. He had, to put it mildly, a disciplinary problem. To blend in, he had stopped speaking with his Salvadoran accent and avoided using colloquialisms like *vos*. *Vos* is a way of saying *you*, but the more common term, especially among the Chicano and Mexican youth, was *tú*. Saying *vos* revealed Alex's origins and exposed him to more ridicule.

Still, he was starting to make friends. Some of them claimed to be in gangs. They mentioned the Playboys and the Alleyboys. He went with them to the beach or to "ditching parties," gatherings at empty houses for those skipping school. Alcohol flowed. Alex liked the escape it provided. He also liked being liked, and often stole liquor from the corner store for his friends.

It was at one of those ditching parties that he saw the mara in the parking lot below. The gang, if you could call it that, caught his attention because they were listening to heavy metal. Something about the way they acted—music blaring, heads bobbing, hair bouncing, arms waving with their fingers spread like two little devil's horns, made an impression. They were strange, but they were free.

He didn't think too much of it until the next year when he met some of them through a friend of a friend who, like him, had stopped speaking with a Salvadoran accent. Alex was now in junior high, his fourth school in four years.

"Vos sos de El Salvador?" his friend's cousin asked.

The questioner's blunt use of *vos* jolted him.

"Sí, soy de El Salvador."

"*Toda la mara* hangs out over here," he told him flatly. "You should come."

Alex was curious. This kid wasn't just proclaiming his heritage, he was wearing it as a badge of honor. Later, his friend's cousin called him over to meet some other members of the group—two boys and a girl. They told him they called themselves the Mara Salvatrucha Stoners 13 or MSS13.

7.

Soon Alex was listening to Pink Floyd, Judas Priest, Ozzie Osborne and Metallica. The music drove his mother mad, but it helped him form deeper connections with his new friends who listened to AC/DC, Iron Maiden, Megadeth and others. These mostly heavy metal rockers infused Satanism into their lyrics, costumes and showtime antics. The Salvatruchas began to refer to themselves as *la bestia*, or "the beast," a euphemism for the devil, and adopted the spread-finger devil symbol as their own.

They also added 13 to their name because, they told Alex, it was a sign of "evil." The 13 would take on more meaning later, when the group became part of the Sureños, a collection of gangs operating in Southern California under the auspices of the Mexican Mafia prison gang. The Sureños use 13 to connote the *M* in Mexican Mafia—*M* is the thirteenth letter of the alphabet—but that was still a few years away.

The word *Salvatrucha* is often described as a neologism—the *Salva* is short for Salvadoran and *trucha* means "watchful," "savvy," or in some interpretations "be careful." However, *Salvatrucha* also carried historical significance. In the mid-nineteenth century, a soldier of fortune from Tennessee named William Walker and his small army overran parts of Central America, including the Salvadoran isthmus. The Hondurans who battled against him called themselves Catrachos; the Salvadorans called themselves Guanacos or Salvatruchas.

Just over a hundred years later, the Salvatruchas were back, fighting a new battle, this time in Los Angeles.

"Any time anyone fucked with one of the members, the three MSS guys would jump up and protect them," Alex said.

Alex's escapades with the Stoners eventually got him in trouble with his parents. One time, when he was twelve, he stumbled into the house drunk, and his little sister jumped on his lap and smelled the alcohol before telling his mother, who brought him to see the church elders. They spoke to him solemnly, warning him of the dangers that lay ahead if he continued to stray towards the devil. But Alex did not stop. He was becoming a *marero*, a member of the mara.

By the time Alex officially requested to join, the MSS13 was fractioning into cliques and co-opting established rituals from other Latino gangs. One of the most important of these rituals was *el brinco*, the "beating-in" ceremony. In later years, el brinco would become an elaborate affair, complete with a long, drawn-out count to thirteen by the clique's leader. But in those early years of the mara, el brinco amounted to a fight with another member of the gang.

"You're going to get down with Sleepy," one of the leaders told Alex.

The two squared up.

"Pégale," the others prodded. "Hit him!"

The two traded punches. Then they wrestled, exchanging blood, and it was over.

Alex was given a *taca*, or "nickname." From then on, they would call him Rebelde, "Rebel." Alex was now a member of the Catalina Locos, a small clique; in all, there were about forty MSS13 members in Los Angeles. His Salvadoran accent grew thick, and he started using *vos* again.

I can't hide it, he told himself. *I won't hide it.*

It was beginning.

2

NORMAN'S WARS

1.

NORMAN'S FIRST BRUSH WITH THE COLD WAR came at some point in the mid-1980s when members of the Salvadoran army, trained and funded by the United States, arrived at his house. Norman was a kid, no more than ten years old. His memory of the day itself is foggy, but the events that transpired changed the family's trajectory during that tumultuous decade.

The army was, by then, desperate for recruits. They would seize teenagers from buses and classrooms, beaches and cantinas. Mostly, however, they targeted decrepit areas like Norman's where they knew poor kids were bountiful. According to one count, as many as thirty-three boys per day were forcibly recruited during the latter stages of the war.

On that day, the army hauled two of his brothers—Miguel Ángel and Juan David, who went by his second name—to the barracks. Norman's mom, Clara, scrambled after them and pleaded with the military officers to release her sons. She was a single mother, she told them, with five other mouths to feed. She needed her sons to survive.

The army would take others from the neighborhood over the years: Choco, Walter, Crazy and Zorro, to name a few. "There are certain things you just don't forget," Norman told me solemnly years later.

The army commander who took his brothers to the barracks was sympathetic to his mother's dilemma. He gave Clara a choice: David or Miguel Ángel. It was an impossible decision, she told the military official. Undaunted, the commander told her that if she refused his offer to pick one of them, he would take them both. She cried and pleaded, but the commander did not budge.

David was sixteen at the time—sturdy and disciplined. Years later, Norman said that when David was home it was like having a military commander in the house, complete with smacks to the head for failing to follow directions. Miguel Ángel was tall and looked older than David, but he was only thirteen, barely entering puberty.

Clara considered her options. Both boys were unprepared for what lay ahead, but Miguel Ángel was still a baby. The army would destroy him, she thought. The three of them cried, and Miguel Ángel and Clara went home, leaving David in the army.

2.

Norman was born in 1975, in a small hamlet between the country's capital, San Salvador, and the Guatemalan border. He was the youngest of seven kids. After his father left his mother for Norman's cousin on his mother's side, his mom did her best to rear them. They were, like so many Salvadorans, cobbling together a life amidst a growing local and global conflict.

At the time, a guerrilla army was organizing. Colonel Arturo

Armando Molina was the president when Norman was born, but to families like Norman's, it made little difference which army officer was taking his turn at the top. The ideological battle being waged through the Cold War governed their lives.

From the Middle East to Asia to Latin America, the US had established a military and political presence to support regimes—civilian or military—whose purported function was to keep communism at bay. But beneath the surface maneuvered the icy hand of imperialism, a twentieth-century version of Manifest Destiny.

In Central America, US imperialism had begun as plunder at the hands of William Walker, the soldier of fortune from Tennessee. Walker claimed he wanted peace and democracy, but, as the historian George Black describes, Walker and his mercenary army targeted Nicaragua to expand slavery and the US's plantation economy. (His soldiers, Black also notes, were attracted to "the legendary sexual allure" of its women.) After getting an invitation to help one of two political parties that were battling for control of the country, Walker took advantage and overran the government altogether in 1855, then installed himself as president whereupon he declared his intention "to place a large portion of the land in the hands of the white race."

The US government recognized Walker's regime, but he was soon expelled from Nicaragua. Walker kept trying in other regions, including El Salvador, where the Salvatruchas fended him off. In 1860, he was executed in Honduras.

Thereafter the US routinely allied with traditional, wealthy landowners who used the local military as a proxy army to keep labor in check. Local allies of the US also partnered with local politicians to keep taxes and regulations at a minimum and to maintain favorable conditions for foreign investment. And they controlled the judicial system to make sure they were never prosecuted for crimes ranging from land theft to murder. "Interests and imperial rivalry, not morality and consistency, drove US policies," historian Walter LaFeber once wrote.

El Salvador epitomized this dynamic. The country was long ruled by "the fourteen families," a euphemism for the land-owning elites who controlled the levers of state power. When threatened, the families responded in extreme fashion. In January 1932, for example, when faced with a national strike of coffee growers led by the charismatic head of the Communist Party, Farabundo Martí, government forces slaughtered nearly thirty thousand people. Thousands more were displaced, initiating a process of urbanization and eventual migration—first to Honduras and later to the US—that has yet to slow. The event became known as *La Matanza*, "The Massacre."

La Matanza suppressed one type of rebellion but sparked another, which was bubbling over by the time Norman was born. Agricultural cooperative heads, union bosses and students began to connect and organize. Although their objectives differed, their enemy was the same. These groups began to arm themselves, forming the beginnings of a guerrilla coalition that would eventually take the name of La Matanza's most famous victim, the Farabundo Martí National Liberation Front (Frente Farabundo Martí para la Liberación Nacional, FMLN).

They followed the ideas of Marx and Castro, Maoism and Ché, and they received some monetary support, weapons and training from Cuba, the Soviet Union and eventually Nicaragua. But they were also influenced by the Second Vatican Council meetings of the mid-1960s and the Latin American Bishops Conference in Medellin in 1968, during which high-level Catholic officials reinterpreted the Church's central mission. In El Salvador, hundreds of priests and catechists were heeding the call for social justice through the principles of what was termed Liberation Theology. This was not a guerrilla movement—the vast majority practiced peaceful resistance—but Liberation Theology split the country's most revered institution, leaving even its most venerable members vulnerable to attack. For many Catholics, though, the new theology was a religious permission slip to challenge authority and push back against repression.

"Inspired by the principles and the social doctrine of the Church, they had converted into loyal followers of Liberation Theology and what they pursued: social justice," a guerrilla named Mario Alberto Mijango, aka Raúl, would write years later of the insurgency's origins. The theology, as Mijango discovered, would prove to be a double-edged sword. Its adherents, he wrote, were "promoting and cultivating dogmatism that served as inspiration…heroic action and revolutionary commitment, but that dogmatism was also [a source of] tremendous political miscalculation and military errors."

Mijango himself would later become a victim of that very dogmatism.

On the other side, those entrenched in Cold War logic shared a similarly dogmatic approach. The Cold War had put into motion the machinery of battle, which was difficult to stop. Even President Jimmy Carter, whose administration during the late 1970s cut aid to several countries because of human rights concerns, never followed through on its threats to do the same to El Salvador. That would have required the Carter administration to upend a decades-old colonial arrangement, one dependent on the blood of young soldiers willing to shoot their own neighbors.

In fact, aside from the ideological veneer, little had changed since 1932. Those responsible for La Matanza were US allies, and they remained in power. Army officers so often ran the government that the military academy was nicknamed the "School of Presidents."

And so, as Norman's family cobbled together a life in their small hamlet between San Salvador and Guatemala, they paid little attention to which military general was in power. Their names were different, but their uniforms were the same. The United States supported these regimes, however illegitimate or antidemocratic they might be. After all, they argued, the alternative was communism.

3.

A few years before Clara was forced to choose between her sons at the barracks, she collapsed from depression. The thought of her husband cavorting with their niece was too much to bear. She strung a rope from a joist, fastened a makeshift noose around her neck and let her feet slip from the edge of the bed. A loud snap sounded from the house's foundation, and Alejandro, Norman's eldest brother, rushed in, where he found his mother in her room, legs flexed, feet kicking frightfully in the air. Alejandro jumped on the bed and hoisted her from the rafters.

Norman was just a toddler and did not remember this event, but Laura, Norman's older sister, heard the commotion. Terrified, she flung open the door and saw her brother cradling their mother in his arms.

"Mom, don't do that!" Alejandro cried. "Mom, don't do that!"

From then on, Alejandro and Laura became the de facto heads of household. Alejandro was working at the local Texaco gas station, and he used part of his paycheck to take care of the water and the electricity bills. In addition, he was building his mother a new home because his father was threatening to seize the house and move back with his new family.

Laura became her mother's workhorse assistant at the local market where they sold vegetables and prepared foods. She and her brothers also helped raise the two youngest, Norman and Rodrigo.

"They looked at me like a mom," she told me later.

Norman and Rodrigo were a rambunctious pair, and she mostly just tried to keep them occupied.

"I would make funny voices and put on clown outfits," she said. "[Norman] was always making jokes."

He was their *"loco,"* a little crazy, but in a goofy, lovable way. The nickname would stick. He and his brother Rodrigo started calling her *"ruquita,"* an endearment roughly translated as sage, older woman.

Alejandro tended to the boys as well. He took Norman and Rodrigo to a boxing match once in the capital of the province. Alejandro liked boxing, especially after he saw the movie *Rocky*. Like Sylvester Stallone's character, he jogged the streets in the morning, saluting his neighbors, imagining himself the hometown hero.

But the family's problems continued. Alone, with seven mouths to feed, Clara turned to Jehovah's Witnesses and tried to discipline her children. Some afternoons, she would send Laura home from the market early, so her young daughter could start the cooking, cleaning and laundry. One day, Laura got caught up in a baseball game in front of the house and forgot to tend to the fire. When Clara arrived home and found the beans uncooked, she struck Laura with a mop. The blows were so strong that the shaft shattered across her back.

Clara disciplined all the children using shoes, belts or anything within reach. Laura and Alejandro eventually employed their own versions of corporal punishment when they babysat. Laura says that after a while, she only needed to reach for the mop to get her little brothers to fall in line.

Amidst the tumult, the family found a rhythm. Norman's mother sold corn, vegetables and beans at the market and washed clothes in other people's homes. Over time, she saved enough money to start a small food stall, which later became a restaurant. The whole family helped. One of Norman's earliest memories is of grabbing a large pot of chicken soup and carrying it to market with his brother Rodrigo.

But Norman's father Gabriel and his new family remained a withering presence. David hated his father for leaving his mother and accelerating her suicidal ideations. Laura was hurt when Gabriel—who was making good money as a local transporter—showered his new family with the amenities that he never gave them: new clothes, elaborate meals, and a better house. But Norman's mother did not mind.

"She was very faithful to my father," Norman told me. "She always wanted us to respect him. She never wanted us to have a stepfather."

Despite his neglect, Gabriel could be charming. According to Norman his father was "friendly with everyone" and a "good person." He would call out to people on the streets, "Hey man, how are you?" or "Good morning, my brother." In Norman's mind, Gabriel was not so much a villain as a victim of circumstance, despite the tumult he was causing inside their family. Gabriel had three children with Norman's cousin and was regularly cavorting with other women. His growing desire to place his new family into Norman's home created a major rift.

Once again, Alejandro came to the rescue. He bought a small plot of land and gathered building materials, urging the family to help him source rocks and sand from the river. He hired a builder, and when the house was finished, they visited together. The house had no furniture, no windows. It was a simple structure made of hollow cement blocks, wood beams and a corrugated metal roof. But it was theirs, all theirs. It still is. They would later adorn it with a plaque bearing the family name.

When Norman was ten, his father left his cousin and moved back into their home, bringing his three kids from the other relationship with him. They also established a stall in the central market, just a few spots down from Norman's mother's. It was tense at times. Laura and David remained resentful, and Gabriel's kids would torment their half siblings about what they had and what Norman's family did not. Still, for Norman, they became "a parallel family." Later, these families would coalesce through the Mara Salvatrucha.

4.

El Salvador's war is often dated to March 24, 1980. On that day, a group of heavily armed men met in the Camino Real Hotel in

San Salvador. Soon after, two of them left in a red Volkswagen Passat and three others in a Dodge Lancer. They took different routes to the same destination—a hospital chapel in northwest San Salvador, where Archbishop Óscar Romero was to administer mass.

The archbishop was slight and soft-spoken with a crew cut and thick, black glasses. In some respects, he was conservative, spending much of his time praying for change rather than organizing for it. While he spoke on behalf of victims of violence and injustice, the archbishop chastised some of his colleagues who were helping to organize more radical religious groups and helping unions.

Yet for right-wing forces and their death squads, Romero represented a major threat. During his popular weekly radio homilies he regularly denounced the government's human rights abuses. His words inspired activists and guerrillas, and they provoked the ire of his enemies. Romero regularly received written death threats scrawled with swastikas. His enemies dropped pamphlets on the street comparing him to Iran's Ayatollah Khomeini. "Be a patriot! Kill a priest!" a flyer from the time famously said. Many took the challenge seriously. In the three-year period Romero was archbishop, eight priests were killed. Another sixty went into exile or were recalled.

Romero was unbowed. During his homily on March 23, he'd proclaimed that "no soldier is obliged to obey an order against the law of God" and ended with what would be a dramatic but ultimately empty plea to the death squads, the army and their progenitors to "stop the repression!"

The hospital chapel stood on a quiet residential street. The Passat pulled up just before 6:00 p.m. and waited until mass began. Shortly thereafter, a man, later described by the Truth Commission as "a bearded stranger," raised his rifle, shooting a single .22 caliber[5] bullet that hit the archbishop mid-service. The

5 The Truth Commission said it could have been a .223 caliber.

sound shook the church and left Romero with a five-millimeter hole in his right thorax. He died, slumped in a pool of his own blood at the base of the chapel pulpit.

The public outrage that followed forced the government to mount an investigation. A few months after Romero's assassination, police raided a farm where they arrested twelve active and retired military personnel, and twelve civilians, who were allegedly planning to overthrow the government. They confiscated weapons and documents tying the men to the killing of the archbishop.

Among those arrested was Roberto d'Aubuisson, a dashing, chain-smoking former military intelligence officer and the farm's owner. D'Aubuisson—who a US Ambassador once described as "a pathological killer"—had founded several death squads, including the White Warriors Union, which targeted outspoken clergy.

But d'Aubuisson was a slippery target. He maintained a deep relationship with the military and led a nascent extreme-right political movement, which would become the National Republican Alliance (Alianza Republicana Nacionalista, ARENA).

After a series of terrorist threats, authorities released d'Aubuisson. The first judge assigned to the Romero case survived an assassination attempt and fled the country. A subsequent judge fumbled a US extradition request for a key participant in the murder, and El Salvador's congress refused to lift d'Aubuisson's immunity, who was by then a powerful ARENA congressman.[6]

As the investigation dragged on and the atrocities continued, Washington remained largely silent. Just a few months after Romero's assassination, a death squad raped and shot a group of US nuns. The US ambassador to the United Nations later suggested the nuns were "political activists." The crime was never

---

6 His son would become an important politician in his own right, and three of his nephews would become some of the most important and prolific chroniclers of El Salvador's street gangs, including the MS-13.

solved. As the bodies of union leaders, political opponents and clergy piled up, the State Department blocked human rights groups from visiting.

Meanwhile, war began. In October 1980, four rebel factions came together to form the FMLN. In January 1981, the guerrillas launched what became known as the "final offensive," an ambitious but ultimately ill-fated attempt to topple the government. Days later, President Carter asked Congress for $5.7 million in military supplies for El Salvador, and US Special Forces flew in from Panama to train several crack units in El Salvador against the guerrillas. They called them Rapid Deployment Infantry Battalions (Batallones de Infantería de Reacción Inmediata, BIRI).

5.

David, Norman's brother, became a bitter government soldier, at war as much with his family as he was with the guerrillas. Norman said his tour took him to the Guazapa volcano, a traditional stronghold of the FMLN, where he and several others were taken captive. The rebels, Norman said, tortured them for months until the army arranged a prisoner swap. The experience cemented David's ire toward his mother and, by extension, his family.

When David returned home around 1986, Norman hardly recognized him. Norman was becoming the clown of the family, a reckless kid who sought attention amidst a sea of siblings and half siblings. But David was serious. He imposed a strict curfew on Norman and his brother Rodrigo, who was also unruly. Norman described Rodrigo as the "more sinister" and "ambitious" of the two. But, he added, he had a "good heart" and was a "good brother."

"If he has money, he'll give it to you without thinking twice," he told me. "He wants people to like him."

Others in the family also tried to create structure for Norman and Rodrigo. Norman's other brother, Gabrielito, could see his younger siblings were in need of guidance, so he tried to impart good habits, forcing them to shine their shoes, for example, before going to school. When Rodrigo and Norman would fight, Gabrielito would intervene. Norman felt protected by Gabrielito, who became a kind of surrogate father.

"He was the one who always had my back," he told me.

Gabrielito would sometimes pick up Norman and Rodrigo after school. At the bakery he would buy them sweet bread and a soft drink, then bring them to the car repair shop where he worked. The garage specialized in fixing and reselling cars that had been in accidents. At the shop, Gabrielito would teach his younger brothers the basics of car maintenance. There they absorbed the culture that shaped young men: talk of women, drinking and partying; struggles with bosses, strict fathers and religious mothers; bravado and violence.

Norman's other brother, Miguel Ángel—who escaped the army the day David was forced into service—became a *cobrador*, collecting bus fares. On Saturdays, he would sometimes take Norman and Rodrigo to the capital of the neighboring province, where they would eat *tamale de sal*, a salty version of the Central American staple wrapped in plantain leaf, and *elote*, a smoked ear of corn.

Between them, Norman's siblings tried to keep an eye on him and Rodrigo. The only physical abuse from his childhood that Norman mentioned to me came from David, who would slap him on the back of the head when he didn't know the answer to a question on his homework. Norman's mother didn't approve.

"How do you expect him to get smarter if you keep hitting him?" she would ask.

David didn't care. He barely spoke to his mother after she left him at the barracks. Instead, he drowned himself in alcohol. At one point, Norman found an Alcoholics Anonymous pamphlet buried in his brother's stuff. He had obviously gone to a meeting, but he'd kept drinking anyway.

One day, while on leave, David came home drunk. Norman's dad was at the house and an argument ensued. David and his father started to fight, while his mother cried. After his father left the house that day, David could not hold back his anger.

"Why did you leave me in the army?" he screamed at his mother. "You don't know how I suffered!"

6.

In early December 1981, the Salvadoran army sent the first of its US-trained BIRI to Morazán, the northwest province along the border with Honduras. The battalion was named the Atlacatl, after an indigenous leader who led a resistance army against the Spanish conquistadors. Their mission was to hunt leftist insurgents. They were trained to shoot at anything, the *New Yorker*'s Mark Danner wrote in his detailed account of the events that would follow that December. Decorated in skull and serpent insignia, they reportedly murdered animals and drank their blood. The ritual culminated with a fight song:

We are going forth to kill.

A mountain of terrorists!

The fight for Morazán pitted FMLN Commander Joaquín Villalobos against Lieutenant Colonel Domingo Monterrosa. Villalobos, who, with his skinny frame and angular face looked more school teacher than guerrilla commander, had created an insurgent radio transmission called *Radio Venceremos*—roughly translated as "We Will Win Radio." Monterrosa, who was often photographed with aviators spread across his wide jowls, looked like a poster child of a Latin American military dictator and was obsessed with *Radio Venceremos*. He would expend more than a few helicopters to destroy it; and eventually, it would lead him to his final, fatal mistake.

The December 1981 government offensive was dubbed Operation Rescue. Trucks, airplanes and helicopters carried as many as four thousand soldiers to the region. According to the CIA, a third of El Salvador's army participated. Support troops corralled the zone, blocking passage to the south, while the Atlacatl pressed north, deploying from the helicopters in small batches.

The government began operations in Perquín, a guerrilla stronghold, banging on doors and carting suspected rebels and collaborators into the woods to interrogate them. Forces then spread to the neighboring villages: El Mozote, Los Toriles, Arambala and La Joya. When I visited the region years later, two survivors from La Joya recalled the way the army spent two days laying camp, creating security perimeters and sending scouts to scan the neighboring towns.

Few believed a massacre was imminent, even though El Mozote and La Joya were guerrilla strongholds. One of the survivors of the La Joya massacre remembered the first time she saw what they euphemistically called *los muchachos*. They were gathered on an open field where the locals played soccer. She had seven young children, and the guerrilla leader told her that if she gave his forces beans and rice and a little bit of money, they would not take her children to war. She obeyed, relinquishing a few dollars per month from her earnings washing hammocks. A year later, the guerrilla leader recruited her eldest son anyway. "The war," he told her coldly, "will not be won with food or money. It will be won at the end of a gun, and if you want to try and take him back, you will take his dead body."

These guerrillas—who were under the command of Villalobos—called themselves the People's Revolutionary Army (Ejército Revolucionario del Pueblo, ERP). The ERP was a faction of the FMLN.

Raúl Mijango was part of the ERP operating in and around Morazán. A mid-level commander, he was known for his stamina, his stealth operations and his surprisingly accommodating political positions—he was not like those dogmatic Marxist-

Leninists. He was a Trotskyite, with a dash of social democrat. But in war, he was a fierce soldier. He'd trained in Nicaragua and Cuba and carried an AK-47 assault rifle he claimed was a gift from Fidel Castro himself.

The ERP operated in small groups—about forty to forty-five—concentrating in areas like La Joya where the army presence was sparse. When soldiers did come, they could expect hostilities—ambushes, booby traps and snipers. Just a few months prior to Operation Rescue, for example, the guerrillas had ambushed the army in La Joya, forcing them to retreat. The attack, as the United Nations Truth Commission later noted, was embarrassing.

By December 1981, the Salvadoran army no longer attempted to distinguish between rebel combatants and non-combatants in the territories held by the FMLN. There were only insurgent states and non-insurgent states. Morazán was an insurgent state, as were its villages, from El Mozote to La Joya.

7.

One night, Norman's mother woke him and Rodrigo and told them to pack. It was 2:00 a.m. They were going to visit David, who was stationed in the Arce Battalion in San Miguel, one of the headquarters of the infamous BIRI. To get there, they'd have to traverse more than half the country by bus. Most of the trip was uneventful, more adventure than danger. Norman had never left his state, and his excitement was palpable. "I was happy because I was going to see my brother," Norman recalled.

Along the way, their mother met a young man who helped them switch buses. On the next leg of the journey, the man climbed to the roof of the bus. The boys chased after him, riding for a while with the duffel bags and the sacks of rice strapped to the metal girders. It was exhilarating, unforgettable.

They had just passed a dam along one of the country's main

waterways when a guerrilla unit stopped the bus at a checkpoint. Death squads and rebels frequently extorted buses, a practice the gangs would later co-opt. The guerrillas also set up impromptu checkpoints to surprise their enemies. With large weapons, "men with beards," as Norman described them, forced everyone off the bus. They split the men from the women and began checking IDs. The man who had helped them switch buses made sure Norman and Rodrigo were set aside and not checked.

Norman remembers standing next to the bus with Rodrigo while the guerrillas rifled through the passengers' wallets. When they reached Norman and Rodrigo's traveling companion, they found his military ID. He was a soldier. The rebels dragged him behind the bus as the boys looked on. A guerrilla raised his weapon and fired a single gunshot that scattered the man's brains across the pavement.

"I remember his hair moving," Norman told me later. "I started to cry."

As the journey continued the boys were haunted by what they had seen. Rodrigo obsessively recounted the incident, and Norman relived the moment in his dreams. The guerrillas. The guns. The hole in the man's head. The mass of flesh that had spread across the hot asphalt. The memories, he said, "Do not go away. They will never go away."

8.

In late December 1981, *Radio Venceremos* began to issue special reports from northern Morazán. Their interview with Rufina Amaya, a dark-haired middle-aged woman from El Mozote, was bone-chilling. She was the sole surviving witness of the Atlacatl's incursion into town.

Amaya—who would go on to tell her story in nearly exactly the same way to numerous local and foreign correspondents, including the *New Yorker*'s Danner—said the Atlacatl soldiers rounded up the villagers in the town plaza. A short interrogation followed, but it was, according to the Truth Commission, perfunctory. Soldiers separated the men from the women and children, who were placed in houses adjacent to the plaza. Not long afterward, Rufina heard pleading and screams. The soldiers began marching the men blindfolded toward neighboring hamlets in groups of five or six where they were shot. When two men, including Rufina's husband, tried to run, the soldiers gunned them down, then pulled out machetes and hacked off their heads.

The killing continued like this for several hours until there were no more men. The soldiers then removed the youngest girls from the plaza at the point of their bayonets. They were taken to the edge of the village where they were raped and killed, their bodies piled into the houses around the plaza like sacks of coffee.

Rufina, who died in 2007, told Danner that the women in her small group, who were marching to their deaths, saw these bodies and started screaming, clutching each other and falling to their knees. Amidst the chaos, Rufina said she slipped behind a tree and hid, while the soldiers finished the job with her neighbors and burned their lifeless bodies along with the rest of the village. The remaining children were killed inside the houses or dragged to the church, where they were shot and macheted to death just feet from the pulpit. Of the 143 victims forensic doctors exhumed from the area in and around the church, 131 were children under the age of twelve.

"In all instances, troops acted in the same way: They killed anyone they came across, men, women and children, and then set fire to the houses," the Truth Commission wrote.

Other survivors emerged later, including Dorila Márquez, who told me when I visited that she and her family had survived by fleeing to the outer edges of El Mozote. There, they saw the smoke coming from the town center. "It was a strange smell," she said, still haunted by the scent.

José Santos Sánchez, a survivor I met in La Joya, was also scarred by the atrocity. In tears, he recalled what he found five days after the massacre at his mother's house. "A bunch of, I mean, without a head, like when someone weeds a garden and cuts, a bunch of weeds, like that," he tried to explain to me, his voice trailing off. "I buried eleven."

In all, the Atlacatl soldiers had murdered twenty-one of José's relatives at his mother's house, including José's wife, sixteen children, and one pregnant woman. They'd raped at least one of José's in-laws, whom he found with her skirt above her head, her underwear torn off. They'd killed the animals, hacked away the orange trees and destroyed the papaya plants.

Before they left, the gang of soldiers scrawled a message on the wall of their home: "the Atlacatl was here."[7]

On January 27, 1982, after some extraordinary reporting, the *New York Times* and the *Washington Post* published front-page stories of the massacre within a few hours of each other. In all, hundreds had been killed. "The road was littered with animal corpses, cows and horses. In the cornfields behind the houses were more bodies, these unburned by fire but baked in the sun," Alma Guillermoprieto wrote in her gripping account in the *Post*. "In one grouping in a clearing in a field were ten bodies: two elderly people, two children, one infant—a bullet hole in the head—in the arms of a woman, and the rest adults."

The response to early reports was first incredulity and then obfuscation. "Civilians did die during the operation," Assistant Secretary of State Thomas Enders told a congressional committee in February 1982, in what would become the standard US response to the atrocity. "But no evidence could be found to con-

7 In the *New York Times* account of the massacre from 1982, a survivor told the reporter, Raymond Bonner, there was graffiti that said, "the Atlacatl Battalion will return to kill the rest."

firm that government forces systematically massacred civilians. Nor does the number of civilians killed even remotely approach the number being cited in other reports about the incident."

It would take years of international investigations, exhumations, forensic study and an international court to vindicate the early accounts that the army had massacred nearly one thousand people, most of them women and children. The massacre would become, what Danner called, "a central parable of the Cold War." As many as ten US advisors were working directly with the Atlacatl Battalion, and most of the weapons studied by international forensics teams had, according to the Truth Commission, "Discernible head stamps, identifying the ammunition as having been manufactured for the United States Government at Lake City, Missouri… All of the projectiles except one appear to have been fired from United States–manufactured M16 rifles."

Mere hours after the stories of the massacre appeared in print, the Reagan administration—as part of its obligation to assure that the Salvadoran government was "making a concerted and significant effort to comply with internationally recognized human rights" prior to sending further aid—sent a note to Congress certifying that the government was "achieving substantial control over all elements of its own armed forces, so as to bring to an end the indiscriminate torture and murder of Salvadoran citizens by these forces."

Some in Congress protested forcefully, but it was largely lip service, since neither the Democrats nor the Republicans wanted to be blamed for "losing" El Salvador to Marxist-inspired insurgents. During his testimony, Enders told Congress the Reagan administration was about to sign an executive order to allocate $55 million in additional military assistance to the country, adding to the $25 million in military assistance and the $110 million in economic aid that had already been authorized. El Salvador was poised to become the third largest recipient of US aid behind only Israel and Egypt.

9.

Norman's wars, both inside and outside of the home, continued throughout the 1980s. When I spoke to him, he remembered the firefights, how the gentle *pop-pop-pop* of an automatic rifle would rise in volume and fury as it came closer to the house, then fade as the guerrillas fled back into the hills. His mother would rush the kids to their rooms where they would hide under their beds until the shooting drifted away or came to a sudden stop.

The war penetrated the town more permanently in other ways. The military established the Civil Defense, a civilian paramilitary group that carried machetes, handguns and rifles as they patrolled the poor neighborhoods, searching for insurgents. The Civil Defense worked as government informants and sometimes as their proxy death squad. Some Civil Defense members leveraged their positions to steal land or seek revenge on neighbors.

Norman vividly recalled when death squads began roaming his village, searching for "communist" sympathizers. As it was in other parts of the country, the war in Norman's state had divided its citizens into two camps: insurgent and not insurgent. One night, while the family was eating dinner, a group of armed men dressed in all black burst through the back door. Startled, the family leaped from the table with their hands in the air. The men barked orders and then asked the whereabouts of a neighbor.

Norman's brother David was home, and at first, they took him, thinking he was a guerrilla. As they dragged him from the house, David explained that he was an army soldier. They released him and left the house in search of the neighbor who was never seen in the area again. Norman said he didn't know if he'd escaped or had been killed. What he did know is that the neighbor's son would later become a member of the Mara Salvatrucha.

3

THE MAKING OF A STREET GANG

1.

THE FIRST MARA ALEX SANCHEZ REMEMBERS getting shot was a guy they called Cujo, an homage to the Saint Bernard from the Stephen King book turned popular movie. Cujo was the leader of Alex's clique, the Catalina Locos. It was 1985, and the Stoners were evolving from zealous music fans into a criminal street gang. They'd developed a reputation for tenacity but lacked serious weaponry. Their rivals, however, were upping the ante. Cujo took a bullet in a drive-by. The Mara Salvatrucha were stunned.

What do we do? Alex remembers them asking each other.

The answer was, in a word, nothing. Cujo survived, then disappeared from the gang. The Catalina Locos ultimately disbanded, and its former members drifted toward other cliques in the MSS13. The gang was dynamic, not invincible.

Alex floated toward a clique named the Normandie Locos. Normandie Avenue is one of the main north-south arteries of Central Los Angeles, and Alex lived a few blocks away. He knew one of the clique's budding leaders, and a friend from his mother's Jehovah's Witnesses congregation was already a member. While the Catalina Locos were disintegrating, the Normandie were setting themselves apart—keeping close watch on their territory and effectively exploring new revenue streams, specifically around the sale of marijuana and crack cocaine.

The crack epidemic exploded in the 1980s and altered the criminal dynamic in the city. Not since prohibition had a drug engendered such urban violence. This was in part because crack was such a democratic drug—bountiful and cheap, there was a low barrier of entry into the trade. And it was highly addictive, making sales brisk and returns immediate.

The explosion of drug use led to the presumption that drugs were at the heart of gang violence. However, drugs were just one in a confluence of factors that caused homicides to rise throughout the 1980s. Weapons were more available. And new tactics—most notably, drive-by shootings—were increasing across the city.

Some of these murders were related to gang matters: recruits, territory, snitching, drug deals. Others were seemingly more trivial but led to violence all the same: a perceived slight; a long gaze at someone's girlfriend; the wrong colors, tennis shoes or baseball cap; an accidental collision at a party. Violence was not so much a game of logic as a fight for vengeance, after which the chains of retribution spread like spiderwebs.

Alex's new clique, Normandie, was becoming entrenched in this complex, multilayered intergang conflict. The first Mara Salvatrucha Alex knew who got killed was nicknamed Rocky. Alex looked up to Rocky, who was a few years older. When Alex got into fights, Rocky noted Alex's fearlessness with a gentle pat on his back and a whisper, *"Firme."* It was the gang's way of saying *you're a fucking badass.*

About a year after Cujo disappeared, Rocky was lured into what Alex said was a classic trap: a ditching party with girls, liquor and marijuana. When the Crazy Riders saw Rocky go into the building where the party was, they gave chase, weapons drawn. Rocky spotted them and ran, but he was shot from behind, then killed with a blast to the face.

The murder drew the Mara Salvatrucha further into the violent vortex of drugs, guns and vengeance. After Rocky's murder, the Normandie traveled to the heart of Black gang territory in South Central, where the Bloods and the Crips were fighting their own war. They couldn't afford an Uzi, the gangster gun of choice at the time, but they managed to acquire a handgun.

To pay for it, they sold marijuana, $12 a dime bag. But dealing drugs never became a Mara Salvatrucha mainstay. Alex, for instance, says he hated it, in part because the profit-sharing was skewed and the potential jail time for the sellers significant. Those slinging the drugs—and taking the greatest risk—made $2 a bag. The other $10 was split between the gang leader and the wholesaler. So Alex and many of his mara friends just smoked it. "It's like what's the point?" he told me later. "You're barely getting shit."

Around the corner, on Fedora Street, a rival crew known as the Fedora Locos was making good money. Alex told me they weren't so much a gang as an organized group of drug peddlers, or what the Mara Salvatrucha called *traqueteros*.[8]

It's an important distinction. The Mara Salvatrucha was not primarily a moneymaking enterprise. Instead they borrowed and stole from each other. They consumed the products they were supposed to sell. They didn't show up for work. Few wanted to expose themselves to high-risk drug deals or work long hours walking the streets. And they weren't receptive to customer complaints. They floundered, stayed just above breakeven. And in most cases, drug dealing became an individual hobby rather than a gang-wide enterprise.

8 Sometimes spelled *traketeros*.

In contrast, traqueteros were specialists. They set up regular distribution points, had valued customers and made plans for steady expansion. They had a variety of products to satisfy the market—marijuana, cocaine and crack, to name a few. Alex said the Fedora's main distribution point looked and worked like a drive-through with cars lining up for service, and the Fedora guys handing the drugs through their windows. Over time, the Fedora also obtained guns and set up security. They began to contract small-time peddlers, who would pose as day laborers, positioning themselves at the same corners where crew chiefs would pick up underpaid illegal workers for construction and landscaping jobs.

For a while, Alex says the mara coexisted with the Fedora. The Fedora sold the Normandie marijuana or sometimes just gave it to them to sell. This went on for a few years, until some Normandie started stealing from the Fedora. In retribution, Alex says the Fedora killed a Normandie leader named Rata in an alleyway shootout.

Rata was a mentor to Alex, but he was in juvenile detention at the time, helpless to react. His counterparts, however, gathered more weapons. They shot Fedora members, chased them from the neighborhood and redefined terms with the peddlers: *You no longer work for the Fedora; now you work for us.*

By the time Alex got released from juvenile detention, he says the Fedora were dead or banished, and the mara were collecting taxes, *renta*, from local drug dealers. It was the new normal. The Mara Salvatrucha was bad at selling drugs, but it was good at collecting money from those who did.

2.

By the late 1980s, gang violence in Los Angeles was reaching historic levels. According to a study in the *Journal of the American Medical Association* (JAMA), between 1979 and 1994 gang violence killed over 7,200 people. At the tail end of the 1980s and the early 1990s gang-related homicides represented over a third of all the murders in the county.

To deal with this rising violence, the Los Angeles Police Department (LAPD) changed its tactics. Instead of trying to establish a permanent presence, police engineered quick strikes and designed missions to intimidate and overpower entire neighborhoods. They created additional special units, the most notable of which was Community Resources Against Street Hoodlums, or CRASH. CRASH quickly became an effective, albeit blunt means of finding and incarcerating suspected gang members. The group would later earn a notorious reputation when some of its members began to set up a gang-like operation of their own. The police were not the army, but they sometimes acted like they were.

The transformation had begun years earlier. In 1950, the LAPD named Bill Parker as its chief. Parker, a World War II veteran, created a new, military-style training facility complete with drill sergeants and pressed uniforms. Recruits had to meet height requirements and learn tactics like the chokehold. In Parker's police, "No one dared being labeled a sissy boy, snitch and traitor," Joe Domanick wrote in his history of the LAPD.

The macho ethos was passed from generation to generation. Parker's bodyguard and chauffeur was Daryl Gates. Gates, like Parker, was square jawed and thin-skinned—the hard-charging, unapologetic sort that became the prototype of the department and the perfect man to carry on the legacy of his mentor when he became police chief in 1978.

"We went after crime before it occurred," Gates told *Frontline* after he left the force. "Our people went out every single night trying to stop crime before it happened, trying to take people off the street that they believed were involved in crime. And that made us a very aggressive, proactive police department."

In many respects, Parker, Gates and other police chiefs significantly improved the LAPD, making it the envy of other cities.

Corruption fell as they raised standards for recruits, paid higher wages and improved benefits. The LAPD were among the first to create intelligence divisions and Special Weapons and Tactics (SWAT) teams, both of which would become standards in police forces across the US. Plus they knew how to market themselves, lending their name and services to countless television shows and movies over the years.

In 1988, around the time the Normandie's fight with the Fedora was heating up, Gates initiated Operation Hammer, which included widespread gang sweeps and the use of military-grade hardware in dense urban spaces. The police centered their resources on the Black and Latino neighborhoods. The LAPD has fewer police per square mile than most big cities in the United States, forcing it to be more strategic about its use of resources. A report by the Police Foundation published in 1991 noted that LA had just fifteen sworn officers per square mile. By comparison, Chicago had fifty-four; Detroit, thirty-seven; Philadelphia, fifty-one; and New York City, eighty-nine.

Crime was higher in the predominantly Black and Latino areas, as was demand for the police. It was part of the difficult balance the LAPD had to strike in these neighborhoods: communities of color wanted more uniformed officers in their neighborhoods, but many bristled against them when they arrived in force. Gates saw it as a double standard. In a letter to the *Los Angeles Times* at the time, he claimed that the newspaper and "special interest groups" wanted it both ways. "You seemed shocked by the apparent lack of control our community has over gangs and the streets," he wrote. "I am one leader who has aggressively addressed this very problem."

Still, a show of force did not necessarily beget results. Gates once famously piloted a tank with a fourteen-foot battering ram into the side of a house, all with the media in tow. When the team rushed in, they found two women and three children eating ice cream.

It hardly mattered. In 1988, a *Los Angeles Times* poll found that 61 percent approved of Gates's performance. Operation Hammer lasted years, during which city-wide sweeps led to the arrest of thousands, including one notable weekend in which over 1,400 people were taken into custody.

Throughout, violence crept higher and cries of abuse grew. Routine traffic stops often became exercises in humiliation, especially when Blacks and Latinos were spotted in White neighborhoods. Police would often force them to kneel, then to lie on their stomachs with their arms spread out or behind their back—something they called a "prone-out" position. As a federal government commission later wrote, "The practice has created a feeling among many in Los Angeles' minority communities that certain parts of the City are closed to them."

It was a legacy that dated back to the Zoot Suit Riots. Los Angeles had been built on the backs of cheap, nonunion labor—a combination of Blacks coming from the South, unemployed Whites arriving during the Depression, a steady flow of Mexicans, and later, Central Americans. Most police officers were White, including the top brass. The LAPD integrated only in 1961 and spent most of the next two decades struggling to attract officers of color. In the early 1980s, the city mandated that at least 25 percent of all new recruits would be minorities or women. Later, the police faced accusations that it stymied these same new recruits.

In 1994, the American Civil Liberties Union said 83 percent of LA policemen lived outside the city. It was little wonder why many residents perceived them as an occupying army. Gates's own statements often made it worse. Early in his tenure, he suggested Blacks' "veins or arteries do not open up as fast as they do in normal people," after a study found that a disproportionate number of Blacks were dying because of the chokeholds the police had learned at the academy. Indeed, between 1975 and 1982, the LAPD would choke fifteen people to death, more than any other department in the country.

3.

One day, just after Alex turned fifteen, his mom got a phone call from his school. Alex had missed class, again. Furious, she stormed into his room.

"I'm going to send you home!" she screamed, referring to El Salvador.

By then, Alex didn't want to go back. He had friends, access to drugs and alcohol and was enjoying himself in Los Angeles. He was fed up with his mom's rants, her beatings and the Jehovah's Witnesses that hovered around their house. Although he had a broken arm at the time, he grabbed her car keys, tumbled from the second-floor window into the urine-stained driveway, and drove away.

Alex spent most of the next few years on the streets, only returning to his mother's apartment for short stints when he was released from juvenile hall or, later, from prison. Alex was not alone. He said there was a steady group of about a dozen mara bouncing from place to place.

Homelessness was common in gangs, a natural byproduct of broken homes, abusive guardians and traumatic childhoods. The abuse often intensified on the streets. For a while, Alex said he lived with other Mara Salvatrucha in the basement of a man's home. In lieu of rent, the gang members offered the owner stolen items, which he could resell. The mara attracted girls, many of whom were also runaways, and the group in turn attracted older men who solicited sex from the girls and the boys. A mini-criminal economy formed.

It did not last. A gang member would see a man trying to pick up his girlfriend, and the mara would jump him. The owner also grew tired of the Mara Salvatrucha because they destroyed his basement. As the gang decamped to abandoned homes and empty apartment buildings a pattern emerged: the mara would create a mini-criminal economy, make a little money, party and eventually destroy the property. Toilets overflowed. Empty milk cartons and hot dog packages piled up in the corners. Crack pipes and liquor bottles were strewn across the hallways. It was time to move on to the next *destroyer.* The name caught on, eventually becoming a catch-all. A destroyer is still a crash-pad, a party-place, a meeting spot, a stash house, a torture chamber, a brothel or all of the above.

On the streets, Alex's run-ins with the police multiplied. He and a fellow gang member began robbing people who had jewelry or looked like they might have money. When that didn't work, they went into the local grocery store and shoplifted ham, cheese and bread. When they got caught, the security guards would sometimes call their parents, other times call the police.

Some police officers were worse than others. The Rampart Division in Central Los Angeles had a particularly violent reputation. Alex said he and other mara would commit crimes in Rampart, then run to another territory because they didn't want to be captured by that division. "They would beat the shit out of us," Alex said. "And they would take us to rival neighborhoods and just drop us off and, on the loudspeakers, say who it was. 'Hey, you're so and so from MS!' And then they would just take off and all of sudden you would have people coming out and you wouldn't have a choice but to run after the cop car."

The division was attempting to wrest control from an area spinning out of its grasp, but its violent tactics were a problem. In one case chronicled by a federal commission, police chased down a twenty-four-year-old Latino suspect who'd hidden under a stairwell after crashing his car. Incensed, the police pounded the suspect into submission, and he lost an eye because of the excessive force. The victim sued the LAPD for $177,000.

A report about the division by the LAPD described what it called "Rampart culture." This included hazing new arrivals—getting them to wash the squad cars, load shotguns and make sure other equipment was ready—as well as a slow indoctrination in the harsh ways of dealing with suspects. Between 1994–1998, the period the LAPD studied, Rampart police pursued suspects at double the rate of other divisions and injured them at three times the rate. Their use of force rate was higher, and their suspects were injured in these cases 59 percent of the time, the highest percentage in the city.

Questions about their tactics were often dismissed with the mantra: *It's the Rampart way*. Rampart officers collected mementos from their forays into gang territory—hats, T-shirts and other paraphernalia—a kind of war-time booty. Some division officers even designed their own logo: a skull and a spread of cards they called The Deadman's Hand. "What separated the Rampart culture from the rest of the department was the frequently heard chorus, 'We do things differently here,'" the LAPD report read. "Though not unique, this type of mentality was significantly more pronounced and pervasive at Rampart than in other divisions."

The rough tactics didn't affect Alex and his mara friends. In some ways, it made them more brazen. On the street, getting arrested and beaten by police was a badge of honor and a rite of passage. Alex was in and out of juvenile hall throughout the 1980s. Assault. Robbery. Breaking and entering. Defacing property. One time, he got out in the morning after a 14-month stint in prison and was in jail again by that evening, captured in the act of spray painting a wall with the words "I'm back."

4.

In 1987, Los Angeles County filed the first gang injunction against the Playboy Gangster Crips in what was then known as the Cadillac-Corning area. Other injunctions followed—including one against the Mara Salvatrucha in Hollywood. California was becoming the testing ground for antigang measures that would later be implemented across the country and eventually abroad.

The Youth Justice Coalition called the injunctions a kind of "group restraining order." They established curfews, restricted the use of beepers, prohibited associating with known gang members or wearing certain colors or clothing considered gang paraphernalia in designated areas. These practices were later copied by other states because they gave police more power to interpret and enforce the law as it suited them in areas where crime was the highest.

The injunctions had an immediate, if not long-lasting impact on crime rates, which in Los Angeles were double the national average. Indeed, the Police Foundation study from 1991 showed that Los Angeles officers dealt with nearly twice the number of crimes than their New York City counterparts. In some respects, Los Angeles's residents sympathized and appreciated the effort: the study said the LAPD had the second fewest citizen complaints among the big cities, and a 1988 *Los Angeles Times* poll revealed the LAPD had a 74 percent job approval rating.

But some criticized the measures, saying they created a kind of generalized stop-and-frisk policy, effectively criminalizing already marginalized neighborhoods. Mass arrests that swept up innocents became commonplace. Family members were sometimes prohibited from contacting or spending time with one another. Critics also noted how injunctions worked in tandem with gentrification—injunction areas frequently abutted areas with increasing property values or those undergoing revitalization, as was the case of the injunction against the Playboy Gangster Crips in Cadillac-Corning.

What's more, the injunctions were also seen as racial profiling, since the gangs they targeted were almost exclusively Black and Latino. The irony was that determining who was a gang member was largely ad hoc—a combination of intuition, interrogation and observation. Some gang members were relatively easy to identify. Alex, for instance, had *Mara*, in small letters, and *Salvatrucha*, in large letters, inked across his chest—a marker that would haunt him in later judicial proceedings. But others were subtle, making gang designation more of an art than a science. Over the years, states would struggle with this question. By 2016, there would be forty-four different definitions of gangs in state laws across the country.

There were additional questions regarding gang affiliation: Just who was a gang member, and when did a member become a member? For the Mara Salvatrucha, it was the formal "beating in" initiation known as *el brinco*. But for many police and prosecutors, gang affiliation started well before then, when wannabes "posted up"—doing surveillance, acting as couriers and performing other errands to prove their loyalty and gain the confidence of the gang. The gang's network stretched well beyond these *postes* or *paros*, as these lookouts were known in mara lingo. Family members, friends, taxi drivers, mechanics, bus drivers, waiters, politicians, prosecutors, police and many others all did favors, willingly and unwillingly, for the gang, which begged the question: Were they also gang members?

The confusion about what constituted a gang and who was a member did not stop the crackdowns. In 1988, the California state legislature passed the Street Terrorism Enforcement and Prevention Act. The STEP Act effectively criminalized "gang affiliation"; it required those convicted of gang offenses to register using fingerprints and photographs, and to notify authorities whenever they moved; and it set up "gang enhancements," which added years on sentences for many crimes committed in service of the gang.

To prosecute alleged gang members, the act legally defined what a gang was for the first time in California. "Any ongoing organization, association, or group of three or more persons, whether formal or informal, having as one of its primary activities the commission of one or more of the criminal acts," referring to a list that included robbery, assault, extortion, and money laundering. It added that the gang should have "a common name or common identifying sign or symbol, and whose members individually or collectively engage in or have engaged in a pattern of criminal gang activity."

In a dangerously flawed attempt to fit the gangs into a recognizable category, lawmakers seemed to be drawing from commonly used definitions of sophisticated organized crime groups. However, as the case of the Mara Salvatrucha illustrated, gangs had different origins, purpose, hierarchy, recruiting, and modus operandi than groups like La Cosa Nostra. Unlike mafias—who controlled unions, got government contracts, and ran sophisticated multinational enterprises, among other elaborate schemes—the Mara Salvatrucha could barely manage the traqueteros in the neighborhoods under their purview. A gang is, as Joan Moore once wrote, "an adolescent group, not a unit in a massively organized crime syndicate."

California's definition was not just a linguistic mishap. It was yet another fundamental misunderstanding of who the gangs were and another accelerant in the vicious cycle of gang violence and state repression.

The Mara Salvatrucha's battles on the streets were about to make it even worse.

5.

In late 1989, there was a party on the second story of an apartment building near the corner of Normandie and Martin Luther King Jr. Boulevard just a few blocks southwest of the University of Southern California. Some Mara Salvatrucha went; so did members of the 18th Street.

At the time, the two gangs coexisted despite the violence swirling around them. The 18th Street were an established brand. Founded in the 1960s by Chicanos, they dressed a little like pachucos with fedoras and oversized suits, and drove low riders through the wide Los Angeles thoroughfares. For a time, the 18th Street opened its doors to other immigrant groups, recruiting a mix of Latinos, Romanians, Samoans, Whites and Blacks. Later it restricted its membership to Latinos only, becoming one of the few gangs that had a mix of local and recently arrived Latinos of various nationalities.

The Mara Salvatrucha, on the other hand, were carving their own path. With their long hair, heavy metal music and ripped jeans, the mara were impetuous, rambunctious, irreverent and ferocious.

Still, the two were born next to each other—18th Street is a short, three-block stretch between Arapahoe and St. Bonnie Brae in Pico-Union. Both gangs drew from the same refugees to fill their ranks, and the mara eventually also opened their doors to Latinos from various countries. They'd grown up together on the same playgrounds, went to school together and dated each other's sisters. According to journalists Carlos Martínez[9] and José Luis Sanz, who have documented the origins of the 18th Street/Mara Salvatrucha rivalry, gang members sometimes even shared territory, swapped colors and shared each other's signs—the *E* for *18*, and devil horns for the mara. "If the Mara Salvatrucha ever had a brother in Los Angeles, his name was Barrio 18," Martínez and Sanz eloquently write, using the Spanish-language name of the 18th Street.

At the time, the city was focused on violence in predominantly Black neighborhoods, which had the highest homicide rates. Yet, according to the JAMA study cited earlier, more than 56 percent of the victims of gang violence during this period were Hispanic. And 40 percent of the gang-related homicides happened in the central district, where the Mara Salvatrucha,

9 One of three nephews of Roberto d'Aubuisson, who has become a prolific chronicler of gangs in the region.

the 18th Street and dozens of other Latino gangs were most prevalent.

In this environment the main organizing principle was violence. The mara was using whatever weapons they could find to wield power, including machetes, which they hid beneath their clothes. The fierce metal blade had an added psychological impact on their would-be rivals. Most kept their distance, fearful of how it could carve a deep hole into their shoulder, their thigh, or their skull. Machetes had other advantages as well: they were cheap and legal.

The mara also had experience with guns and military tactics. Some were ex-soldiers, including at least one former member of the Atlacatl battalion, who was appropriately nicknamed El Soldado (The Soldier). Others were ex-guerrillas. They could manage weapons and munitions, and they understood how to control physical space, obtain and use intelligence and counterintelligence, and spread propaganda.

But mostly, the Mara Salvatrucha were just relentless. And when they lost, they could draw replacements from the near constant flow of Salvadoran refugees to LA, many of whom were coming from broken families and suffering from severe trauma—near perfect mara recruits. By 1989, the gang counted numbers in the hundreds. The marabunta—that inexorable army of ants—knew how to overwhelm any rival.

In Central LA in particular, the mara were squeezing against other gangs. In his seminal work on the Mara Salvatrucha based on years of observations and interviews, the anthropologist Tom Ward says the mara and the 18th Street were beginning to fight over recruits during this time, and, in some cases, over members who wanted to switch from one gang to the other. By the late 1980s, renta from drug dealers and others was also rising. Central Los Angeles was an extremely crowded gang market.

"Enemies are usually created by proximity," Ward noted.

Alex Sanchez didn't go to the party on Normandie and Martin

Luther King Jr. that night, but he remembered that tensions were rising between the two gangs, in part because the 18th Street felt the Mara Salvatrucha "were disrespecting them." As a legacy Chicano gang, the 18th Street looked down on the mara. It wasn't so much a relationship between brothers, like Sanz and Martínez described it, as it was an experienced uncle viewing with contempt his upstart nephew.

The gathering itself was nothing special. Alcohol and marijuana flowed freely with a lively mix of music amongst what Moore might describe as "an adolescent group." Yet these are typically the spaces where conflict is hypercharged, and the chains of retribution explode.

In their book *The Hollywood Kid*, Óscar Martínez and his brother Juan José[10] say tensions began when the Mara Salvatrucha arrived at the party to find one of their former members had joined the 18th Street. They didn't mind, they said, as long as they could beat him out of the gang—a kind of reverse version of el brinco. The 18th Street assented, then watched as the mara pounded him. The fight escalated from there: an 18th Street challenged a marero to a one-on-one. After they fought to exhaustion, another fight followed. This time El Soldado, the former Atlacatl member, badly beat an 18th Street member.

There are, of course, variations of this story. Numerous mara told Martínez and Sanz that it started over a woman, who was at the center of a heated discussion between two gang members from opposite sides of Pico-Union, one of whom was a Mara Salvatrucha named Shaggy. Ward also says he heard the same story about the party and the fight over a woman, among other theories, although in his version the mara was named Scrappy. (It should be noted that Ward used pseudonyms and composite characters in his book.)

All the versions align on one central fact: at some point in the evening, a group of 18th Street members retrieved an automatic

10 The other two nephews of Roberto d'Aubuisson.

weapon and sprayed the Mara Salvatrucha, leaving Shaggy to bleed to death.

The multiplicity of accounts here reflects the larger complexity of inter-gang dynamics. Gang violence cannot be easily distilled into simple narratives, and motive is almost always slippery. Ultimately the muddled beginnings of this fight have serviced the gangs. Predecessors no longer know why they're fighting, but the rivalry has provided meaning and purpose to these gangs and fueled their expansion.

"I hate, therefore I exist," Martínez and Martínez write in their book, *The Hollywood Kid.*

Word of the attack spread quickly, in part because of the familiarity between the two groups. One gang member told Martínez and Sanz that the Mara Salvatrucha responded by picking up an 18th Street member who was walking through Normandie territory, and torturing and killing him in a destroyer. The 18th Street responded in kind. Alex, who knew Shaggy, told Martínez and Sanz that by the time he and others in the Mara Salvatrucha moved to quell the squabble, four others had already been killed.

In less than twenty-four hours, the 18th Street had gone from family to archenemy. Neither gang would ever be the same.

4

THE GHOST OF WILLIAM WALKER

1.

CORPORAL ERNESTO DERAS PACKED HIS THINGS. He and his military unit were going for some R&R. They needed it.

They had spent the previous week battling FMLN guerrillas around the Guazapa volcano, the rebel stronghold. Just fifteen miles from San Salvador, the wide, sloping, 4,500-foot volcano had become a symbol of government ineptitude and the insurgency's fortitude. Despite two major offensives that included as many as 10,000 troops and aerial bombardments, as well as regular assaults by smaller battalions like Ernesto's, the military could not dislodge the estimated 1,500 communist fighters from the volcano.

"The guerrilla force," the Associated Press declared at the time, "has established itself as a virtual parallel state—providing security, education and health services."

The fight was exhausting, and Ernesto and the others in his unit were in a good mood as they made their way to the barracks. But word was trickling through the ranks that the FMLN was planning to strike the capital, San Salvador. The date was November 11, 1989. The FMLN and the army had been trading volleys for nearly a decade, and the war had reached a stalemate. If the Guazapa volcano was a symbol of the army's impotence, San Salvador was a sign of the FMLN's limits. The guerrillas had decided that an assault on the capital city—another so-called "final offensive" nearly ten years after their first "final offensive"—would jolt the ruling class, who had ignored a series of demands the rebels had made shortly after the election of Alfredo Cristiani, the right-wing ARENA party presidential candidate.

Ernesto and his unit arrived at their base only to get new orders: *shower, clean your weapons, pack your gear and prepare for battle*. From there, they went to a town on the eastern edge of the city, where their job was to cover the perimeter of San Salvador.

Ernesto considered himself a solid if not spectacular soldier. He was skinny but sinewy and wily. He took pride in being part of the army. He was, he said, "committed," so much so that he'd tattooed the name of his battalion to his arm.

Ernesto was just settling into his cot, drifting into a slumber when he heard the first shots. It was close to midnight. He grabbed his US-made assault rifle, and scrambled out the door with his unit. Some groups headed west toward the glow of the city, but his went east toward the darkness and the sound of the gunfire.

As they reached the edge of town, the sergeant slowed the unit to a virtual crawl. Ernesto didn't like the sergeant. Few did. Years later, he would tell me this was normal in the army, especially when the commanders had risen through the military academy without having first spilled blood on the battlefield. Under different circumstances Ernesto might've held his tongue, but on this night, his frustrations boiled over.

"You know what, Sergeant, when you say something, they have to do it. Why don't you take point? Are you afraid? Come on!"

2.

The FMLN offensive was as much a political assault as it was a military one. Behind the scenes, third parties—including high-level officials from the Catholic Church, and foreign leaders from Costa Rica and Mexico—had been pushing for a cease-fire. In September 1989, the government and the FMLN had signed the first of what would become the Chapultepec Peace Accords, named for the Mexican castle where they were forged.

The signing of these first accords signaled the beginning of the end of a war that had torn the country to pieces. Thousands had died. Tens of thousands more had resettled in the cities, causing rapid, forced urbanization that would have lasting effects on the region's security and stability. In 1970, El Salvador was 60 percent rural, 40 percent urban. By 1989, it was nearly 50–50; by 2020, it would be 70 percent urban.

At the same time, US businesses and politicians were agitating for free markets and deregulation, which, in theory, would create opportunity and bring wealth to a wider subset within poor countries like El Salvador. Ultimately, this series of economic policies, known collectively as the "Washington Consensus," modestly lowered poverty rates and decreased inequality. But the Consensus would also leave countries like El Salvador even more dependent on foreign investment, multilateral bank loans and remittances, which some argued were the real reason inequality and poverty dropped.

Yet for people like Cristiani and his right-wing supporters, the policies allowed them to become stewards of the neoliberal service economy promulgated by those forging the Consensus. A graduate of Georgetown who'd married into an elite coffee-growing family, the finely cut, well-dressed, English-speaking president was a near perfect emissary for this transitional period. At the behest of his US patrons, he began preparing to privatize state entities, lower tariffs and create lucrative incentives for foreign investment, which had plummeted during the war. His Central American neighbors were doing the same.

There were positives to neoliberalism. In this new paradigm, dirty wars of the type waged in El Salvador were bad for business. ARENA, for instance, chose Cristiani over Roberto d'Aubuisson, the charismatic, popular major-turned-congressman who'd founded the party. D'Aubuisson's blunt politics and death squad connections made him an international liability, even for the US government. While many Salvadoran elites privately supported d'Aubuisson's tactics—and the bodies of activists, union leaders, students and catechists continued to pile up—the Reagan administration subtly sought to undermine the volatile leader. When Vice President George H. W. Bush visited the country in 1983, for instance, he condemned the death squads and demanded the removal of army officers connected to human rights abuses. After the visit, d'Aubuisson, never one to back down, allegedly hatched a plot to kill the US ambassador.

War was also expensive. By 1989, Washington was providing about $1.5 million a day to El Salvador's security forces, its deepest involvement in a conflict since Vietnam. In all, the US had spent close to a $1 billion during the previous decade of fighting. At the same time, El Salvador had become a domestic burden for the US. The refugee crisis was beginning to have residual effects in Los Angeles and beyond as the Mara Salvatrucha added handguns to its stockpile of machetes.

Los Angeles had long since implemented its own version of neoliberalism: nonunion labor, limited government regulation, lax zoning laws, the steady erosion of the social safety net and an aggressive police force. Now the system was going international. Capital was about to get a visa. Workers, meanwhile, were going to get fewer benefits, less job security, and, when they tried to cross into other countries to find work, treated like criminals. It was little wonder, perhaps, that LA had more street gangs than anywhere else in the United States. For those paying attention, it was a preview of what was to come in El Salvador.

The fight over El Salvador's neoliberal soul began on Halloween, 1989, when right-wing forces exploded a bomb at the San Salvador headquarters of FENASTRAS, one of the country's most powerful unions. The blast killed ten, including a union leader named Febe Elizabeth Velásquez. The FMLN would commemorate the offensive in her name.

3.

The first dead man Ernesto ever saw was next to a coffee farm. Coffee was the nation's top export, and Ernesto had grown up in Santa Ana, the Salvadoran epicenter of the industry. For a time in the 1970s, El Salvador was the world's fourth largest coffee producer. By the mid-1980s, when Ernesto found the dead body, the industry was in a downward spiral. Exports had dropped an estimated 20 percent since the fighting started.

The war was by then a central part of Salvadoran life. Ernesto would hear the artillery and gunfire in the distance and see the soldiers pass by his house. It was around then that he saw the dead man lying next to the coffee farm. The man showed signs of torture: his fingers were cut off and burn marks singed his naked corpse. Things got worse. Ernesto says death squads left three heads on a spike. The torsos were never found. He also heard about a woman who'd had her breasts cut off.

To survive, Ernesto and his family lived in a bubble of their own making. They clung to the belief that if you were tortured, your head placed on a spike, or your breast sheered off with a knife, you were obviously guilty of something.

"My family, we just knew that the people they killed were

part of the guerrillas, were doing something wrong," he told me later. "And us? Well, we just had faith that we weren't involved in any of that."

Ernesto was the youngest of eight children. His father died of cancer when he was seven, leaving his family rudderless. Ernesto started skipping school and stopped doing his homework. When he took a weapon to school, the administrators expelled him.

By then, Ernesto had started hanging with what were broadly termed maras, El Salvador's primitive version of the street gangs of today. They had disputes over territory, but the maras—which did not yet include the Mara Salvatrucha or the 18th Street—were still relatively harmless by today's standards. Ernesto's mara was about twenty strong. They named themselves the Mara San Juan after their neighborhood.

At first, Ernesto says he and his friends fought other maras with slingshots, but eventually they graduated to chains and, in some rare cases, machetes. When I talked to him, Ernesto played down the violence. He claimed it was more about finding friends than the thrill that came from fighting.

"It was just normal. I mean you have friends, and you hang out with them," he told me. "You play soccer. You go to dances. You *hang* with them."

But Ernesto liked the fighting, and from a young age, he wanted to be soldier. When he played war with his friends the bad guys were always the guerrillas. He loved the uniforms, especially the camouflage pants, and the idea of a shared vision. The army could offer affirmation and community.

After joining the military, Ernesto became a member of BIRI, the rapid deployment umbrella force sponsored by the US. There were, in fact, six BIRI, including Ernesto's group, Belloso, which trained at Fort Bragg, North Carolina, earning it the nickname Gringo Battalion. Like the Atlacatl, the army used the Belloso for its dirty work and also like the Atlacatl, it was linked to several civilian massacres, including one in 1983 in Chalatenango.

There, according to the *Boston Globe*, "The troops killed hundreds of civilians, torched villages, burned crops and chased thousands of peasants into the mountains, where they survived on tortillas and, when necessary, leaves."

Ernesto joined the Belloso a few years after the massacre at Chalatenango and went through a three-month basic training in El Salvador, learning how to manage his US-made M16 assault rifle, an M60 machine gun, and an M203 grenade launcher. The army also got him into physical and mental shape. He would eventually tattoo *BIRI* across his bicep—a knife cutting between the I and the R—and *Belloso* on his upper deltoid.

In battle Ernesto operated a .50 caliber machine gun. The gun was so heavy it had to be broken into pieces—each piece carried by an individual soldier—but its potency made it worth the effort. The rounds, which were over two inches long, could tear through a guerrilla's body at a distance of a quarter mile. Being part of the .50 caliber rifle detail might have saved him. Ernesto lived most of the war from the safe distance the rifle afforded him.

But on the night of November 11, 1989, as the first cracks of gunfire marked the guerrillas' final offensive, Ernesto felt vulnerable. Traversing the dark mountainside behind their shaky commander, Ernesto decided to take point. As his unit made it to the top of a ridge overlooking the cornfields, he scanned the horizon, spotting a group dressed in camouflage in the distance.

"What are they?" he asked the soldier behind him.

It was an important question. His unit was alone—a dozen men led by an inexperienced sergeant. The other unit in the distance looked to be about one-hundred strong.

4.

To organize the attack, FMLN commanders had gathered in Managua, Nicaragua. It was a fitting backdrop. Nicaragua was where William Walker, the infamous soldier of fortune, had bullied his way into the presidency in the mid-1850s, setting the stage for decades of US intervention in the region. Nicaragua was also the first domino to fall when Sandinista rebels overthrew a US-backed dictatorship in 1979. The Reagan administration spent millions trying to dislodge the Sandinista government, and by 1989, the country had become the epicenter of the Cold War in Central America.

Among those in attendance in Managua was rebel commander Joaquín Villalobos, the professorial-looking guerrilla commander who'd led the ERP faction against Lieutenant Colonel Domingo Monterrosa's Atlacatl in Morazán. Villalobos had proven to be an expert strategist, goading his enemies into serious military blunders. For years after the massacre in El Mozote and La Joya, for example, Monterrosa continued his quest to destroy *Radio Venceremos*, and in 1984, appeared to have achieved his goal when his troops captured what looked to be a transmitter after a skirmish with guerrillas. As Monterrosa packed the war trophy into his helicopter, Villalobos's forces watched and waited. Once the helicopter flew into view, the rebels detonated the bomb hidden in the fake transmitter, killing Monterrosa and thirteen others on board.

Another attendee in Managua was a stout rebel commander named Salvador Sánchez Cerén. Sánchez Cerén was head of a hardline faction of the FMLN and El Salvador's future president. Guerrillas like Villalobos and Sánchez Cerén were astute historians and political analysts, and they could smell a weary foe. An offensive, they felt, was a way to accelerate peace talks and to establish a strong position at the negotiating table. (Sánchez Cerén would employ the same tactic years later against street gangs.) The FMLN command had divided the country into four major areas, each with a strategic headquarters, and the rebels decided they would target battalions in each, as well as launch a full-frontal assault on San Salvador and its periphery.

The battle was also ideological. The Berlin Wall fell in early November 1989, just days before the offensive began, leading to a mini-existential crisis within the leftist FMLN. Even the

Sandinistas in Nicaragua, which until then appeared to be in a strong political position, were about to be ousted from power. To prepare their troops for battle, the FMLN commanders created a refrain: *"Hasta el tope y punto."*

"To the end, period."

And then they went, in groups one-hundred strong toward the city, where units like Ernesto's spotted them. Ernesto grabbed a pair of binoculars. It was dark, but he could see there was something different about the soldiers in the distance. It wasn't just that their uniforms were a mishmash of different shades of green. A couple of them had rocket-propelled grenades (RPGs) slung over their shoulders. Only the guerrillas used RPGs.

Ernesto guessed they were planning to attack a nearby air force base. Indiscriminate bombing had become a hallmark of the Salvadoran Air Force and thus a favorite target of the insurgents. But before he could react, he felt the whiz of the first bullet go past his head. Ernesto and his unit scrambled to lower ground, but the guerrillas were coming from the other side as well.

As they cowered, the gunfire continued. Rocks and dirt fell on them, and it was difficult to get a shot off. Ernesto and his unit were more accustomed to battling in the mountains, where heavy brush protected them from the rebels. From afar, you could shoot at will, which created a false sense of security. The Salvadoran soldiers would expend hundreds of rounds firing blindly into the foliage, Ernesto told me, in the mistaken belief they were killing rebels by the bushel. On the other side, the guerrillas seemed to be mocking them, using their sparse supplies of munitions to inflict maximum damage, then carting their dead away to keep the army from enjoying their small victories.

Ernesto's unit was now in a full-scale panic. They called for reinforcements, and the army sent helicopters. But the gunfire from the helicopters was nearly hitting them, so they requested they halt the air fire.

Meanwhile, the guerrillas kept them pinned down. The rebels had a sharpshooter, and every time Ernesto raised his head, the sniper would fire. Army soldiers shot back and launched grenades to push the sniper from his position, but they still couldn't escape.

At one point, a bullet grazed Ernesto's leg. Frightened, he raised his arm to fire. This time he felt a powerful blow to his shoulder that knocked him down. Luckily, the bullet went through clean. He was bleeding badly, but ground reinforcements were finally coming.

They had been fighting for three hours, and other soldiers were beginning to arrive on foot, pushing the guerrillas from their positions and taking casualties along the way. By the time the rebels had retreated, a soldier in his unit was dead, and the rescue team had lost as many as four.

5.

The government had expected an offensive, but it did not expect to get humiliated on the world stage. The FMLN attacked the presidential palace and fired shots at Cristiani's residence. They assaulted military barracks in a half-dozen provinces and sent troops into gated communities in the northern part of the capital. By morning the FMLN had overrun Ciudad Delgado, Soyapango, Mejicanos, Apopa, and other areas surrounding San Salvador, and reporters in and around the city were broadcasting the offensive from the rebels' vantage point.

Inside the government, there was panic, frustration and anger. The Salvadoran Air Force began strafing Mejicanos and Apopa. The bombing left buildings in ruins and the casualty rate was high. Wary of the public's reaction towards the indiscriminate bombing, the government scrambled to censor local media and imposed a curfew. By some estimates, as many as 13,000 of the war's 75,000 fatalities came during the twenty-day FMLN final offensive in 1989.

Still, other casualties were harder to hide from public view. Death squads had been active for years. In the aftermath of the war, the National Security Archive and the Human Rights Data Analysis Group published the Yellow Book, a database of just under two thousand targets the army had deemed "delinquent terrorists": people connected to unions and opposition parties, as well as alleged members of the FMLN. For the death squads, there was no distinction between these categories. According to the organizations that published the book, many of those on the list had been "killed or disappeared and never seen again; others were captured, tortured, and later released."

The government often tried to pin these deaths on the guerrillas or justify the use of force on innocent civilians by claiming they were rebels or insurgent sympathizers. It was part of a long-standing pattern. The US government backed the Salvadoran regime and its military, including its US-trained military battalion, even when, as it was a decade earlier, their targets were carrying Bibles, not guns.

6.

Around midnight on November 16, five days after the offensive began, the military deployed Atlacatl troops to the Central American University in San Salvador. Known by its Spanish acronym, UCA, the university is run by Jesuits, and, at the time, it was home to considerable leftist activity. Numerous guerrilla soldiers and commanders had emerged from the UCA, and a few student organizations were openly sympathetic to the FMLN.

From the military's perspective, the professors, namely the Jesuit priests, were the ideological forefathers of the leftist movement. The military would later claim that the priests were providing the rebels with logistical support by helping to store and smuggle weapons during the offensive. No evidence ever supported this claim, but former soldiers like Ernesto still cling to this accusation—even conflating events that happened at other universities—as a means to justify myriad barbarities like the one that would happen at the UCA that November night.

"Those, what do you call them, priests, they faked weddings. The people would pretend they were getting married and the presents they brought were really weapons for the guerrillas,"

Ernesto told me, mistakenly referring to something that occurred at the National University. "It was from that university that the militias came, the protestors, and others who tore the city to shit. All that was political. It wasn't religious."

Right-wing ideologues in the ruling ARENA party echoed this view. Just hours before the Atlacatl Battalion entered the university gates, Roberto d'Aubuisson held a press conference. There, according to a later released CIA memo, d'Aubuisson stood at a chalkboard and "berated" the UCA rector and two other Jesuits by name, claiming the Spanish-born priests had "only come to take power in El Salvador."

"Everything will be taken care of," he reportedly said, without elaborating.

The UCA resembles a US community college. A chain-linked fence surrounds low-rise buildings, rotundas and curvy walkways. Roads wind through a leafy campus. The government had closed the university once the offensive began, so as the soldiers moved between buildings, there were few witnesses. At least one of the soldiers carried an AK-47 confiscated from guerrillas.

The soldiers arrived at the main Jesuit residence around 2:00 a.m. and banged on the door with the hard muzzles of their automatic weapons. One of the priests opened it, perhaps believing it was just a follow-up from an army search and seizure done a few days prior. The soldiers burst in and searched the residence before dragging six priests, the housekeeper, and her sixteen-year-old daughter to the backyard for a summary interrogation.

The incident would mark a chilling culmination to a war that had begun almost ten years earlier with a single bullet piercing the thorax of an outspoken archbishop. We often think of war as two militaries squaring up, when in reality it is this: a group of young men, taught to embrace the power and finality of violence, shooting a group of defenseless people over perceived transgressions.

In the distance, fighting continued and sporadic gunfire echoed across the campus. The soldiers lined up the priests, their housekeeper and her daughter. The gunmen forced the group to lie face-down in the grass—a kind of Salvadoran-style prone-out position—then executed them. Afterwards, they sprayed the residence with gunfire, launched rockets and grenades, and wrote on a piece of cardboard: "FMLN executed those who ratted them out. Victory or death, FMLN."

7.

The ghost of William Walker stalked Central America for more than a century after his death. US intervention became doctrine. Sometimes, as it was in Nicaragua and Haiti in the early part of the twentieth century, the US sent large military contingents to exert control. Other times, as in the case of Guatemala in 1954 and Chile in 1973, they fomented a military coup d'état. With El Salvador, the US trained the military, then covered for their numerous atrocities.

So it was perhaps eerily fitting that the US ambassador to El Salvador during this time was a man named William Walker, who sought to distance his Salvadoran allies from the incident. The obvious preliminary conclusion was that right-wing forces had perpetrated the massacre. But Walker took a different tack. Following the killings, the ambassador wrote a memo to Washington, noting that the university rector "sympathized with FMLN positions." Then, strangely, he blamed the guerrillas. "We cannot discount...that FMLN extremists may have murdered [Rector] Ellacuria et al in order to salvage their hoped-for popular uprising."

When it became clear that the guerrillas were not behind the murders, US officials, communicating via secret diplomatic cables and internal memorandums, began talking more about "rightist extremists" in the ARENA party and made direct references to d'Aubuisson. At the same time, they distanced their ally, Cristiani, from the murders. In a November 19 memo, Walker called the killings "a barbarous and incredibly stupid action," and said President Cristiani was "a decent human being" who could not have been privy to the plan.

The US Embassy spent the next several weeks on the defensive. By then, the US was a regular target itself. On the day of the UCA massacre, an armored embassy vehicle was struck by gunfire. The Salvatruchas had expelled one William Walker some 140 years earlier and helped secure his execution. The new William Walker was now himself under fire.

The war was not over, but the murder of the Jesuit priests and the guerrilla offensive opened the door to its final phase. Its relationship with the military untenable, the US joined the Catholic Church and neighboring nations and urged further negotiations for peace. Cristiani acceded and talks began in earnest. But while the guerrillas and the government were coming to the negotiating table, the country was still falling apart.

Ernesto felt it. After recovering from his injuries, he was sent back to battle and his division spent the next month fighting in Guazapa. They had arrived near the same time the rebels were having a large cookout for themselves and their followers. The guerrillas were celebrating. They thought the fight was over, that their offensive had won them the space they needed to end the war and start negotiating a favorable settlement. But there were still battles to be fought, and El Salvador was far from peace.

Ernesto witnessed these deep divisions as well. Regardless of how the peace process played out, healing would take a long time. There were strong reasons to stay in El Salvador. His mother and much of his family were there. He had a girlfriend and his first child on the way. But as he left the army in early 1990, he feared for his life, and his mother urged him to go to the United States.

"They're going to find you and kill you," she had told him over Christmas vacation after the offensive.

There were rumors that the guerrillas were already looking for him in Santa Ana. They had even kidnapped his cousin before realizing they had the wrong Deras and released him. Three of his sisters were already in the United States, and one of them had the money to pay the coyote.

Ernesto packed his things.

PART II

GETTING SERIOUS (1990–2010)

5

LOS SEÑORES

1.

IT'S A GRAINY AMATEUR VIDEO, AND THE TIME stamp reads "7:39 p.m. 4/29/92." The camera is focused on the feet of a man who lies flat on his back on the side of a busy thoroughfare. You cannot see his face, just the side of his arms, which are spread across the pavement. Cars flash across the screen and quickly out of sight. Trash is littered about, and pedestrians walk in front of the lens. The crowd rumbles softly in the background.

"They straight up kill thugs," a male voice suddenly jumps in, referring to the man sprawled on the street.

"Is he dead?" a female voice asks.

"He ain't dead yet, but he gonna die," the male continues. "They spray painted his nose, poured oil in his mouth. He gonna die. He needs immediate help."

The man on the ground was Fidel Lopez, a Guatemalan migrant and self-employed construction worker. Lopez had been stopped and beaten as he tried to drive his truck through the intersection of Normandie and Florence four-and-a-half hours after a nearly all-White jury had acquitted four police officers of excessive force against Rodney King. The verdict came despite the fact that a neighbor had video recorded the officers striking King more than fifty times while he lay on the ground after a reckless car pursuit. When the news broke about the verdict, parts of Los Angeles had erupted, starting with this busy intersection.

The police quickly retreated, leaving the area and innocent passersby like Lopez to the whims of a raucous crowd. Even as the violence escalated, Chief Daryl Gates told the press they were dealing with the situation "calmly, maturely, professionally." Then he went to a fundraiser in the upscale neighborhood of Brentwood.

The riots, looting and the estimated one billion dollars in damage that followed were the products of years of bottled-up frustration over what many viewed as the city's failed security strategy. The government had implemented gang injunctions and set up gang databases. Prosecutors were charging gang members under laws designed for Mafia dons. And police were executing massive raids and huge sweeps that incarcerated thousands. It was not an anti-communist war—which in the case of El Salvador included forced disappearances, mass displacement, and widespread extrajudicial executions—but LA's fight against the gangs had taken on the contours of a counterinsurgency effort.

The aggressive tactics played well in places like Brentwood but alienated the police from communities of color who bore the brunt of the war. In one particularly famous raid in August 1988, as Gates's massive antigang Operation Hammer kicked into full gear, the police smashed through two apartment buildings on Dalton Avenue and 39th Street in South Central, destroying living room furniture, toilets, sinks, family photos and mirrors, then spray painting "LAPD Rules" on the wall. They arrested dozens but charged no one. Following the raid, the city had to pay $4 million in damages and endure weeks of bad press.

By 1992, gang-related homicides in LA County would peak at 618. Drive-by shootings accounted for more than a quarter of these homicides, which only heightened people's sense of vulnerability. The aggressive law enforcement tactics were not only seemingly ineffective, they were heightening racial divisions.

Two weeks after the Rodney King beating, a grocer and a fifteen-year-old Black girl got into a tense physical tussle as the girl was trying to pay for a $1.79 bottle of orange juice. The grocer, a middle-aged Korean woman, thought she was trying to steal, and when the teenager turned to walk away, the grocer grabbed a handgun from the top of the counter and shot the fifteen-year-old in the back of the head. The jury found the grocer guilty of voluntary manslaughter, and prosecutors recommended sixteen years in prison. But the judge sentenced her to a $500 fine, four-hundred hours of community service and probation.

"I know a criminal when I see one," Judge Joyce Karlin said in an interview afterward, justifying her decision.

Karlin's sentencing became a rallying cry, especially when, five days later, a Glendale woman got thirty days in jail for animal cruelty.

"You shoot a dog, and you go to jail," one *Los Angeles Times* columnist wrote. "You shoot a black kid and you get probation."

The King riots began at the police headquarters in Parker Center. Protestors chanted "Guilty, guilty, guilty" as a row of anti-riot squad guarded the entrance. The protest quickly spread to South Central, and escalated into a riot on the corner of Florence and Normandie. First, crowds shouted invectives at the police. Then, after the police retreated, protestors started throwing rocks and bottles at random passing cars. Some of the drivers abandoned their vehicles and ran away on foot. Others crashed as they tried to speed away.

Throughout, news crews and witnesses took videos, which since the King video, had become the go-to way to chronicle police abuse. This time, however, they captured the unraveling of common decency and the frustration of a city.

At 6:39 p.m., a half-dozen men—among them a nineteen-year-old, solidly built, light-skinned Black man who was later identified as a Crip gang member named Damien "Football" Williams—pulled Reginald Denny, a White truck driver, from the driver's seat and hit him repeatedly, before Williams threw a brick at Denny's head from close range, knocking him to the pavement. The attack was captured live from a cameraman in a helicopter.

Denny's beating would dominate the news coverage, but an hour later Fidel Lopez's attack was also caught on tape. As many as twelve people joined in the beating, including Football Williams, who dropped a stereo on his head. Others spray painted his body. In the video, as one of the assailants walks away, his fist held high in the air, Lopez can be seen in the background, bloodied and sprawled on the street.

Among the audience, watching on TV from penitentiaries across California, was the Mexican Mafia, the state's most powerful prison gang. They didn't know Lopez, but they saw Black men—and at least one Crip—beating a Latino, and spray painting his face, and they stirred.

2.

Ernesto Deras remembers when the riots started. He was in North Hollywood with his new army, the Mara Salvatrucha, who like the rest of the country was glued to the TV. When they saw people openly looting liquor, televisions and stereos, they decided to join the fray.

Ernesto, the former Salvadoran soldier, had traveled a long way only to find himself in a different kind of war. Just months after the FMLN's final offensive in November 1989, Ernesto and his brother arrived in Los Angeles as the city was in the throes of the worst spate of violent crime in its history. Latinos were getting hit more than others: 55 percent of the victims of gang-related homicides were Hispanic.

Ernesto said he had no intention of staying. His sister cleaned houses. Other relatives were doing similarly menial jobs. In Salvadoran terms, the jobs paid well. But Ernesto wasn't longing for the American Dream. His life followed a more modest formula.

"I didn't go to [America] to work or to study. I had no idea why I was even going," he recalled. "For me, it was like a vacation, nothing more. Two years, and I was going back."

Two years, and I'll go back. It was a familiar migrant refrain.

Ernesto got a job making guitar cases, and he bought a used car for $300—a "Chevy with nice rims"—but his life felt empty. He didn't miss the army. He missed the comradery, the purpose it gave him, the devotion it required and, of course, the uniforms. He liked telling stories about his army days and sharing photographs. In one, his hair was pushed back by a makeshift headband that read "fuerzas especiales" (special forces). His arms were taut as he gripped a US-made M16 with a grenade launcher. A cross hung from his neck. He looked like a teenage Latino version of Rambo.

It was an apt image. Ernesto was a displaced soldier searching for a purpose. And when his nephew complained that the neighborhood gangs were bothering him, Ernesto stepped in.

"Llegó la mara," his nephew whispered.

Ernesto was curious.

"Cómo?" he asked. *"La mara?"*

Ernesto looked outside. The group reminded him of his old gang, the Mara San Juan in Santa Ana. Ernesto asked for an introduction, and a few days later, his nephew arranged a face-to-face via a friend. This was his first contact with the Mara Salvatrucha. They bonded.

"It's just, these are my people," he told me when I asked him how he felt when he met them. "Whoever was talking about the Mara Salvatrucha was talking about my blood, you know what I mean? The place where I'm from."

Ernesto quickly devoted himself to the mara. Anyone outside his Salvadoran bubble became his enemy.

"They want to finish us off," he told me, referring to the Mexican gangs who dominated the Valley and who his nephew said were threatening him.

The mara understood this logic. It breathed it every day.

Ernesto said his courtship was short, his initiation a bloody blur. As his four opponents circled him he caught one of them in the eye with a punch before feeling a deep jab to the ribs that sent him to the ground. Although he was writhing in pain, the others kept kicking and punching him without mercy. After the brinco, he was baptized Satán (Satan) of the Fulton Locos. He would need three days to recover.

Gang life suited Ernesto. As a member with a bit more experience, he knew when he could relax, drink and smoke marijuana, and when he had to harness a focused sense of rage. After all, this is what gang life is: huge spates of downtime, followed by small spurts of extreme violence and mayhem.

Ernesto understood how to take advantage of those chaotic moments, searching for enemies, beating back challengers and gaining the respect so sought after inside the gang. He also used his military knowledge—positioning the mara to corral rivals, looking for destroyers on dead-end streets, scouting escape routes, doing recon of the enemy, collecting renta from the traqueteros, and showing the mara how to manage weapons. This became his hallmark: Satán knew how to take territory, and the Fulton grew to be one of the most powerful cliques in the city.

Ernesto started seeing a woman who was also in the gang.

They rented an apartment in a two-story stucco building they used to plan assaults, and to store weapons and drugs. He lived across the street from an abandoned house that became the Fulton's go-to destroyer. Eventually, he started wearing a uniform: a long raincoat that could conceal his shotgun.

By the time South Central exploded in riots two years later, Ernesto was a budding leader of the Mara Salvatrucha. As the riots spread to other parts of the city, and the Hollywood police headed south to provide backup, the Fulton Locos made their move. Using a stolen truck as a battering ram, they smashed the windows of storefronts.

"Let's get all the homies some Nikes," one of them shouted, before they broke into a prominent shoe store.

They unloaded their booty at the destroyer and headed out again. It all seemed so easy until the police stopped their car at a surprise checkpoint. Ernesto was caught with stolen gold chains and brought to the Los Angeles County Jail.

3.

Others in the gang remember the riots as well. Alex Sanchez, who was in prison at the time, eventually got a pair of stolen Nikes from the melee. They were a welcome gift for the troubled gang member. At that point Alex had been in and out of prison for years. But what had started as a rite of passage had become a humbling education.

The first time he was sent to LA County Jail, for instance, he thought he was ready. He was coming directly from juvenile hall, and his experience there had taught him that the initial seventy-two hours were the most crucial. In those first few days, you were labeled *punk* or *not punk*. There were, of course, other designations. The Spanish word is *culero* or *culerito*, which is closer to *faggot*. But punk or not punk—or the more popular modern alternative, *bitch* or *not bitch*—was the most important.

The designation could make the difference between being abused, physically and sexually, or not at all. Anywhere between four and thirteen percent of inmates are raped or sexually assaulted every year in the US penitentiary system, according to US Department of Justice surveys of inmates. And as they carted him past the first layer of holding cells, Alex told himself: *Those motherfuckers will have to fight me. I'm not getting raped.*

He was eighteen, with thick arms and a powerful core. He was hitting his physical prime, but he was still vulnerable, in part because he was wearing the uniform he'd been issued at juvenile detention. After they put him in a holding cell with several others, Alex stood on a bench taunting anyone who dared look his way.

"Dude!" he screamed at one of the others. "Look somewhere else!"

"Youngster!" the man responded.

"What!"

"Calm down," he told him. "Come here."

"What do you want?" Alex asked with a snarl.

The man eyeballed his shirt, smiled, then asked: "You coming from juvenile hall?"

"Yeah."

"Órale," the man responded.

It was an entreaty. Alex—who was beginning to understand that gang life was as much about politics as it was about brute force—took the offer. The two sat down and began to talk. Class was in session.

County, as everyone referred to it, was controlled by the Mexican Mafia. The Mafia came together in the late 1950s at the behest of about a dozen Chicanos in the Deuel Vocational Institution, then a juvenile facility in Tracy, California, where gangs from East Los Angeles and the San Fernando Valley united to protect themselves. At the time, La Cosa Nostra was in the news, so the group modeled themselves after the Sicilian Mafia, employing their symbols, copying their structure and stealing their name.

As the original members made their way through county, state and federal penitentiaries, they held tight to the ethos that Chicano gangs should stick together. Over time they added a more formal system with strict rules, initiation rituals and a coded language. They exercised together. They ate together. They got stoned together. They dealt drugs together. And when they were threatened, they fought together.

Their numbers were few—in the dozens rather than the thousands—creating the feel of an exclusive club. These members were called Made Men, Big Homies, Carnales, or Los Señores. Below them were associates, high-level operatives who controlled the crews inside and outside of prison. And below them were soldiers, low-level gang members who did the bidding of Los Señores and their crew chiefs.

Rivals emerged—White and Black prison gangs—and on the other side of the prison yard stood another Mexican gang, Nuestra Familia (NF). The NF were cousins, sometimes literally, but they were made up of more recent arrivals from Mexico, more farmworkers than city dwellers, more *campesino*, or peasant, than *cholo*, the urban Chicano style of pressed white T-shirts, baggy plaid button-downs and oversized Dickies. The war between the Mexican Mafia and NF eventually engulfed most of the California state prison system, but the Mexican Mafia held the upper hand. By the mid-1970s, the FBI considered the Mafia "the strongest prison gang in the California Prison System."

California's war on gangs increased the Mafia's power. Between 1980 and 1989, felony arrests of Hispanic males in the state increased by 100 percent. In Los Angeles County alone, that number more than doubled, reaching a record 86,843 felony arrests of Hispanic men in 1989, which accounted for nearly half of all Hispanic male felony arrests in the state. LA County Jail became the crossroads of gang operations. The Mafia understood: control County and you control all of Southern California's gangs.

With this surge of prisoners came the construction of new penitentiaries and juvenile halls. And new facilities meant new battles, which often played out in bloody prison yard brawls in a process sometimes referred to as "opening up" a prison.

Throughout, authorities tried different tactics to quell the rising conflicts. In a strategy that El Salvador would implement a few years later, California segregated its prisoners by gang affiliation. Authorities sent Mafia members to Folsom or San Quentin, and NF to Deuel, which had been converted in an adult prison. They isolated prison gang leaders and associates in what were later termed Secure Housing Units, or SHUs. They limited visits. Still, communication and criminal activities continued. In addition, prison assaults with weapons spiked during the 1980s, an indication of the surging racialized violence raging between the Latino, Black, and White prison gangs. In the early 1980s, inmate-on-inmate assaults were fewer than five hundred per year. By the end of the decade, that number had nearly doubled.

What's more, the de facto recognition of power only emboldened leaders, including those in the Mafia who solidified their hold on the Latino gangs in Southern California. Soon, it was not just Mexican-American gangs, but all Latino gangs who coalesced under the Mafia banner. The grouping became known as the Sureños. The NF, meanwhile, gathered the Northern California gangs into what they called the Norteños.

Inside the prisons, the Sureños became the Mafia's soldiers. They passed the coded messages known as *huilas*, "kites," between cells, cellblocks or to the outside world. They made weapons from razor blades and cardboard, then planned and executed attacks on their enemies—who they called *chavalas*, "little girls"—during meals, recreation time or transition periods.

They moved money and contraband, including drugs and alcohol fermented from mess hall fruit. They controlled prostitution and internal prison sex rings, a powerful and underappreciated point of leverage. And they organized mass protests over excessive abuse, institutional neglect, visit restrictions or anytime they felt the need to reassert control.

It was in this highly charged context that Alex had landed in County for the first time. His mentor who called him down from his perch to talk was from a rival gang, but when the two sat in the holding cell, Alex listened intently: to survive, he had to fall in line with his kind—the Latinos who were tumbling into the prison system in record numbers.

It was the beginning of his education. The MS had yet to join the Mafia's umbrella group, the Sureños, but pressure was mounting on both the inside and the outside for them to do so. To be sure, the Mafia was preparing an audacious strategy, which would require every Latino gang—even the rambunctious, machete-wielding Salvadorans—to be on board.

4.

The video is steady, but the picture is a little fuzzy. A mustached man in a plaid shirt gestures toward a large group of young men. They look at him intently, squinting in the California sun. Some are gathered in a tight circle, and others are in the baseball stands behind him. One of them steadies a baby stroller.

The man in the video that day was Peter "Sana" Ojeda. He had been a Mexican Mafia member since the 1960s, making his name from the inside of a prison cell as a Big Homie. Ojeda was released in 1987, and in January 1992, he was filmed by local police talking to the young men in Santa Ana, California's El Salvador Park.

Ojeda was acting as a Mafia emissary. At the time, the Los Angeles underworld was undergoing a seismic shift. Police crackdowns left cliques leaderless, and internal fights escalated. The squabbles were disrupting the Mafia's lucrative drug business inside and outside of the prisons. Put simply, the Mafia needed peace to sell more drugs, and during the meeting, Ojeda reportedly called for an end to drive-by shootings, issuing a warning to those in attendance: heed the Mafia's call or face the Mafia's wrath. In the video of El Salvador Park in Santa Ana, the gang members listen, then break off to consult with their own.

The city's two most prominent Black gangs, the Crips and the Bloods, were also talking peace. For the Mexican Mafia, a potential truce between the Black gangs was cause for alarm. A unified front of Black gangs might mean more competition for drug markets inside and outside of prison. Ojeda and Los Señores felt threatened enough to take action.

The El Salvador Park gathering marked the beginning of a series of historic gang meetings in Los Angeles. As the Rodney King trial spun the rest of the city into a state of volatility, the gangs found a more stable pose. In late April 1992, just days before the King verdict was announced, the Bloods and the Crips reached a truce in the Watts neighborhood. The detente led to a modest drop in homicides.

The Mexican Mafia scrambled to keep pace by pushing for truces in their own neighborhoods. And by August, seven months after that first meeting, a Santa Ana Latino gang truce had been forged. Ojeda read its contents aloud to about five hundred gang members who'd gathered again in the El Salvador Park. As the *Los Angeles Times* reported, violators of the truce were warned they would be treated "as a child molester, a rat, a rapist, which all mean a coward."

"This is a historic moment," Ojeda reportedly told the gang members. "It's something that we all want."

5.

From the moment Ernesto stepped into County after being arrested during the Rodney King riots, he became a Mafia target. The Mara Salvatrucha was still not completely under the Mafia's control, and Ernesto and his mara counterparts paid for it dearly. On one of his first days in jail, a group thrashed him after he told them he was Salvadoran. He received a transfer to another area, but got beat up again. After a third move, he said his cellmates forced him to sleep on the floor, and he contracted chicken pox. It may have saved him. Prison authorities sent him to the hospital for most of his thirty-day stint in jail on petty theft charges.

Others were not so lucky. The Mafia was squeezing the Mara Salvatrucha from the inside out, beating them up in prison and calling on the Sureños to attack them in the streets. According to former mara, the Watts truce had accelerated the Mafia's timetable.

The Mafia started organizing more truce meetings in Los Angeles, Riverside, San Bernardino, and San Diego Counties, during which they called for an end to drive-by shootings. The meetings were always punctuated with the same threat Ojeda had issued: heed the Mafia's call or face the Mafia's wrath. Most obeyed.

"We can control those gangs," Rene Boxer, a high-ranking Mafia-member-turned-government-witness told an interviewer a few years after the truces. "We've displayed it. What law enforcement, [government] administrations, all the resources of the federal government can't do, we can do. We can control gangs. And as quick as we can say don't do drive-bys we can say, 'Start shooting at cops'... The power of the Mexican Mafia is vast."

Back inside prison, things were anything but peaceful. Following the brutal beating of Lopez, the Mexican Mafia fomented a series of riots against Black gangs throughout the California prison system. Richard Valdemar, who was working in prison intelligence at the time for the Los Angeles Sheriff's Office, told me that his unit intercepted messages between Sureños calling for retaliatory attacks on Black inmates. Spray painting Lopez's face, Valdemar said, was a particularly egregious offense because of the symbolism related to claiming territory. The Mafia imposed new rules on the inside: Sureños were not allowed to interact with any Black inmates. No meals. No hustling. No drug deals. No contact of any kind.

The Mexican Mafia also gave the order to attack the Latino gangs that were not under its Sureños umbrella, among them the Mara Salvatrucha. The gang had long enjoyed its reputation as an outlier, but under the new regime, there was no escape. The beatings, as Ernesto Deras discovered when he was arrested, were constant and brutal. In the Mafia's mind, if you were not part of the Sureños, you were the enemy. The incarcerated Mara Salvatrucha began pleading with their counterparts on the outside to find a way into the Mafia. It had, in short, become a matter of life and death.

6.

The mara began negotiating their entry into the Sureños by volunteering to put in what the Mafia terms "the work," to show "commitment." The words would later become part of the mara lexicon, euphemisms for extreme violence in the name of the gang.

One of their first jobs as Sureños soldiers was to lead the charge against Black inmates. Violence in the penitentiaries is not disaggregated by gang, but according to former LA Sheriff's intelligence officer Valdemar, there was a noticeable uptick in Mara Salvatrucha participation in prison assaults. His team also intercepted a kite in which the mara volunteered to kill Football Williams, the man who had thrown a brick at Reginald Denny on national television and had participated in the public assault of Lopez an hour later. Prison officials put Williams in protective custody, which Valdemar says probably saved his life.

Still, it took months for the mara on the outside to make overtures to the Mafia. At first, the mara sought an interlocutor—an intermediary gang with whom it had a working relationship. But none of them were willing to risk their own contacts with the Mafia by vouching for the volatile Salvadoran gang. The mara then looked for a direct contact, which proved even harder.

The Mafia, like the Mara Salvatrucha, has a hierarchy but it is a diffuse organization with no central governing board or leader. It's not even entirely clear who is a member and who isn't. To this day, authorities talk in round numbers, estimating there are between 100 and 120 Big Homies nationwide. ("Pocos pero locos," small but fierce, they like to say.) In other words, you don't find the Mafia, the Mafia finds you. After weeks of sending out feelers, a marero got a call. The Big Homie on the other end invited the gang to a meeting in Elysian Park in Central LA. The rules were simple: come ready to deal, but no weapons.

The Mara Salvatrucha held an internal meeting and designated two members from each clique who would attend. On the night of the gathering, they piled into three cars and drove to the park. Hundreds of gang members had converged from different corners of the city. LAPD helicopters circled above, shining lights. Police in plainclothes sat in their cars on the edge of the park taking pictures and scribbling notes.

From a distance the Mara Salvatrucha leaders watched as Mafia associates and Sureños helped to park cars and collect firearms. But instead of handing over their guns, the mara left them in their cars and headed to the meeting.

As they approached the circle where most of the gang leaders had converged, they heard whispers. *The MS is here. The mara. The Mara Salvatrucha.* Slowly, the other gangs turned to face them.

A Mafia leader then asked two of them to step into a tighter, smaller circle. Mara enemies began to shout at them, screaming about the gang's transgressions. The Mara Salvatrucha leaders barked back. It went on for a while like this: the gangs airing grievances, the Mafia mediating. It was a catharsis of sorts but designed more for the Mafia to show its power than for its Sureños soldiers to resolve their differences.

After some tense back and forth, the Mafia leader intervened again, this time with another simple instruction for the mara leaders: "Alright, this is what's going to happen: you guys are going to give us five thousand dollars and five weapons."

It was an official offer: pay renta, and the Mafia would stop brutalizing the mara in and out of prison. The gang had become, in other words, a part of the Sureños. From now on, they would be called the Mara Salvatrucha 13, or MS-13. There was no cheer, no celebration. This was business. Mafia business.

7.

Not long after the mara became Sureños, William "Blinky" Rodriguez approached Ernesto. Blinky's son was killed by gang violence in 1990, and he had started forging gang truces in the San Fernando Valley. He was working with a former Mafia member named Donald Garcia whose broad build and blunt talk had earned him the moniker Big D.

Ernesto was, by then, a leader in the Fulton clique and not easily impressed. He had little incentive to talk peace. He had quit his job. He had a place to live. He had a girlfriend in the gang. Fulton was carving out large swaths of territory in the Valley, collecting as much as $2,000 per week from the traqueteros, more than their MS-13 counterparts in Central LA. The LA cliques were tough. The Valley cliques were smart *and* tough.

But Blinky and Big D had a way about them. Blinky, a former kickboxer with surprisingly soft facial features, came at you with compassion. He talked about God and love and brotherhood, furrowing his brow with each probing question. Blinky had famously forgiven his son's killer, who had been sentenced to thirty-seven years in prison for shooting Blinky's son as he sat in a car. Big D, on the other hand, came at you with the harsh truth, trying to scare gang members into leaving. He talked about brutal ways to die in prison and on the street, and about rape—especially about rape. One of the first things he liked to tell gang members, for example, was that they would, one day, be incarcerated and that in jail they would be forced to "suck dick."

Ernesto was impressed, and shortly thereafter he got word that the Mafia sanctioned the truce efforts. He had to make peace or they would make war. After an internal meeting with his clique, he and forty of his Fulton members went to Pacoima Park in the Valley, well armed and ready to forge a truce or, if necessary, to provoke a fight.

Blinky met Ernesto on the edge of the park, then accompanied him and about ten other mara to the middle of the meeting where other gang leaders awaited. As the invectives flew between them, Blinky kept the peace, reminding Ernesto—who wore a skullcap that read "Fuck Everybody"—and the other leaders of the consequences of war.

"Aquí no hay pleito." Here, there's no fight.

One by one, they aired their grievances. Past conflicts over girls, tit-for-tat murders, endless battles for drug corners. And respect. Always respect. Little by little, the spiderwebs of retribution were wiped away or at least swept under the rug.

Blinky led a prayer. The reward for adhering to the peace was clear, as was the price for going back to war. God would absolve them. The Mafia would fuck them.

6

THE DEPORTED

1.

FOR NORMAN, LIFE IN THE MARA BEGAN WHEN El Jefe (The Boss) returned to his town after being deported from the United States.

El Jefe lived in front of Norman's school near his home in El Salvador, and one day, as Norman left, they bumped into each other.

"What's up, Loco?" El Jefe said, using Norman's childhood moniker.

Norman did a double take. El Jefe was dressed in oversized Ben Davis, the thick workman trousers that had become a cholo standby. The end of his belt hung below his knees. An enormous plaid button-down was draped like a curtain over his shoulders. His arm was covered in tattoos. "He was ready to roll," Norman would tell me later.

"Jefe?" Norman queried, hesitantly.

"They don't call me Jefe anymore," he replied, his head slightly cocked. "Now I'm Little Man."

El Jefe had gone to grade school with Norman. He liked to give orders, even when they were kids, so Norman and his friends facetiously called him El Jefe. He'd left for the US before the end of the war; so had dozens of neighbors and nearly all of Norman's family. It was part of an exodus without precedent, El Salvador's version of the Irish Potato Famine. As much as 25 percent of the country, or an estimated 1.5 million people, fled during the decade-long war, most of them to the US.

By the late 1980s, Norman says the townspeople were too afraid to venture into the night because the warring sides or death squads could confuse civilians for combatants. The firefights had also increased in frequency and duration. The war had cut into the family's income and education. Norman's mother stopped fetching vegetables from the farmers at dawn; curfews and gun battles led schools to cancel classes.

Inside Norman's home, a discussion ensued. For some of the boys, another world beckoned. They heard it repeatedly—*el norte*—on the streets, in the car repair shops, waiting for the bus, at the grocery store. The United States promised a different future. And money. For Norman and his siblings, it would also get them away from their turbulent home life. Throughout the war, his parents had continued their on-again, off-again relationship, and their parallel families started to have parallel problems. Eventually, several of Norman's half siblings would follow his path toward the gang.

Other townspeople had already traveled to the United States, among them El Jefe.

"He always wanted to be someone," Norman remembered.

The easiest way to be someone was to go to the US. From there, evidence of success trickled back to the Salvadoran countryside. Families built an extra room, upgraded their roof or got a better car. One neighbor, Don Alberto, got a telephone—the only one in the neighborhood. Whispers and envious chatter followed, and the jingle of the landline constantly reminded his neighbors of the possibilities.

The 1989 rebel offensive had accelerated the exodus. Buses burned. Firefights raged. Guerrillas took entire villages, and Norman's family remained inside for days. Norman says they ran out of food before the Red Cross finally spirited them to a nearby school where they stayed for four days until the fighting died down.

"It seemed like the war would never end," Norman said.

Peace talks may have been in motion, but the army trucks were still doing the rounds, looking for more soldiers. It was only a matter of time, Norman's brothers said, before the army took them to battle, just like they'd done with David, whose drunken rages and isolation served as the family's cautionary tale.

The first to leave were Miguel Ángel and Gabrielito. The whole family went to the bus stop next to the local credit union where they all shook hands. Norman took a long look at Gabrielito. As the bus rolled away, he felt like someone was punching him in the gut.

"There, watching my brothers go, the family started to disintegrate," he told me.

After a few weeks, Gabrielito and Miguel Ángel reached Los Angeles. Norman said he doesn't know how they got there, but he remembers they called Don Alberto's phone, and the family sprinted to hear their voices from what seemed like the other end of the world.

By the time El Jefe, now known as Little Man, was deported back to El Salvador, Norman's house was barren. A few months after Gabrielito and Miguel Ángel went to the United States, Laura had hopped a bus like her brothers and headed north. Norman remembers they received a letter from Mexico City a few weeks later, and after three months, she too called Don Alberto's phone. She had made it to the United States. She eventually joined a church and got a job. She would soon start lobbying for Norman and others to join her.

Rodrigo was still in his teens when he left El Salvador. He went to Los Angeles to join Gabrielito and Miguel Ángel. Gabrielito tried to get him a job at the garage where he'd found work, but Rodrigo drifted toward the Mara Salvatrucha—whose name was just beginning to circulate in Norman's house.

By then, Miguel Ángel was already a member of the mara. He'd connected with the gang while waiting for day work on a street corner. One of the laborers who sold drugs recruited Miguel Ángel to the gang. Rodrigo's initiation soon followed.

To be clear, the vast majority of Salvadorans steered away from gang life, including the rest of Norman's immediate siblings. But for the tiny percentage of those who began running with them, a pattern was emerging. Flight. Dislocation. Desperation. Initiation. Arrest. And ultimately, deportation. It would accelerate as the years passed, setting the stage for the next round of wars.

2.

Little Man was Norman's age, but to Norman, he looked older, more knowledgeable, more experienced. As they spoke, Little Man shook a can of spray paint. While the ball bounced up and down inside the can, Norman asked him if he was going to return to school. Little Man scoffed, turned to the wall and sprayed the letters *MS-13 Little Man*.

Norman, meanwhile, was helping to provide for his family. In the morning, he went to school. In the afternoon, he worked at a factory that made brick tiles for floors. He was hanging with a local mara, but the gangs in El Salvador were not what they are today. They stole. They fought. They partied. But Norman's mara were more mischief-makers than predators.

Little Man threw parties and put on music he'd brought from California. Gang members would smoke, drink and dance. Hip-hop. Rock 'n' roll. A million and a half Salvadorans had gone to the US. Now the US was coming to El Salvador. Little Man and Norman would also watch Disney movies. *Bambi* was one of their favorites, Norman told me.

Language shifted as well. They didn't drive a truck, they drove a "troka" *(troh-kah)*. Car breaks were "brekes" *(breh-kez)*. To hang out was to "hangear" (*hang-ey-ar*). A meeting was a "mirin" *(meeh-reen)*. Acting as a lookout, or posting up, became "postear" *(poh-stey-ar)*. Bastardized gringo nicknames also proliferated: Chivoy (Shy Boy), Chory (Shorty), and Gánster (Gangster), among them.

The foreign cachet attracted women. Norman met several, and one became pregnant with his first child—a boy who he would not recognize as his own until years later. He met another woman not long afterward during a visit to the beach. Her name was Carla. She would remain with him for years, becoming his emotional pillar and rearing their four children.

The mara's favorite musical group was the Tavares, an all-Black band whose songs blended elements of R&B with soul and a touch of disco. The gang mimicked the group's choreographed dance moves and mouthed the words. Norman also liked break dancing and quickly found that for the first time his small stature and low center of gravity were an asset.

"It all began there," Norman would tell me. "It wasn't like, 'You want to be in a gang?'"

The group had talent. Some members entered a local contest that landed them on a weekly television variety show. They won, and took home $35. They grew tighter.

It was beginning.

3.

When the Irish arrived in the US during the potato famine in the 1840s, there was no nationwide immigration policy. And when the

Irish created legendary New York City gangs like the Dead Rabbits in the Five Points district of lower Manhattan, there were no special antigang laws or gang enhancements. Their arrival marked the beginning of a messy, violent experiment in social integration during which the new immigrant class, and many others, charted their own "queer ladders of social mobility"—as the sociologist Daniel Bell wrote—to become prominent American citizens. These White settlers, as Bell noted, "Ignored, circumvented or stretched the law when it stood in the way of America's destiny, and their own—or, were themselves the law when it served their purposes."

By the time Salvadorans began arriving en masse just over 130 years later, the US government had already begun to criminalize immigration and to militarize the fight against gangs, truncating any potential "queer ladders" Salvadorans might have climbed to political, economic and social stability. As yet there are no Joe Kennedys in Salvadoran lore, men who straddled legal and illegal worlds and opened the door for the next generation to become presidents and attorneys general.

Salvadorans faced a different law enforcement apparatus. In the mid-1980s, the Immigration and Naturalization Service (INS), the precursor to ICE, began working with the Los Angeles antigang CRASH unit to find and deport suspected gang members. One of Alex Sanchez's friends in the gang was deported this way after the two were caught shoplifting. By April 1989, the joint task force trumpeted 175 deportations of Mexicans and Salvadorans. In a *Los Angeles Times* article, the force claimed to have "decimated" the Mara Salvatrucha, deporting as many as 20 key leaders. It was a bold assertion. Alex's friend, for example, came back within a month of his deportation.

Much of the focus on deporting Salvadorans was part of a larger political calculus related to US foreign policy. Asylum applications from Nicaraguans fleeing the Marxist Sandinistas were accepted at far higher rates than Salvadorans fleeing the

US-backed Salvadoran government. Immigration officials during the Reagan administration were also more likely to designate Salvadorans as "economic" rather than "political" refugees. Salvadorans, it seemed, were the wrong color, from the wrong the country, fighting the wrong war.

Still, there were glimmers of hope. In the 1990s, the US government gave Salvadoran immigrants Temporary Protective Status (TPS), a designation that offered ephemeral "relief" from deportation for reasons ranging from natural disasters to war. But when the El Salvador peace accords were signed in 1992, pressure mounted for the US to eliminate TPS and any special provisions for the country's refugees. Asylum claims were once again limited, and the numbers of criminal deportees increased.

In this complex geopolitical swirl, members of US gangs like Little Man got sent to Norman's hometown. Others followed: Chino and his brother Vago; Luther and El Maldito. Smokey, Rebelde, Santos, and Chepe Furia, among others, landed elsewhere in El Salvador.

One member, Borromeo Henríquez Solórzano, alias El Diablito, came from the legendary Hollywood Locos. Wiry but formidable, El Diablito had arrived looking just as cholo as Little Man, but he was much more ambitious, strategic and intelligent. He'd long blurred the line between the personal and the communal in ways that others gang members never did or could. In the early 1990s, for example, El Diablito was already moving stolen cars, largely for his own personal gain, a business he would expand over the years. Car culture was essential to Latino gangs in Los Angeles, including the MS-13. A *ranfla*—slang for lowrider—became synonymous with the mara leadership council.

Norman first met El Diablito at the beach in 1994. It was, by Norman's account, a typical gang encounter: they drank, talked and schemed. El Diablito wanted Norman's help. "They needed drivers," is the easygoing way Norman would describe it later. "I had no idea the cars were stolen."

A few days later, Norman and several others boarded a caravan of minibuses and traveled to La Hachadura, a rugged town along the Guatemalan border where the stolen cars were being stored. El Diablito's crew gave Norman fifty colones, or about $5 to drive one back. It was his first venture into high-end MS-13 criminal life.

Soon afterward, another leader, who was also from the Hollywood Locos, told Norman the MS-13 was ready to beat him into the gang. Norman did not talk about his jumping-in with me, but by then the mara had begun to formalize their initiation. It would last thirteen seconds, an homage to their new masters inside the California prison system, the Mexican Mafia.

By then, the MS-13 had essentially copied the Mafia's rule book. No theft. No rape. No snitching. No leaving the gang. Gang meetings were compulsory. Orders to kill, so-called luz verde, had to come from the top, and any member who spotted a rival in the 18th Street gang had the obligation to attack them. Failure to follow these guidelines would lead to *corte*, "court," the gang's internal justice system. Depending on the infraction, the mara meted out physical punishments in increments of thirteen, going up to thirty-nine seconds, an eternity for a beat-down in any gang world.

The new recruits were enthralled: the mythology and the structure, the rituals and the comradery. It was unlike anything in El Salvador. Yet it was reinforced by something Salvadorans understood very well after a decade of war: violence. They gained entry by attacking someone else. Then they beat each other into the gang. Then they attacked other people. And when they made mistakes, they attacked their own. Such cyclical violence reflected the larger systemic and political turmoil that encompassed their world.

Norman and his mara friends who'd been jumped in soon had the makings of a clique. They thought about naming themselves Hollywood, an homage to their new conquering heroes from

California. But there were rules concerning this sort of thing as well. Norman and his cohort would have to name themselves after something local. Sonsonate *(Szon-zo-nah-te)*, they thought. It was the name of their state and had a melodious ring to it. What's more, the fare collectors had long ago linked it to a similar sounding city name in the United States.

"Cincinate!" (Cincinnati) young men hanging on the edge of the buses yelled as they leaned out from the doors in search of passengers. "Cincinate!"

Cincinate, Norman and his friends said, the Cincinate Locos.[11]

4.

On December 24, 1994, a few months after Norman's initiation, someone shot and killed Norman's brother Gabrielito. The report I got from the police department years later said he was found in a park along a byway in the northwest part of the city, "lying face down" with a "severe head injury."

Gabrielito had moved to the same city as Laura and was trying to reconcile with his wife who'd separated from him. He drank and was abusive, Laura later told me. Norman's family suspected the beatings had led to his murder by someone in his wife's family, but ultimately no one was prosecuted.

"We don't know what happened," Norman said, his voice trailing off.

After he'd left, Gabrielito had kept in touch with Norman, sending him gifts from *el norte*, including a racy pair of high-tops with the brand—LA Gear—emblazoned on the side. The city name lent them a special allure in the gang world.

"It was devastating," he would say of Gabrielito's death. "It was something… I don't know. A void."

On December 27, a Christmas card arrived from Gabrielito

---

11 As it is with the rest of Norman's story, this name has been changed. There is no Cincinate Locos of the MS-13.

addressed to Norman, which he'd sent before his death. When he opened it, it began playing holiday music—a squeaky version of the synthesized Christmas carols popular in Central America. In the days that followed, Norman heard the carols in his head, often triggered by the real carols playing on the streets. It was both maddening and soothing—stirrings from the beyond.

"I can hear the music," he told his mother. "But it's not coming from the card."

He asked her if she heard it. She didn't, so he went to the neighbors.

"Do you hear it?" he asked.

They just looked at him.

After Gabrielito's funeral, Norman threw himself into gang life. Like many cliques, Norman's had an unassuming beginning. They spent their time hanging out in the town's central plaza because there was little else to do.

Norman's girlfriend Carla had their first child, and Norman's second, a girl, in 1995. But by then, the mara were his real family, and their battles with other gangs, in particular the 18th Street, were intensifying.

Norman says it was about a year after they had launched their Salvadoran clique, when the first 18th Street leaders arrived. Like the leaders of the MS-13, they'd been deported from the US, bringing with them the same swagger and bravado that Little Man and El Diablito boasted. Both the MS-13 and the 18th Street used this cachet to usurp most of what remained of the local gangs. Then, like they had in Los Angeles, they turned their ire on each other.

Fistfights soon broke out at the plaza. These quickly gave way to knife fights. They began to sketch out territories—the unofficial, invisible map that would come to dominate urban life in El Salvador. Norman was at the center of these early battles, honing his fighting skills and gaining respect, climbing the gang's own "queer ladders" of mobility.

Eventually, Little Man declared, they needed a gun. He collected some money, but the gun never appeared. The others in the clique started asking questions, and they decided to hold a meeting in a small city on the Pacific near Norman's hometown. During the meeting, Little Man gave them excuses. They gave him grief but nothing further. There were rules but not yet stiff consequences, especially for leaders with the power that came from being deported.

After the meeting, Norman and about ten others decided to buy a bottle of rum and drink it at the beach. As a soft buzz settled in, they bought another. Darkness fell, and they were still drinking. After they finished the second bottle, the clique went to the bus station, but the last bus had left. Worse still, the 18th Street were waiting, armed with machetes.

Their rivals gave chase. Norman says he ran as fast as he could but at some point felt a piercing blow to the top of his head. It knocked him to the ground. Dazed but aware that he had just taken a machete to the skull, he could feel the warm Salvadoran pavement beneath him and the blood flowing down his face. His heart was racing as he awaited the next, and what he thought would be final blows from the long, sharp blade.

Instead, he felt a tug at his feet. He glanced down. The attacker had tucked the bloody machete he'd used on Norman under his arm and was fiddling with Norman's shoes, unlacing the LA Gear high-tops Gabrielito had sent him from the US and scrambling to push them off his taut, flexed feet. Norman understood. Anything with LA on it was the ultimate prize.

Then a truck drove by, or a car. Norman does not remember exactly. What he does know is that the vehicle sped past them and startled his attacker who panicked and ran.

Gabrielito was looking out for him, again.

5.

After recovering from the machete blow to the head, Norman collected $2,000 from his brothers and sisters, and contacted a coyote named Marcelo. He said goodbye to his girlfriend and his newborn daughter, then caught a bus with his parents to Totonicapán, a western province of Guatemala. There, he and about twenty-five others from El Salvador and Guatemala gathered, and Norman took leave of his parents.

From Totonicapán, the group went by bus to a town along the Mexico-Guatemala border, then made their way into San Cristóbol de las Casas, Mexico, the picturesque colonial city. Once in Mexico, Norman said they hopped mostly from minibus to minibus. At one point they split into groups of four, and Norman's group boarded a larger passenger bus. The driver removed the bathroom's wall mirror, and Norman and his group climbed behind it, where they continued their journey, bouncing underneath the toilet for hours.

After nearly two weeks, they congregated in a small hotel in Matamoros, along the US-Mexico border. The next day, Marcelo instructed Norman and the others to place their belongings—their clothes, pictures of their families, gifts from their relatives, toiletries and jewelry—in securely tied garbage bags. Then they waded through the Rio Grande. The water reached Norman's mouth. He couldn't swim, but he could stand on his tippy-toes and flail his arms and legs as needed. He was an athlete, a dancer and, most of all, a fighter.

On the other side, they split up again. Most headed west toward California. Some went east toward Washington, DC, Maryland and Virginia, the so-called DMV. Norman secured a ride to his sister's house. There, he got a job at an old-school Tex-Mex restaurant, complete with a neon sign, multicolored margaritas, faux wood panels and high ceilings. At first, he washed dishes. Then the cook got him to cut vegetables for nachos and *pico de gallo*. Soon, he was promoted to assistant cook. He made $5.25 an hour, plus tips. And when he worked overtime, he got paid extra. Norman also started to go to church with his sister, Laura, and her husband. For a time, it looked as if Norman might escape the mara's grip.

But what he had left in El Salvador kept pulling him back. His girlfriend and daughter were still in his home state, living with his troubled parents. Norman began to send a hundred dollars every couple of weeks to El Salvador via Western Union. But when his mother had gallbladder issues, Norman decided he had to go home. His sister, Laura, begged him to stay, to keep earning so they could bring his family and their mother to the United States, but after less than a year, Norman decided to return to El Salvador. There, the MS-13 awaited, and so did the 18th Street.

6.

Norman said he arrived in El Salvador again sometime in 1996. Reunited with his family, inspired by the church and whipped into shape by his sister, he said he tried to keep clear of the gang. But the mara was there, pestering him, calling him and reminding him of the risks of going it alone. The 18th Street's presence had grown, and the fighting between the two gangs was getting worse. *They are going to get you*, his friends warned him. *They don't care if you left the gang. They don't forget.*

Norman slowly reintegrated himself. He is vague on the details, but it was clear that this was his pattern. Regardless of his status as a "former" gang member, he could not avoid a confrontation. The town was small. The plaza was smaller still. Soon enough, he bumped into a group from the 18th Street. One of them pulled a knife, Norman said, and slashed his stomach. It had been less than a year since he'd returned, but already he began to feel that he would never be safe in El Salvador. What's more, his mother had recovered, so he decided to return to the United States.

The coyote for his second trip was named Eduardo. The family—resentful but resigned to help the youngest—once again scraped together the money, but this trip was more arduous. When US authorities surprised the group at the US border, everyone scattered, and Norman found himself alone in an arid mountainous pass. He economized his water but could move only at night. Without the sun as a compass, the desert was boundless and confusing.

After two days, Norman was tired and dizzy. He had blisters on his feet; his water was running low. He thought he might die. Desperate, he made his way to a road. It was the middle of the night, and he does not remember how long he was there before a vehicle passed. When I asked him to describe it for me, he just said that it was "an old truck with an old man."

The man pulled over, and the two exchanged an awkward hello. The old man spoke no Spanish, and Norman hardly any English, so the old man simply gestured for him to hop into the truck and began driving. Norman managed to tell him that he wanted to go to where his sister lived, but the old man said he wasn't going that far. Instead, he took Norman to the closest mid-size city and dropped him at a shopping center along the side of the highway. Norman said he gave the old man a twenty-dollar bill and thanked him. He had probably saved his life.

Back in the US, Norman once again moved in with his sister, Laura, and began working in construction. He had a plan, he told her, to make money and bring his girlfriend, who was now pregnant with their second child, to the US with their kids. But by 1997, Norman was not the same diligent dishwasher that he was in 1995. He was jumpy, impatient, and was again feeling pulled toward gang life.

Laura tried to keep him away from trouble the only way she knew how: by bringing him to church. The elders embraced

Norman, even baptized him, dunking him in the ocean and blessing him with the Holy Spirit. But Norman was drifting. He could not keep a job and began talking about going to Los Angeles. He was also drinking, staying out. After a while, Laura asked him to move.

Norman went to Los Angeles where he reunited with his brothers and got a job doing quality control for a blue jeans stitching line in a factory in the heart of the fashion district on Seventh and Alameda. But there were distractions. His brothers Miguel Ángel and Rodrigo were by then very active in the gang. He met more mara at the factory.

Norman has no criminal record in the United States, and he claims he did not run with the gang during this period. But it was clear where he was headed, until he got word that his girlfriend had given birth and was suffering from preeclampsia, a condition marked by high blood pressure and, in the worst cases, seizures. His sister told him to stay, to stick to his original plan. But Norman decided to go home again, and this time there would be no escape.

7.

As decisions go, Norman's choice to return to El Salvador the second time was the responsible one. His wife and kids needed him, and soon Norman was working again. But things got more complicated when his brother Rodrigo was deported back to El Salvador and slid into gang life. The pressure mounted for Norman to do the same, especially since the fight with the 18th Street escalated. *Why is he always running?* the other gang members would ask Rodrigo. *Does he think the 18th Street is gonna forgive him?*

By then, deportations had gone from a trickle to a flood. In 1996, new federal legislation in the US increased the number of crimes for which undocumented migrants could be deported. Local and federal authorities also increased their cooperation, adding databases that tracked alleged gang members and their immigration status, so they could remove them under nearly any pretense. In California, the statewide database would eventually include over 200,000 purported gang members, 133,000 of which were Hispanic. Other databases were established in cities, municipalities and states across the US. They took on similar acronyms: LEADS, GRIP and GREAT, to name a few. From Orange County to New York City to Albuquerque, the era of big data in fighting gangs had begun.

Yet the databases were deeply flawed. There was still no consensus on what constituted a gang member. Law enforcement simply used the lists at their discretion, creating their own criteria and determining who fit, some of it ad hoc. By 2012, for example, 11 percent of all Blacks and 4 percent of all Hispanics between the ages of twenty and twenty-four in Los Angeles County were included in the gang database. A later audit by the California state government found that forty-two people in the database were placed on the list as infants.

The implications of these lists were significant. They were used to determine motive in courts and apply sentence enhancements. Federal and state agencies would consult them before offering employment. And authorities would use them to accelerate the deportation of suspected gang members.

Over the next twenty years, close to one hundred thousand ex-convicts would be sent to El Salvador and hundreds of thousands more to its Northern Triangle neighbors, Guatemala and Honduras, strengthening the already growing gangs in the region. Nicaragua, meanwhile, was spared. For every thousand ex-cons deported to Nicaragua, the Northern Triangle received thirty thousand. These deportees were coming home and bringing with them their grudges, their trauma and their wars.

By then, the gangs had gotten guns, including Norman's clique. One of the leaders, Malvado, carried a Llama Max .45 caliber pistol in his black Toyota. Malvado had a thick build and generous jowls. He was one of Norman's closest friends and in the summer of 1999, the two got together at a hotel to have a drink. It was 10:00 a.m.

At some point during the day-long binge, two other men joined them, and then a woman. When that bar closed, the five of them decided to go to a Texaco. There was a food stall that sold liquor next to the gas station where they could sing mariachis and keep pushing the evening along. Others mingled at the Texaco, including the husband of a woman who would later tell authorities she and her husband had drunk "forty beers and two bottles of liquor" that night.

One person verbally provoked another and the man, his wife later told authorities, grabbed a knife. She said she tried to stop him but couldn't. She was "lost" in a drunken haze, she later testified.

One of the gang members went to the car, described as "a Toyota with tinted windows" in the case file, and got the Llama Max .45 caliber. Shots rang out—six by the count of the private security guard who watched the whole thing but couldn't, or refused, to identify any of the MS-13 members later as assailants. Then Norman, or someone else in his crowd, or various members of his crowd, took the knife and stabbed the man several times.

When police arrived, they found the man on the ground with the bloody knife next to him. Officers drove the victim straight to the hospital in their squad car, where he was pronounced dead from his wounds. The five bloodied suspects fled the scene in the Toyota, but the police stopped them a few blocks away. The officers pulled them from the vehicle and started beating them.

"Kill me!" Norman remembered screaming as they beat him and his friends into the pavement with their fists, batons and rifle butts.

Inside the car, the police found the Llama Max and blood stains.

At the station the police asked the wife, "Who did it, who killed your husband?"

The inebriated woman pointed at Norman.

7

"WE GO TO WAR."

1.

AS HE DROVE THROUGH THE CITY ON THE MORNING of June 24, 2009, Los Angeles Police Detective Frank Flores was pleased. Under the umbrella of the FBI's special MS-13 unit, Flores and the head of the unit, Jon Bauman, had pieced together what they believed was a landmark case.

The case came, in part, from their work on a significant drug and murder conspiracy investigation involving an MS-13 leader named Nelson Comandari.[12] The wiretaps in that case picked up voices of gang leaders in Los Angeles and El Salvador, among other places. On many of these wires, they heard a nickname, Rebelde (Rebel). The conversations also featured a Camarón (Shrimp) and a Zombie. But the FBI was focused on Rebelde.

They had recorded the calls for years. In all, they had some

12 His name is sometimes written in official documents as Commandari.

seventy thousand telephone communications on file. They also gathered testimony from numerous gang members who talked up Rebelde. And as they deciphered the conversations and the testimonies, two things became clear to them: Rebelde was Alex Sanchez, and Sanchez was still a gang leader in the MS-13.

Were it true, the discovery would shake the city. In the mid-1990s, Sanchez had been deported to El Salvador, had returned illegally and then distanced himself from gang life. Part of this pivot was paternal—he had a son, and he wanted to be a good father. Part of it was therapeutic—he'd begun working with a gang-intervention program called Homies Unidos. The organization received substantial political backing and city government funding. Alex himself had become a cause célèbre, denouncing police abuses and fighting against his own deportation.

There were skeptics, among them Flores and Bauman, who questioned Sanchez's commitment to his new life. Sanchez argued his status as a former gang member was what made him an effective counter-gang specialist. But the approach had rekindled a debate: Were gang leaders using non-governmental organizations (NGOs) as facades to camouflage their criminal lives?

Flores and Bauman thought they had the answer, at least as it related to Sanchez. In one of the calls, Sanchez told his gang counterparts, "We go to war," an illustration, investigators said, that Sanchez was putting a murder plot into motion.

The caravan pulled in front of Sanchez's apartment complex in Bellflower, a predominantly White, working-class area filled with one-story bungalows and sunbaked lawns. It was 6:00 a.m. The twilight was creeping over the tree line. Across the city, police were conducting similar raids related to the same racketeering indictment. In all, the government would charge twenty-four members of the MS-13 with crimes ranging from murder to gun charges to robbery.

But for Flores, this suspect had taken on special meaning. He'd had a pair of handcuffs engraved for the occasion in honor of two other officers who'd left the force—in large part because of a lawsuit Alex had filed against them for harassment. He gave the cuffs to Bauman.

Bauman's team surrounded Sanchez's house and Sanchez opened the door.

"Put your hands up! Walk backwards! Turn around!"

As Sanchez lowered his hands behind his back, Bauman placed the cuffs Frank had given him on Alex's wrists, then led him outside where Frank was waiting.

2.

Frank remembers the first time he thought about being a cop. He was a teenager playing basketball in Evergreen Park with some friends. A man ran by them, and a policeman gave chase. Frank and his friends stopped the game and watched as the two converged. It was part of living in Boyle Heights, the gritty East Los Angeles area where violent drama often played out like an episode of *T.J. Hooker.* In full stride, the policeman pulled his night stick from his belt, raised it in the air and slung it toward the suspect, hitting him in the legs and sending him careening face-first into the gravel. *Oooohhhh!* he and his friends cooed.

Although he grew up surrounded by some of the most storied barrios in Los Angeles—White Fence, Primera Flats, Cuatro Flats, Mob Crew, VNE and Big Hazard among them—Frank never doubted his path. From the beginning, he was the anti-cholo. He favored crew cuts, dressed in Huskie jeans rather than Dickies, and ducked his head during lunch when the gangs gathered in tight circles, avoiding the fateful question: *¿Qué barrio?*

His family also kept an eye out for him. Frank's mother was born in Texas, his father in Ciudad Juárez, Mexico. When Flores was five, his father left and started another family. His maternal grandparents, who were restaurateurs, became his bedrock.

His uncle was an old-school cholo who warned Frank on more than one occasion that he would have to answer to him if he tried to join a gang. And his godmother would show up unannounced to the park to make sure he was playing basketball with his friends and not smoking marijuana.

Six months after Frank turned twenty, he applied for the police academy. At twenty-one, he became the youngest enrollee, the ultimate rookie amongst rookies. During the simulations, the others in his class made him the "utility guy," dressing Frank in what he described as a red Michelin Man suit. Frank cut an imposing figure, but his counterparts, the female cadets in particular, pummeled him using the punching methods and night stick techniques they'd learned in their six months at the academy. "After a while, that suit just doesn't absorb the punches anymore," he told me with a smile.

After a few years as a beat cop, the police assigned Frank to CRASH, the antigang unit created in the 1970s. Of the twelve guys on Frank's team, almost all had Latino surnames, but most could not speak Spanish very well. This is common among children of first-generation immigrants whose parents and grandparents shun their native language for the same reasons Alex Sanchez avoided the use of *vos*: it was the source of ridicule and discrimination. Frank's Spanish was better than most and put him in a good position to take the lead quicker than he had anticipated. The cases were exciting, kick-in-the-door type stuff. Robberies. Shootings. Drug busts. It was, in his own words, "intense," the type of policing that reminded him of the cop chopping down that suspect in Evergreen Park.

It was also instructive. By the 1990s, CRASH had developed a reputation for pushing the limits of law enforcement. Gang injunctions in particular gave officers wide latitude. CRASH units regularly rounded up suspected gang members and charged them with petty crimes, knowing their sentences would be enhanced by their gang status.

Frank's CRASH unit worked Hollywood, where a few prominent MS-13 cliques were operating, most notably the Hollywood Locos. At the time, the MS-13 was a small part of Frank's CRASH unit portfolio. But he could see the gang was evolving as a criminal organization and growing into a prominent street presence. Their new, powerful parent organization, the Mexican Mafia, was using the mara for its own ends, often under the guise of what Frank saw as dubious gang truces. But the MS-13 were also taxing drug dealers and stealing cars, some of which they sent to Central America, providing the foundation for the gang's budding criminal enterprise in that region. Some cliques matured quicker than others—the Hollywood Locos was one of these.

The Hollywood clique shot caller was Nelson Comandari. He was not a typical mara. According to one former Salvadoran police commander with knowledge of the leader, Comandari had grown up among criminals. Comandari's uncle counterfeited Salvadoran currency, trafficked scrap metal stolen from government functionaries and fabricated tax seals for counterfeiters. Even when this uncle was arrested, he remained active in the underworld, setting up a *motelito*, "little motel," inside the prison where he would rent rooms with romantic music for conjugal visits. The family also had stakes in multinational businesses. Another uncle trafficked stolen shrimp before getting into the international drug trafficking business with members of the Cali Cartel.

Nelson Comandari would later take advantage of these drug connections but not before they nearly landed some family members in prison. The drug war was in full swing in Colombia, and in the early 1990s, the Cali Cartel employed Comandari family members to take out its main enemy, Pablo Escobar, who was at the time in a prison the Colombian government had constructed in Medellin especially for him. The Comandari clan worked its contacts. One uncle secured three oblong five-hundred-pound bombs of the type used on a Salvadoran A-37 Dragonfly during the civil war. An air force officer working on the inside snuck the bombs out with the refuse. Another uncle had the bombs painted yellow with the word *Caterpillar*—the heavy-equipment maker—written on the side and moved them to a port where they were to be taken to Colombia and dropped on the special prison from a helicopter.

However, an informant foiled the plot. El Salvador police seized the bombs and arrested a Cuban, two Guatemalans and a half-dozen Salvadorans. Among those captured were several members of the Comandari family, but through their powerful connections they ultimately evaded prosecution.

Some Comandari family members operated, in part, from San Salvador's vivacious city center, where they had regular contact with politicians and criminal groups. It was there the young Nelson Comandari began smoking marijuana and hanging with corrupt police, car thieves, scrap dealers, gun traffickers, drug dealers and, eventually, gang members.

Nelson got into trouble, often. The police jailed him on numerous occasions, including one time when he was captured with an AK-47, stolen computers and a truckload of stolen fabrics. But like his family, he knew how to skirt justice and was never prosecuted. He would employ this talent throughout his criminal career. One prosecutor I spoke to likened him to Keyser Söze, the elusive villain from *The Usual Suspects*. "No one was ever really sure if they saw him or not," the prosecutor said.

It was during this time period that Comandari connected with the mara. Alex Sanchez told me he met Comandari on the streets. San Salvador's historic city center is home to a pristine Catholic cathedral where where Archbishop Óscar Romero gave many of his most stirring homilies. It's also where some of the country's first Salvadoran MS-13 and 18th Street cliques were born. Comandari began working with members from the Hollywood Locos to steal and resell cars, among other criminal exploits. From the beginning,

Comandari developed a reputation for knowing how to take care of his team. When his colleagues landed in prison, for instance, he would send them money. On the holidays he would bribe guards to give the prisoners a recently slaughtered cow.

After the AK-47 case against him fell apart, Nelson fled to the US. In Los Angeles, Comandari reconnected with the MS-13, specifically with Alex Sanchez, who went to eat with him, then took him to the Valley and introduced him to members of the Hollywood clique. The gang embraced him. He was generous with his new friends, using his underworld connections to bring in marijuana and cocaine, which he readily shared.

His entry into the gang came amidst controversy surrounding his true gang credentials. Gang members would claim he bought his way in, and US investigators said his beating-in ceremony was not a "thirteen-second" affair, but rather a symbolic punch or two from the more experienced mara of the Hollywood Locos, who christened him with the nickname Comanche.

Comandari quickly became a leader. He was sturdy, built like a stack of bricks, and stern. Frank says other gang members he spoke to at the time could barely pronounce his name without stuttering. "He was another level," Frank told me. "He was educated. Smart. Forward-thinking… And what he said he was going to do, he did."

Comandari instilled the gang with more discipline and meted out violent reprisals against those who crossed him. He quelled infighting and ensured the MS-13 did not victimize their civilian neighbors. "He put some chivalry into the madness," one federal investigator told me.

Comandari also established a Mexican Mafia–style operation with wholesalers and distributors, who would pay the MS-13 set fees for the exclusive right to sell drugs at fixed points in their territories. In return, the gang would provide protection. The fees were higher, but for the wholesalers and distributors they were worth it—Comandari's deal ensured predictable returns, and they were rarely stuck with excess inventory. The gang benefitted too. They increased their revenue and reduced their risk of getting caught with illegal drugs.

"It was a win-win," Frank explained.

Comandari employed the system throughout the city, including in Central Los Angeles where Alex Sanchez's Normandie Locos operated.

3.

As it happened, Alex's mother was in the apartment complex the morning Bauman and Flores arrested him. She was staying with his brother, Alvin, who had been diagnosed with cancer. And as the police readied the caravan to take Alex away, his mother glanced out the window where she could see Flores leading him into the back of a police van. It was the first time she'd been there when he'd gotten arrested.

By then, Sanchez had stopped running from authorities and had begun confronting them. After stints in prison for crimes ranging from car theft to illegal possession of a weapon to defacing public property, Alex was deported back to El Salvador in 1994, where he connected with Comandari and others. In 1995, he reentered the US without authorization and kept a much lower profile, working odd jobs and, for a time, staying off the police radar. He had a son with his girlfriend, and he began a journey that eventually brought him into the Homies Unidos's fold, first as a volunteer, then as a staffer.

In the late 1990s, Alex and others began to organize Homies Unidos meetings in places like Immanuel Presbyterian Church. A towering cement structure on Wilshire with ornate, multicolored stained-glass windows and stiff wooden pews, it was an odd choice, but its open-minded pastor was interested in mitigating gang violence. At the church, Homies Unidos volunteers and staff like Alex fed gang members and wannabes and gave them art supplies while trying to convince them to permanently give up the gang life. Some organizers and sponsors complained the kids just came for free food. Alex did not care. Perhaps reflecting on his own youth—how he'd hungrily drifted between destroyers while the Rampart police gave chase—he saw starving teenagers, not capricious, ungrateful gang kids.

Alex's affiliation with Homies Unidos did not stop police from targeting him; it may have accelerated it. He was once arrested after giving a talk for Homies Unidos at a Salvadoran restaurant. At a friend's birthday party, a CRASH officer hit him in the head with a night stick and harassed the other partygoers. On another occasion, CRASH officers picked him up and interrogated him at the station, then dropped him in another neighborhood, a practice to make it look like he was snitching. CRASH officers also stopped Alex and others going in and out of the Immanuel Presbyterian Church before and after meetings. To the police, Alex wasn't a *calmado*, gang slang for "retiree." He was establishing a new persona, helping to expand the gang's power by increasing its political reach and creating, as one of them said to Alex, a "supergang."

"We'll see who wins the court trial—his gang or our gang," one CRASH officer reportedly said to Sanchez, after hitting him in the groin during a routine stop-and-frisk.

According to his lawyers, CRASH focused on Alex because he'd become an alibi in a homicide case. Through the 1990s, CRASH had continued working with INS to find and deport suspected gang members, despite the 1979 Los Angeles City ordinance—pushed by then Police Chief Daryl Gates—that prohibited police from inquiring about the immigration status of suspects. CRASH had also found that it could rid itself of pesky witnesses by handing them to INS. Alex was a pesky witness, claiming that the murder suspect was actually at a Homies Unidos–organized rehearsal for a play.

The police practice of working with the INS came under

scrutiny after several members of the Rampart CRASH unit were arrested and tied to multiple cases of fabricating evidence and testimonies, filing fake police reports, and evidence theft. One member of CRASH had robbed a bank. Another had stolen drugs from a police storage unit. CRASH unit members had also beaten an 18th Street gang member they'd arrested until he'd vomited blood. As one gang member told *Frontline*, CRASH itself operated "like a gang."

In September 1999, as the Rampart CRASH scandal was coming to light, California Congressman Tom Hayden organized a panel at the Immanuel Presbyterian Church to discuss police transgressions. With cameras from local access cable running, Alex, along with prominent lawyers and activists, testified to police abuse. CRASH unit members were standing in the back of the church behind the pews, heightening the tension. In his account of that evening, Hayden said the police muttered threats to the crowd then frisked and arrested several of them when the meeting ended. For his part, Alex escaped out a side door where a waiting car whisked him away.

But the fight was just beginning. In January 2000, a member of CRASH arrested Alex then handed him to the INS for illegally entering the country in the mid-1990s. Against the backdrop of the Rampart scandal, the case to deport Sanchez received outsized political and media attention. Homies Unidos took advantage, organizing a huge group to go to the Rampart Community Police Station and file dozens of harassment complaints. Meanwhile, inside the detention center, Alex helped organize a hunger strike for a group of Cubans who'd been languishing for years in legal limbo—unwanted in both the US and Cuba. Alex and others passed messages on paper plates to spread the word. Some were leery of the Salvadoran cause célèbre, but on the designated day, no one ate. The MS-13 member once branded as Rebelde was now becoming a political insurgent.

During the Democratic National Convention in Los Angeles that summer, Alex's supporters, led by his brother Oscar and Hayden, organized a march of about a thousand people from MacArthur Park to the Rampart police station. The marchers surrounded the station wearing T-shirts reading *Todos Somos Alex* and placards calling for authorities to "Free Alex."

When Alex improbably won his asylum case—in part by getting a judge to downgrade earlier criminal acts from felonies to misdemeanors—he was free to return to his job now as director of Homies Unidos. Undeterred by threats, he remained outspoken against police and federal officials. Sanchez further antagonized the FBI by testifying for defense lawyers in federal and state conspiracy cases against MS-13 members, including in the defense of a marero in the gang killing of Brenda Paz, a gang-member turned FBI-informant, who was brutally murdered in Virginia in 2003. In response, the prosecution brought their own expert witness: LAPD Detective Frank Flores. According to the defense attorney, it was the first time a former gang member had testified, and it helped his client win his case. Alex soon became a regular expert witness; so did Frank.

In the meantime, the LAPD disbanded CRASH. An independent review panel issued a report in March 2000 that highlighted a culture of police corruption that went far beyond Rampart: racial profiling, widespread abuse and harassment, and CRASH's regular use of excessive force. In September of that same year, the city council voted to bring in the US Department of Justice to provide oversight of the LAPD while it implemented reforms. It was the second time since the Rodney King riots that the federal government had to police the police in Los Angeles.

In June 2000, during a press conference at Immanuel Presbyterian Church, Homies Unidos filed a lawsuit against two officers of CRASH, one of the over $100 million in lawsuits against the police following the Rampart scandal. Soon, Sanchez began to receive subtle and sometimes overt threats. And while the CRASH unit had been disbanded, the LAPD continued haranguing suspected gang members, and Homies Unidos continued documenting it. One of the names that kept appearing in the complaints from the gang members was Detective Frank Flores.

4.

Although he began his career banging down doors, Frank insists he was always more of a thinking man's cop. "This is a game of inches," he likes to say, employing one of the many sports metaphors he mixes into his lexicon. "They want something. You want something."

Frank wanted information. To this day, he sees his job as mainly to create opportunities to flip gang members, so they would cooperate with law enforcement. Frank would look for tells and work emotional angles. He always made a point to know about gang members' families, for instance, especially the mothers. When he arrived at a house looking for a gang suspect, he would head straight to the mother. Similarly, if Frank had jailed a suspect, and the mother came looking for him, he saw it as an opportunity to gain crucial intelligence.

"I always know a good gang officer because he knows about the gang member's family, the mom, everything around him," he told me.

Respect, Frank said, was at the core of his approach toward policing. The uniform was not about power, he added, but about understanding. He sought to disarm people by upending their expectations of the police.

"Just because you're wearing the uniform, doesn't mean you have to be that person in the uniform," he told me.

After CRASH was disbanded, Frank began working with the joint police-FBI task force where he could employ his brand of policing. Working sources. Talking to mothers. Consoling and cajoling witnesses. It was nearly a complete reversal from the

CRASH days, but Frank was at home with it, in part because it was at odds with the traditional reputation of the LAPD.

Yet many were not happy with the transition. The Rampart scandal gave everyone a reason to complain. Gang members and activists focused on abuses and corruption they said continued, including in Frank's circles. The city government had to pay for lawsuits. The police said they had been neutered, and a number of community activists agreed, illustrating the common misperception that violent neighborhoods don't want the police—in fact, they often want more boots on the ground.

The former CRASH unit cops—who had put in weekends, late nights and years tracking gang members—were demoralized and started punching the clock. After dropping for nearly a decade, homicides in Los Angeles began to rise again. Among the victims was LAPD Chief Bernard Parks's granddaughter, who was shot and killed in what authorities said was a gang-related drive-by. The police felt pressure to crack down on violence, but there was little appetite for another CRASH.

Instead, the federal government took the lead. Drawing from experience against the Mafia, the bureau formed antigang task forces around the country and developed conspiracy cases against the gangs using the Racketeer Influenced and Corrupt Organizations, or RICO, Act. RICO cases are useful for prosecuting criminal leaders who distance themselves from the organization's everyday activities. By then federal authorities had used it successfully in Los Angeles to prosecute a case against the Mexican Mafia and another against the 18th Street. But the law is easily abused. Defense lawyers like to call it the "Alice in Wonderland statute" because it allows prosecutors to entertain just about any fantasy. There were also questions about RICO's utility as it related to street gangs. The statute had been used successfully against mafias, but gangs like the MS-13 were far less hierarchical, organized or financially solvent.

Nelson Comandari's case illustrated this paradox. By the early

2000s, the FBI said the MS-13 had between eight thousand and ten thousand members, operating in thirty-three states. On paper, it looked like a near perfect drug distribution chain—from El Salvador to the United States, the gang had infrastructure, communications, weapons and access to dealers. Comandari, for example, had a stranglehold on several local Los Angeles markets. He also had international contacts, which helped him secure drugs from South America. He was, according to authorities, "the CEO" of the MS-13, pushing it to new heights.

But from almost the beginning, Comandari had trouble corralling his own members. Other gang leaders were suspicious of Comandari's intentions and jealous of his success. For the gang, Comandari's entrepreneurial endeavors and overt power grabs were disrespectful to el barrio, a mortal sin inside the organization. The tension led to violence. Between 2000 and 2003, federal authorities said Comandari killed at least seven people, most of them in the MS-13. In one clique alone, the Coronados, Comandari targeted four of its members. In 2004, Comandari targeted one of his lieutenants. Gang leaders told me the death toll was much higher and included murders in El Salvador where Comandari maintained his hitman networks.

Comandari also faced logistical challenges. MS-13 members were, to put it simply, not good criminals. With their distinct tattoos and peculiar style of dress, they were highly visible. They lacked discipline, and their internal codes pushed them into public confrontations with other gangs that could lead to their capture and force them into cooperating with law enforcement. They were inexperienced and naive, talking on phones that authorities easily tapped. And they were clumsy operators, pulling their guns when they didn't need them, and shooting when they didn't have to.

This sloppiness was what the FBI and Frank depended on to build their case against Comandari. After being captured in 2000, a Comandari lieutenant flipped. Authorities began recording his phone calls with Comandari, as well as to gang leaders up and down the East and West Coast. Comandari was attempting to consolidate the gang's power and leverage its reach for a nationwide drug trafficking initiative. Authorities captured additional MS-13 members who also flipped. Investigators like Frank logged phone numbers then tapped them, and the case expanded.

Comandari began moving his operations outside the gang, working more regularly with the Mexican Mafia, which continued to rule the MS-13 from the prisons. In a diagram of the hierarchy drawn up by authorities, Comandari is directly below his two Mafia sponsors, and parallel with a Mafia fixer and two other gang operators from the Sureños's umbrella group. Below him are telephone facilitators, a drug dealer and two maras, who appear as "associates," the only MS-13 members on the chart.

Comandari started operations as far away as New York and Texas, but his ambition was getting the best of him. Soon, East Coast investigators started to track his movements and listen to his phone calls. Comandari was wily and often dropped off the map. But he was also increasingly isolated from his support networks, and in March 2005, authorities captured him in Houston at his mother's house.

Under normal circumstances, arresting the CEO of the MS-13 would have inspired fanfare. However, US prosecutors buried the news. The silence was a sign: Comandari, like his lieutenants and others in the MS-13 before him, were talking, and investigators like Flores and the FBI's Bauman were debriefing him. What's more, with Comandari's testimony, the MS-13 conspiracy case was widening yet again. Flores and the FBI didn't just want the criminal arm of the organization, they wanted the political one. Specifically, they wanted Alex Sanchez. And Comandari—and others—were giving him up.

5.

The *United States of America v. Jose Alfaro et al.* was part of a multilayered, sixty-six-page RICO indictment against twenty-four members of the MS-13. In the indictment, "Alex Sanchez, aka Rebelde," was the twenty-second person mentioned, nestled between Jute and Tears. The indictment had a long description of the MS-13, a necessary precursor in RICO cases. For there to be a conspiracy, there must first be a criminal organization that binds the players.

It was also a story of the gang in Los Angeles in the late 1990s and early 2000s—a dizzying array of criminal acts: sales of crack, cocaine, meth and heroin; a forced overdose; a body dumped on the side of the 110 Freeway; assault with a deadly weapon; loitering in front of a Subway sandwich shop; shooting two gang members in a parking lot. It went on for 33 pages, chronicling 127 events. And that was just Count 1.

Prosecutors connected Alex to two specific crimes. First, the indictment enveloped him in a drug trafficking conspiracy, claiming he was part of what was essentially Comandari's petty drug dealing operations—control of wholesalers and dealers collecting renta from the traqueteros; taxes and payouts to the Mexican Mafia. Second, they listed him as one of four participants in "a series of phone conversations…during which they conspired to kill Walter Lacinos, aka 'Cameron' [*sic*]."

Lacinos, or Camarón (Shrimp), was once one of Alex's protégés in the Normandie. Alex had been in the group who'd administered his brinco, which, under normal circumstances, engenders a special bond. But in 1997 Lacinos was captured, tried and sentenced to ten years on felony weapons charges. He believed that a fellow Normandie, nicknamed Zombie, had informed on him, leading to his arrest.

Authorities first sent Lacinos to Los Angeles County Jail. There, he seethed, imagining the type of revenge he would take against his snitches. He was eventually moved to a Supermax prison in Florence, Colorado, a brutal, mountainside penitentiary where he spent twenty-three hours a day in solitary confinement and began to mentally deteriorate. The mara sent him money and correspondence, but no one from his family visited, Alex told me. He was, in essence, alone. The isolation sent him into a tailspin from which he never recovered. "He went crazy," Alex said.

It was there, Alex says, that Lacinos decided he would kill not just Zombie, but also Alex and two others in the Normandie who Lacinos believed were informants for the police and the FBI. Alex says he heard about Lacinos's threat on his life on May 6, 2006, as he was walking through Koreatown with his son. By then, Lacinos had been released and deported back to El Salvador where he'd requested that leaders green light Alex, Zombie and the others.

Alex says he was not in a charitable mood that day and wanted "to settle" the matter, so he dropped his son at home and went to talk to some local gang leaders. The group was drinking when he arrived at the apartment where they'd gathered, and he says he decided to join them. The alcohol loosened his lips, he told me, and he began talking more "shit" than he probably should have.

6.

Frank Flores is a traditionalist, a conservative at heart. He wears a suit and neatly pressed shirt over his beefy body. He's always clean-shaven and seemingly well rested. He wants stability, order. When he was little, for example, his Japanese neighbor used to take meticulous care of his garden, coifing his boysenberry tree, and occasionally dropping fruit into Frank's young hands. It was a beautiful gesture that Frank thought of as a symbol of living in a true melting pot of cultures and communities. But as he got older, the neighbor stopped caring for the garden, and the boysenberry tree withered and died.

The gangs, Frank says, were at the heart of the city's demise. They had become more sinister, more reckless than his uncle's brand of cholos. "It was not about the neighborhood," he said, using the English for barrios. "It became about money and drugs."

The gang may have had an equally ferocious vendetta against Flores both for his counter-gang actions as a policeman, and, if the complaints compiled by the Homies Unidos were to be believed, his abuse of MS-13 members. In two of the intercepted calls in the Sanchez case, gang leaders from the Hollywood Locos discussed assassinating the detective, even going so far as to select the weapon to do it. Frank identified one of the voices on a wiretap, and police picked up the suspect, thwarting the plan. Frank would soon be called again to decipher the wiretaps at the heart of the case against Alex.

Those wiretaps started with a call on May 6, 2006, the same day Alex said he heard about Lacinos's request to green light him and several others. After a few beers with the other mara at the apartment, Alex and about ten MS-13 members got on a speakerphone; a Normandie leader, Moisés Humberto Rivera, alias Santos, picked up his phone in a prison in El Salvador.

"Hello!" one of the LA mara says.

"What's up?" Santos replies.

"What's up, homie, how are you?" the LA mara says.

They continue briefly, until Alex jumps in.

"What's up, man!"

Alex and Santos then go back and forth for a bit. At the heart of the issue was a document Lacinos had taken to Santos. Lacinos said the document proved Zombie was the snitch who'd landed him in prison. But Alex repeatedly says the document is a forgery and blames Comandari, the jailed former leader of the MS-13, for its fabrication. As they continue, Alex gets noticeably more agitated. Eventually, his anger overflows.

"And you know what?" Alex says. "All the cliques over here still have a lot of respect for me, and now I'm going to show these papers to a fucking bunch of homies from other cliques, to show them what a liar this motherfucker is. And you know what? You know what, man? Tomorrow he has to face the consequences."

Alex then apologizes to Santos for getting tense, and the two continue to talk like this until the call drops. Rivera calls back, and they go back and forth until the call drops again.

Rivera calls back a third time, and this time patches Lacinos into the call. At first, Lacinos is desperate to clear himself. But no one in LA believes him, and tensions rise.

"No! [call breaks] the motherfucker!" Alex says to Lacinos. "Can you see that? *You see who you are!*"

Background voices drown out the next words, before the transcriber picks up the conversation again.

"If you want to start something, we are going to start something, man," Alex says to Lacinos.

Seemingly frustrated, Lacinos tries to exclude Alex from the conversation, or perhaps needle him.

"You get involved in things, when you're no longer active, man! You see? Better yet, what you should do is to be careful with 'Homies Unidos'[13] and not, not get involved in our things, you see?" Lacinos says.

The call breaks, then returns with Lacinos saying, "because you are no longer active, see what I mean?"

"I have never, I have never worked with those motherfuckers," Alex responds, referring to the accusations he'd talked to police or the FBI. "And I can assure you that the day I fucking screw up with the barrio, I'll kill myself!"

The call ends without any clear resolution, but the next day Alex talked to Zombie. From the transcript, it is never clear who Zombie is, and he's not identified by name in the call records. What's clear, though, is that something has been decided.

---

13 The translated transcript reads, "United Homies," which was a reference to Homies Unidos.

"The thing is this, you see? This dude is, is already..." Alex pauses. "The—the—the homies over there, man—right now—as I was told, man—are going to stop all the activities this guy is involved in, in the barrio, man. You see? Because this guy, this guy is doing something against the whole clique, against all of us. He is threatening us, talking shit about us, and now all of us have answered."

Zombie and Alex go back and forth a bit before Alex breathes the words, "We can defend you—we are all doing that. And we have said, we go to war."

Alex goes on.

"You see, every time this guy would send a threat they would respond here, you see what I'm saying? But not now. That's it, man. You see? Because we wanted to deal with this thing, but we wanted to take it easy, you see? To do what we needed to do but taking it easy."

In the call, Alex adds that they once respected Lacinos, helped him while he was in prison and refrained from talking "shit" about him.

"Until now," Zombie answers.

"So, the thing is that this dude has made it public. You see what I mean?" Alex responds, "So, now we find ourselves in a position where we have to do it that way. You know? We not only have to do that on our own, but it's now a barrio thing."

A barrio thing it was. A little over a week later, a marero named Zombie killed Lacinos.

7.

About a month after he was arrested, Alex was in court, shackled and dressed in white prison garb, for his bail hearing. His family, his colleagues, other gang prevention specialists, academics, politicians and supporters packed the courtroom. Over one hundred people had written letters on his behalf, including

Congressman Hayden, a former assistant agent-in-charge of the FBI's Los Angeles office, and political aides who had worked with Homies Unidos.

Alex's brother, Oscar, was again leading the call for his brother's exoneration. Oscar's path had been surreal. After his tumultuous youth taking beatings from his mother and watching his brother go in and out of juvenile hall and prison, he'd decided to study criminology. In a cruel twist of fate, he'd had an internship at the Rampart Community Police Station where he told me he could sometimes hear the screams of the suspects the police were torturing in "the dungeon," a holding cell on the floor below his office. Soon afterward, he said he dropped criminology and got into environmental preservation. Now he was back by his brother's side.

The powerful outpouring of support for Alex did not cow the government. The lead prosecutor said that while those who had written letters were "well intentioned," they had been "duped" and didn't know about Alex's "double life." To prove her point, she showed a photo of Alex after his arrest, his chest visibly tattooed with *Mara Salvatrucha*. She then showed a photo of Alex and another man flashing gang signs she said was taken during a break in a gang prevention conference in San Francisco ten years earlier. "Rebel and Laughing Boy. MS-NLS-13," was written on the back, the *NLS* a reference to the Normandie clique.

Then she turned to the wiretaps and Frank Flores's interpretation of them, which she said showed that Alex was "an active participant in agitating for the retaliation against Walter Lacinos." For Flores—whose testimony in front of the grand jury about this and other telephone calls had secured Alex's name on the indictment—phrases such as "face the consequences," "all of us have answered" and "we go to war," were calls to put a murder plot into motion. Santos, the Normandie leader on the other end of the phone, was a shot caller, and just as he had the power to green-light Alex's murder, so too could he green-light

Lacinos's murder. What's more, Frank claimed the phrase "taking it easy" meant that Alex, who he said was a shot caller, was just lying low, waiting for the right moment to attack his rival.

The defense had not seen the phone call transcripts nor heard the audio, but they would soon submit a detailed response to them by Father Greg Boyle. Boyle is a cherub-faced, healthy-bellied Jesuit priest and founder of Homeboy Industries, a prominent gang intervention program. The priest had worked in Boyle Heights for decades and could describe in intimate, and often lighthearted detail the inner workings of dozens of Los Angeles barrios.

Boyle's affidavit contradicted Flores's in nearly every way possible. While Flores said Alex was a shot caller, Boyle said he was a mediator. Where Flores referenced Alex's push that Lacinos "face the consequences" as a call to violent action, Boyle said it was simply Alex's way of pushing for a more thorough examination of the paperwork Lacinos was using against him. When Flores said "we go to war" was an order to kill, Boyle said it was "encouragement," so that Zombie would speak up and address Lacinos's lies. When Flores said "taking it easy" meant they were lying low, waiting for the right moment to strike, Boyle said it meant nothing.

"There is no 'coded' or gang language specific about the phrase 'taking it easy,'" Boyle wrote, adding that, "'We go to war'…is a figure of speech."

Boyle finalized his testimony by stating that no plot to kill anyone stems from long, drawn-out conversations on an international line in which the two sides confront one another in search of a resolution. In fact, murder plots are planned and executed with short, straightforward communications. What's more, at no point did Alex say there was a green light, or an order to kill, Lacinos.

Perhaps the most persuasive part of Boyle's affidavit was when he pointed out what Flores did not mention from the transcript.

To be sure, the strongest exculpatory evidence from the wiretaps was Lacinos telling Alex that he is "no longer active" and should not even be on the phone.

"One might, then, logically ask, 'So what is Mr. Sanchez doing on these calls?' In fact, that is exactly what Camarón wants to know. Why is a nonactive member even involved?" Boyle wrote. "He is involved because Camarón has told others Mr. Sanchez is cooperating with the FBI. Given Camarón's allegation that Mr. Sanchez is an informant, Mr. Sanchez has the place, purpose and permission to respond. By participating in the call, Mr. Sanchez is trying to clear his own name, is trying to save Zombie's life, and is seeking to bring a peaceful resolution to a highly inflamed situation. Contrary to Detective Flores's contention, Mr. Sanchez is not plotting to end a life; rather, he is trying to save lives."

The defense had a hard time submitting Boyle's affidavit. At a later hearing, one judge—who an LA defense attorney once described as a "five-year-old with power"—would call Boyle's submission "irrelevant," apparently confusing it with a letter of support, which Boyle also submitted.

Indeed, the early stages of the Sanchez case were a brutal reminder of just how warped the system had become. Comandari, the former CEO of the MS-13 who was at the heart of the original investigation, had disappeared into witness protection. Sanchez, the gang intervention specialist who had widespread support for his work, was facing life in jail.

The judge denied bail citing Alex's "risk of dangerousness," in spite of the over $1 million in pledges to help him post bond. Alex was devastated.

"Alex Sanchez looked small as he was led out of the courtroom in his white jumpsuit and manacles," one reporter wrote. "On his way out, he did his best to shoot family and friends reassuring glances. He was okay, his expression said, although he didn't look okay."

8

“WE RULED.”

1.

ALMA[14] ARRIVED IN TEXAS LIKE SO MANY OTHERS had and would in the years to come: on her own. She had just turned fourteen, and she was one of many Unaccompanied Alien Children—or UAC, in immigration vernacular—moving across one of the deadliest borders in the world. Hundreds of thousands of UAC would soon follow in an unprecedented surge that would eventually foment an immigration crisis.

By the time US immigration officials picked her up in June 2010 and took her to a detention center, she had traversed two countries over a two-week period with two dozen people she didn't know. She was, like many of them, fleeing the gangs that had proliferated in El Salvador's cities and spilled into countryside towns like hers.

14 For security reasons, her name and other details of her story have been changed.

In Alma's hometown in an eastern state of El Salvador, the MS-13 had cliques even in the smallest villages. They extorted everyone from auto repairmen to cotton candy sellers. After infiltrating the local tuc-tuc transportation system, they established fierce control over the dirt arteries that snaked into the rural hamlets. They monitored residents, carefully tracking families who received remittances from relatives in the United States, who purchased new cars, who bought cattle or extra chicken feed. They used homes as respites and hiding places, moving into people's living rooms and helping themselves to the contents of their refrigerators.

Development, or any sign of it, simply stopped. No municipal projects went forward until security concerns could be allayed. No new investors came into the area, and the old ones left. No one remodeled their home, lest the gang presume they had some extra cash. People fled, most of them in packs of fifteen or twenty, like Alma and her group had. Other than a cousin she barely spoke to, Alma knew no one on the journey. Her departure had been abrupt, cinematic.

The gang had made it clear they wanted her dead. She had broken one of their rules. A gang wannabe had already hit her square in the head with the butt of a handgun, leaving a deep circular bruise in the middle of her temple, right at the hairline. The scar would stay with her for life.

Her parents saw the injury and knew the implications. Alma was the last of twelve children. Beginning in the early 2000s, they had started sending their kids to the US. By the time Alma went on the run, the family had a few go-to coyotes. The one they contacted was a friend of Alma's godmother, who also knew the power of the gangs—she'd been extorted because of the remittances her children sent to her from the United States. This coyote could make room for Alma on the next bus out of town, he said, and would make sure that she got special care along the way.

Her mom hustled Alma to a hotel in San Salvador with a backpack and some of her clothes. They would not see each other again for years. But when they parted, the two didn't hug; they barely spoke. Her mother left, and Alma waited in the hotel.

It was an agonizing few days. In addition to the bruise on her forehead, she was nursing another, deeper wound. Just days before, during an emotional fight with her parents, she had mutilated her own hand with a knife and tried to close the bloody lesion by burning it with cigarettes. Her arm began to swell, turning deep red with a tint of green, but there was no time to get a doctor. The group had gathered, and she left with them on a bus, heading north.

Alma got as far as the Guatemala-Mexico border before she was overcome with fever. Normally she would have been left behind, but due to the family's long-standing relationship with the coyote, he halted the journey for her. Everyone waited for five days in a hotel until Alma's fever dropped and the swelling in her arm subsided.

They split into two vans and traveled to a village in the middle of Mexico where they checked into a motel in groups of two. Then, they were off again, this time by car, until they'd arrived at Reynosa, along the US border. Although they were just a few hundred yards from the US, this was the most dangerous part of the trip. At the time, Reynosa was a cauldron of organized crime. The two major Mexican criminal groups operating in the area were feuding. Both earned money, in part, by kidnapping groups like Alma's and holding them for ransom. When the families could not pay, the migrants were forced into slave labor, including sex work. Those who refused, got killed.

When I asked her about this part of the journey, however, Alma smiled. She has a wide smile that contrasts sharply with her deep scowl. She described herself as bipolar, a result of a life of abuse and trauma, none of which happened along this treacherous passage. Instead, her group surprised her with a cake. It was her fourteenth birthday. It was the first time she could remember celebrating it, ever.

The next days, however, were difficult. After crossing the Rio Grande in groups of four in small rubber boats, they gathered again on the US side and began walking through what Alma described as a forest. She remembered a waterfall, but mostly she remembered the cacti. Despite the two layers of pants she was wearing to protect her legs, she could still feel the pricks. They rested at daybreak then started walking again when darkness fell. Alma likes to wear high-top sneakers, but she is not athletic. She lasted two more nights, then she was done. The others mildly encouraged her, but she could not move and was putting them at risk. They left.

Immigration picked up Alma shortly thereafter and took her to a detention center. There she called her sister, Magdalena. Magdalena, who had left for the US in the early 2000s, was fifteen years older than Alma. She was living in Virginia and could take her in, she told immigration officials.

Still, the process took months. At various points, immigration officials and others asked Alma about her place of origin, her reasons for fleeing, her plans in the US. She was polite, forthcoming even. She told her social worker things she had held secret for years, things that had led to drastic, life-altering decisions which would tear her family apart. The conversation seemed to cover every topic, sometimes multiple times. But there was one subject the US officials never broached: they never asked her if she was in a gang.

2.

Alma said she couldn't remember a day in El Salvador when she was not physically or verbally abused. Her father beat her, she said, with anything he could get his hands on: a broomstick, a whip, the flat end of a machete. Her mom justified every strike with an insult or a sweeping statement about her worthlessness. "Maybe they were just tired from all the kids they had," Alma told me. "And I suffered the consequences."

Alma's fourteen-member family lived in a small adobe home on the edge of a steep hillside surrounded by maize. Her family farmed the country's basic food staples: corn, beans and rice. She wasn't the youngest. The youngest died after childbirth in the hospital. He was laid to rest in front of the house, beneath a cross that overlooked a lush green valley spread below her family's land.

Alma slept in her parents' room, until the back-to-back 2001 earthquakes cracked the foundation and forced the family to move to the top of the hill. The United States Agency for International Development (USAID) paid for part of the new construction. Alma's older siblings eventually paid for the rest by wiring money from the United States.

In the new house on the top of the hill, Alma's life began to spin out of control. She was almost eight, as she tells it, and was in the fields, helping to gather corn from her family's modest landholdings. Her relatives were around, as they always were, including her paternal stepgrandfather, who was engaged with chores. The family still lives this way—uncles, aunts, cousins, stepkids and other partners residing in adobe and cinder-block homes that dot the steep hills.

At some point, her stepgrandfather grabbed her, forced her to the ground and raped her. She blacked out during the assault and when she awoke, she was bleeding and covered in dirt. She made her way home, ignoring angry calls from her parents at the doorway, who were upset that she was crying and tracking mud into the house. She went straight to the shower. When she emerged, her father beat her, and her mother berated her. They told her that people who take showers while crying go crazy.

She did not tell them what happened, and they did not ask, but from then on, she would never leave the house without a knife or a machete, a practice that would continue even after she came to the United States. The custom would come in handy. Her stepgrandfather, she said, would try to rape her again, but she stabbed him in his hand. When her grandmother threatened to call the police, she threatened right back.

"We'll see who has more to lose," she told her grandmother, who put down the phone. The veiled reference hung in the air for years.

At school Alma was, by her own admission, a bully. She used any excuse to verbally and physically abuse the younger students. She did not feel their pain, and she desperately wanted to escape her own.

"I went [to school] but just to go, to beat up the other kids. I was the worst with the younger kids," she told me. "I was harsh. It helped me get out the shit that I was suffering in my house. I took it out on [the kids] at school."

In the meantime, her older sister—not Magdalena, who by then had gone to the US—began dating a gang leader. El Tigre, as he was known, was part of the most powerful local MS-13 clique in the area. He camouflaged himself with his informal transport business, running people in and out of town in his pickup. This was the gang's way: hide in plain sight.

The family relationship gave Alma an in, and she approached El Tigre. She was nine years old, but for an abused girl in a violent, male-dominated world, Alma's relationship with the MS-13 was a natural fit. When I asked her about it, she started with a refrain I had heard from other gang members: that the gang represented a reprieve from her own abuse, an escape hatch, an alternate community.

"For me, they were my first family. With them, I felt—how can I say this—I felt protected. With them, I felt happy," she explained. "In my mom's house, though, I felt miserable. I wasn't happy there. With [my parents], I didn't feel happy. I still don't feel happy with them."

Large Catholic families like Alma's were once the backbone of the labor force. As rural landholdings grew smaller, large families had extra hands and the same number of hungry mouths. Those extra hands drifted to the big cities, or to the United States or to the gang. Alma was, in this way, collateral damage of a cultural and economic transition, an old Salvadoran way of life colliding with a new Salvadoran reality.

Alma told El Tigre that she wanted to be in the gang. He asked her why, and she told him that she didn't want to be in her house because they all hit her.

"That's how it started. That's how I started to hang with them," she said.

The gang gave her access to alcohol and marijuana, and she began consuming drugs on a nearly daily basis. She loved the drugs. They had the effect she sought: to forget her problems at home, in particular her rape. They also gave her a feeling of invincibility. It was little wonder that she would do whatever the gang wanted.

Beyond an escape, Alma's gang affiliation gave her power. No one outside of the gang messed with her. Not her neighbors, not the men on the streets or the farmworkers, not her fellow classmates. Eventually, even her dad stopped beating her.

The words she used were *andar mandando*. It wasn't typical gang slang, but it aptly described her feeling: roughly translated, it meant, "We ruled."

3.

Like other gang members, Alma is cagey about what the mara asked of her in those first few months, the tests she had to pass to gain respect, the final hurdles she had to cross in order to get in. Alma was part of a second generation of modern street gangs in El Salvador. MS-13's initiation process had escalated from acts of robbery to assault to murder. To move from *poste* or *paro*, "lookout," to *chequeo*, "probation period," to *homie*, the prospective entry-level member had to commit up to five murders. Members typically describe their trajectory in three acts: heady anticipation, initiation and eventually, disillusionment.

Alma's first few months were a whirlwind of drugs and violence. At the time, the MS-13 still accepted women as members. Initiation came via sex or the standard "thirteen-second" beating, she told me. Alma requested the latter. Although Alma's father had sent her sister to live in the US, Alma was still close to El Tigre, who began counting to thirteen. She shielded her chest and face while her mara counterparts pummeled her. When it was over, she took on the nickname La Jefa (the Chief) and soon after tattooed *MS* between her thumb and forefinger.

She was ten years old.

In its first few decades, the MS-13 permitted women to be members. They joined in small numbers and held limited roles. While fighting into the gang—as Alma did—earned you more respect than getting sexed in, women were never officially leaders, and they couldn't become *gatilleros*, "assassins," because male gang members didn't believe they were ruthless enough. Mostly, the gang tasked its women members with intelligence gathering, message sharing or extortion collection. Occasionally, they sold drugs or managed weapons depots.

In general, the mara scorned and abused women. The gang's principal enemies are *chavalas*, slang for "little girls." And *trust no bitch* is a common expression. In this way, the gangs were largely a reflection of Salvadoran society. The country has one of the highest femicide rates in Latin America, and the government has institutionalized control of the female body in extreme ways, such as prosecuting women for abortions, even in cases of rape. While rape outside of the gang was against MS-13's rules, sexual assault and rape of girlfriends and women hanging with the gang remained rampant. What's more, these women lived under a near constant cloud of suspicion. A break in routine. A street-side conversation. An extended absence. A lost telephone. A glance in the wrong direction. For the MS-13, these were all legitimate reasons to kill women. And they did.

One court case in El Salvador that I obtained tracked the exploits of a Salvadoran MS-13 clique from the mid-2000s—the same time period when Alma joined the gang—captured the savage details of this devolution. In the opening pages, two witnesses—one a gang member, the other a gang collaborator—testified that the gang killed a half-dozen women during a five-month stretch for reasons ranging from perceived infidelity to perceived slights, then buried them in shallow graves.

One victim, who'd broken up with a jailed mara, was dragged to a house and gang-raped "in her vagina, her mouth and her anus," the case file reads, before the leader cut her throat. "This is how you kill these bitches," the gang leader reportedly said.

In a second case chronicled in the case file, an incarcerated gang leader had his clique track his girlfriend's movements to a destroyer after she'd visited him in prison. When she disappeared from the house without explanation, questions were raised, then orders were given. The mara later gang-raped and killed her for, as the witness told investigators, "lacking respect for an imprisoned homeboy."

Perhaps the most brutal of these cases involved a fourteen-year-old girl identified as Tiffany. Tiffany was condemned for "playing with the mind" of a gang member nicknamed Baby. "She is flirting with an 18th Street," his counterparts told him. They gang-raped her so many times that one member later complained that by the time he got to her, she was only good "for a suck."

According to the case file, Baby was there when they killed her, wrapped her body in a plastic bag and tossed her into a three-foot-deep grave. Baby was devastated and cried to another mara over his loss. "She was pregnant," Baby told his friend. "It was going to be her first child."

4.

Once in the gang, Alma began to carry a 9-millimeter handgun, which the gang had taught her to shoot. She stored it beneath her pillow in her room in the USAID-funded part of the house where she slept. She continued to carry a knife too, just in case.

She sold marijuana. She was tasked—or volunteered, really—to gather intelligence on the neighbors: who was getting remittances, who had financed a *quinceañera*, or who had remodeled a bathroom. Then she would collect, pressing the cold end of the 9-millimeter to the side of the victim's head, if necessary. Or sometimes, even if it wasn't.

"We would say, 'Those people have money.' And they would have to pay renta. We would collect a little money from them," she explained. "Like, for example, if someone had five kids in the United States, I would see who was in the United States, and I would call that person. 'If you don't pay me such and such, then I will kill your daughter.'"

Alma's godmother had family in the US who sent her money. Alma told the gang. *Call her*, they said. Alma dialed her godmother from a burner phone. When she answered, Alma, in a distorted voice, coldly explained to her the terms of her extortion arrangement: pay or we kill one of your kids.

Her godmother later handed over $2,500. Alma called again when the gang told her to, requesting less money but on a more regular basis. The gang's tyranny spread throughout the countryside, collecting one-time and regular payments from dozens of victims. Alma never identified herself and insisted that her godmother did not know it was her. I asked her what she felt when she did it. "Nothing," she said.

Despite Alma's posturing, the dark underbelly of the gang

was beginning to affect her. She could be a coldhearted bully, but she was also seeking affirmation and fulfillment beyond the gang. She was starting to experience physical attraction to women. When one of her only sexual encounters with a boy led to an unwanted pregnancy, El Tigre gave her pills to induce an abortion. She was twelve.

Although men repulsed her, Alma couldn't say anything about her attraction to women. Being gay in the gang was a death penalty. And being gay in her family was a sin.

Indeed, her torturous relationship with her parents had continued. They could no longer physically abuse her, but they peppered her with Catholic guilt, especially her mother who mumbled to herself that she had "created a monster."

During a particularly charged altercation, Alma says her father grabbed a knife and threatened to cut her MS tattoo from her hand. Alma fought back, and her father hit her. Blood trickled from her nose as she ran to the kitchen. She grabbed a knife of her own and gouged the MS from the fleshy part of her hand between her thumb and forefinger.

"You don't need to rip it out," she told them, as they looked on in horror: she was doing it for them.

She lit a cigarette to suture the wound. Then another. The act put her at immediate risk. Removing an MS-13 tattoo could be a death sentence.

"Kill me, if you want. Kill me," she told them. "I don't want you as my dad. Kill me. I'll be better off in the next life."

After the confrontation, things accelerated. Her father took her to the local ombudsman's office. There a psychologist asked Alma if she was in a gang.

"No," Alma said.

"And do you like men or women?"

"Men."

When they left, Alma told her father that the gang was going to kill her. "Why?" he asked. "Because of you," she told him, "because you wanted me to remove the tattoo, and I did."

Soon after, Alma disobeyed an order to sell marijuana. In the days that followed, she got hit in the forehead with the butt of a handgun, and her parents called her godmother, who connected them with a trustworthy coyote. This was the same woman Alma had extorted for thousands of dollars. She was about to save her life.

5.

Alma called her sister Magdalena from the detention center in Texas. Magdalena began to cry. While they had spoken on the phone a few times over the years, they were essentially strangers. Alma was born when Magdalena was a teenager and searching for her own escape hatch, even while she helped take care of her. Eventually Magdalena moved to San Salvador to clean houses, and later followed their sister Sofía to Virginia. Magdalena and Sofía never returned to El Salvador.

After six months in detention, Alma got Special Immigrant Juvenile Status, a designation that allows minors to remain in the US. Magdalena drove to Texas.

Magdalena is taller than Alma but less formidable. When they hugged, Alma's smile stretched from ear to ear. Still, the road trip back to Virginia was awkward. In the car, Alma cursed her fate and her family. She didn't want to go to Virginia, and she had little idea what awaited her. In short, the Washington, DC, Maryland and Virginia area, or so-called DMV, had become the MS-13's East Coast hub.

In the 1980s, DC was predominantly Black, but Latino communities were emerging. Salvadorans were among the strongest contingent, settling primarily in Mount Pleasant, a gritty half-mile stretch on the edge of Rock Creek Park in the city's northwest corridor. Most had fled from war and were surprised to find that DC was one of the most violent urban areas in the country.

Mount Pleasant was often referred to in press accounts as a "rundown Hispanic neighborhood," but it was really a mix of affluent Whites, low- and middle-income Blacks and low-income Latinos. In 1990, the *Washington Post* called it "the most ethnically diverse [neighborhood] in the city."

"'Black' here means Jamaicans, Haitians, African-Americans," the *Post* wrote. "'Hispanic' describes residents from Guatemala, El Salvador, Cuba, Puerto Rico, Mexico. There are Koreans, Vietnamese, Chinese, Guyanese and numerous white ethnicities. On Sunday mornings, mass is celebrated three times at the local Catholic Church—in English, Spanish and Creole."

But as it was in Koreatown in Los Angeles, the cultures were not melting together as much as scraping against each other.

"While the races live among one another in Mount Pleasant, they hardly live together," the *Post* declared.

Although just a few square blocks, the neighborhood had over twenty liquor stores and a smattering of other low-rent businesses and residences. The city offered few social services and none that catered to DC's newest, Spanish-speaking residents. The local elementary school, for example, was half Latino but had no English as a second language program. The *Post* reported that one building's tenants staged a rent strike to protest rodent infestation; other strikes protested rent hikes. A number of nongovernmental organizations tried to fill the void, but problems eventually spilled from the overcrowded apartments onto the streets.

On May 5, 1991, a police officer shot a thirty-year-old Latino man while apprehending him for disorderly conduct. The officer said the man was wielding a knife, but witnesses claimed he was shot while handcuffed. The man lived, but the incident ignited a three-day riot. Cars were destroyed, storefronts were looted and dozens were injured.

After the melee, many Latinos in the neighborhood headed for the suburbs, filling low-income housing pockets in Maryland and Virginia. These neighborhoods were even less equipped than DC to handle the rush of new residents. Jobs were scarce and schools struggled to integrate new students. Latino gangs proliferated: the 18th Street, La Mara Queens, La Mara Li, Little Locos, Brown Union and, eventually, the Mara Salvatrucha.

By the mid-1990s, small MS-13 cells had emerged in Arlington and Fairfax, Virginia; others in Langley Park, Maryland, and Mount Pleasant, DC. Some gang members came from California, fleeing the state's gang injunctions, databases and deportations. They brought with them the legends and reputations of their storied cliques—Fulton, Hollywood and Normandie. Others came straight from Central America, creating new cliques that paid homage to El Salvador.

By 2000, authorities claimed the MS-13 had close to six hundred members in Fairfax County alone. Their recruits were mostly middle school and high school kids. They were the Alex Sanchezes of the East Coast—recent arrivals from broken homes who'd lost their identity in their long journey to a place where they had few guardians and no connection.

The MS-13 in this region had the earmarks of a criminal group. They collected renta from the small shop owners, restaurants and street venders. Some members stole cars, ran small prostitution rings and sold stolen goods on the black market. But at their core, they remained a rudimentary, violent social organization. And like their West Coast brethren, they reinforced their identity via seemingly senseless acts of violence—against others and themselves. Brute force, rather than savvy intellect, always carried the day in the MS-13.

The gang's presence reached the public consciousness slowly, the violence coming in waves. In July 2000 three kids brutally stabbed a man to death outside of a club in Virginia at the behest of their thirty-four-year-old leader. According to testimony, the main assailant, after facing *corte*, the gang's internal judgment process, murdered the man to redeem himself for his drug abuse. He was still in elementary school when he committed the crime and eventually got twenty-two years in prison. The thirty-four-year-old gang leader decided not to fight his deportation following his prison sentence and would soon join his mara counterparts in Central America.

In another scuffle around the same time, a rival gang member from the Little Locos taunted some MS-13 in the parking lot of a 7-Eleven in Arlington, calling them, in the words of one witness, "girls." Next to being called a snitch, it was the ultimate insult. If you're so tough, "shoot me," the Little Locos member reportedly said. A nineteen-year-old mara got out a gun.

"I'm from MS and what the fuck," he reportedly replied.

Then he pulled the trigger.

6.

The gang continued to grow up and down the East Coast, especially in places like Brooklyn and Long Island where a smattering of cliques was in open warfare with Puerto Rican, Dominican, Black and other Salvadoran gangs. But the MS-13 was also splintering. In the DMV, cliques with Los Angeles roots competed for attention with West Coast leaders. Cliques originally based in El Salvador looked to Central America for direction. Still others were native to the DMV; they sought to build their own reputation.

The disorganization made for a near constant leadership vacuum. Violent intergang reprisals led to police crackdowns—key members would go to prison and cliques would weaken. As new leaders emerged and cliques clawed back power, another violent incident would lead to more arrests and another power vacuum, perpetuating the cycle.

Entrepreneurial gang leaders from as far away as Los Angeles and El Salvador would forever try to make the East Coast theirs. The region became a testing ground for some of the gang's most ambitious schemes, mostly failed forays into drug dealing, cigarette contraband and human trafficking. And the East Coast cliques would always stand in the shadow of their cousins in Los Angeles and El Salvador.

The haphazard nature of the MS-13 in the DMV is what allowed Brenda Paz to lead a double life, splitting her time between the government and the gang. Paz was just fifteen years old when she joined the MS-13 in the suburbs of Dallas. After her boyfriend, a leader of the Normandie Locos, was picked up on murder charges, she fled to Virginia where she was arrested with her new boyfriend for stealing a car. In custody, she became an informant, and for over a year she worked closely with local and national authorities.

At first, she told the police about gang members she didn't like. Arrests followed. Over time, she revealed secrets about murders and how the gang disposed of bodies in abandoned fields as far away as Idaho. She described gang crimes ranging from extortion to prostitution to car theft. She explained the gang's signs, its leadership structure and its guidelines. For the first time, law enforcement and prosecutors began to look at the gang as a serious national threat, one that could evolve into a more sophisticated criminal organization.

But rumors of Paz's status as a cooperating witness began to circulate. Authorities tried to protect her, putting her in a safe house. But she was lonely, and the gang beckoned, so she began a double life: talking to authorities during the day; partying with the mara at night. Emboldened, she even threw parties at her federally subsidized safe house until the Montgomery County Police were called because of the noise.

Authorities later moved her into witness protection in Kansas City and then Minnesota. But she couldn't stay away from the gang. After several more gang-infused parties, this time at a Minnesota hotel, she left the witness protection program. Meanwhile, word about her status as an informant kept reaching different parts of the MS-13. Eventually, a fellow member found her diaries, in which she chronicled her contacts with the FBI and police. A few weeks later, the mara lured her to a remote stretch of the Shenandoah River Valley, where they stabbed her multiple times and slit her throat, nearly decapitating her.

In the history of the MS-13, Brenda Paz's murder remains a defining moment. Soon thereafter, the gang stopped allowing women members. Still, the MS-13 remained a diffuse, leaderless organization, and the East Coast cliques a chaotic mess.

It was this chaos that allowed Alma's tangential, informal reentry into MS-13 circles in Virginia some seven years later.

7.

Magdalena opened up her house to Alma, gave her a bed, food and family support. Alma attended the local middle school. At first, she was depressed and slept through class, but it got better. Alma is sharp—a keen observer, and a quick study, and she began to like school.

"There were other students who spoke English and Spanish. They helped me," she said. "It was good that year. I did well."

Still, she was prone to distraction, and by high school she once again confronted the MS-13. The DMV cliques were rudimentary facsimiles of the cliques she'd known in El Salvador. Many of the key members, especially the older ones, were part-time mara. Most of them worked, had families.

"They don't do shit," is the way Alma described it to me.

The cliques were more fluid: members floated on the edges, then disappeared, only to reappear months or even years later. Alma herself floated on the edges. She didn't exactly rejoin the gang, but she didn't avoid it either. The mara were present in and around the school, and Alma started hanging out with them.

One of her new friends in the US was Cindy Blanco, a recent arrival like Alma. Blanco was younger but hung in the same Salvadoran crowds, something that would catch up with her later. They smoked. They drank. They fought with each other and with others. They took road trips, including to North Carolina where other mara were decamped. They got into trouble, got suspended. Eventually Alma got expelled for selling marijuana in the school.

Alma also mingled with adults, especially when she drank. One of her new, adult drinking friends had a daughter named Paula who was about Alma's age. Alma was, by then, accepting that she was attracted to women. The two girls began to talk. Under a haze of alcohol, they began to steal moments, to kiss and more. For the first time, Alma was falling in love. It was the most powerful drug she'd found yet.

9

ESCAPE FROM ZACATRAZ

1.

ON NORMAN'S FIRST DAY IN MARIONA PRISON, guards probed his body cavities for drugs, paper notes and weapons. He could hear the commotion down the hall, the rumbling of caged men that had become his daily soundtrack. After the search he was led to his cell block. He groaned softly and shrugged to show the guards he needed to be separated. They ignored him, and he raised his voice.

"I got problems in there," he told them.

The guards didn't care. Like any prison, Mariona had a hierarchy. At the time, its leader was José Edgardo Bruno Ventura. Bruno was a legendary thief who'd formed a mercenary army inside the prison system made up of murderers and thieves known as La Raza. Gang members were red meat for La Raza. The guards were but the zookeepers.

"I got problems in there," Norman said louder.

They ignored him again and began to walk him toward the main door. It was 2000, and this was Norman's third prison, so he understood the system. At his first two prisons, he'd been beaten and abused by guards and fellow inmates. But at least those prisons were located close to family so his mom and girlfriend, Carla, could visit. Prison records showed his mother went every two weeks. He later consummated his relationship with Carla—the two were married inside Apanteos, a prison in western El Salvador.

But Mariona, a jail on the outskirts of San Salvador, was entirely different. The prison had three thousand inmates, a third of the entire prison population in El Salvador. And inside, the MS-13 was the minority of a minority. The 18th Street had joined forces with La Raza. In essence, the entire Mariona prison was against the mara. Bruno and his army would not even let them gather in groups larger than two.

"I GOT PROBLEMS," he started to yell before grabbing the bars at the entrance.

The guards pulled out their nightsticks and began smashing his fingers. Norman let go, resigned to his fate.

"If they kill you, we'll take you out," a guard said.

The guards shut the metal door behind him. La Raza pounced, dragged him to a cell and made him take off his shirt. His tattoos bare, they began their interrogation. "Little gangbanger from the MS," they taunted him.

On the other side of the cell, on a bed, two men were raping another mara. Norman remembers him to this day. His nickname was Conejo (Rabbit). He was eighteen years old, and Norman said he'd been there for days, getting ravaged. His face was blank. He'd given up. His life had ended, Norman thought.

"That's what they did with those *bichitos*, with those kids," Norman would say later.

They told him he was next.

"You're going to have to kill me first," he said, the grunts and pounding flesh audible on the other side of the cell.

As it was in the US prison system, sexual assault and abuse was a major part of life in custody in El Salvador. Some 76 percent of political prisoners in the 1980s, for example, reported some form of sexual torture. By the time Norman was in prison, no one was keeping statistics anymore. But Norman told me La Raza would routinely rape other prisoners. To make their victims more compliant, Bruno's gang would slip pills into their victims' coffee or soft drinks.

Like their US counterparts, the Mariona guards did nothing, or worse—they were part of the scheme, facilitating access to the victims and guaranteeing impunity following the assaults. Rape, of course, is not about sex as much as it is about power, and it is a critical organizing principle of prison life. In his book on violence, James Gilligan noted that prison guards systematically allowed rape in US prisons—used it, in fact, "to maintain control of the prison population."

"The officers are entering into an implicit, tacit agreement with the rapists," he wrote, "in which the officers will permit the rapists whatever gratifications they get from raping the weaker prisoners, and the rapists agree in turn to cooperate with these officers by submitting to the prison system as a whole."

Prison, Gilligan concluded starkly, was divided into those who were raped and those who raped.

This appeared to be the system in El Salvador as well. What's more, if the guards resisted, they too could face consequences inside and outside of prison. Authorities in El Salvador provided little cover for these prisoners or guards or their relatives. On visiting days, La Raza assaulted family members of prisoners as well.

"If your woman was good-looking, they would fuck her," Norman told me flatly.

2.

When authorities sent Norman to Mariona in 2000, Bruno's control of the prison was legendary, as were the stories about him. Some claimed he'd married a judge inside prison and contracted Los Hermanos Flores, a Salvadoran cumbia band, as entertainment. Supposedly he kept his dogs inside the prison—Rottweilers, pit bulls, Dobermans and German shepherds—and received stolen goods from the outside, which he sold to fellow inmates. He also allegedly moved drugs and weapons, and he managed most of the transfers and the placement of prisoners in different sections of the prison.

La Raza communicated constantly with the guards, who helped them smuggle in knives and machetes and maintain their brutal regime. Bruno's mercenary army determined where people slept, if they got a thin mattress on the floor or an actual bed. They operated the commissaries and mess halls and could decide if someone got their medicine or not. In this regard, Norman was one of the lucky ones. His mother brought him food on her biweekly visits and medicine, if he needed it. She also came with soap, toothpaste, T-shirts and pants. Some prisoners never got a visit from anyone. Soon, it wouldn't matter as much. The gang would become their permanent visitor.

The demographics inside and outside of prison were changing. The gang population was on the rise. This is what had led Bruno and his mercenary army to ally with the 18th Street. At first, the alliance worked, keeping the MS-13 in check. On Norman's second day, for example, a group of 18th Street and La Raza beat and slashed him and four of his mara prison mates.

In the coming months, the mara begged for their own space. At first, prison officials resisted, but the MS-13 mounted a campaign—lobbying on the inside and writing letters from the outside. Eventually authorities relented, but the battles were only beginning.

The MS-13's new space in Mariona was La Isla, where they housed mentally ill prisoners. In La Isla, the MS-13 had their own twenty-square-foot cement bloc. It was tight, of course, and their mentally ill neighbors—the "crazies," as Norman called them—spent their days screaming in the room next to them. But it was theirs. Soon, they were twenty-five strong, and they began to talk, to organize and to prepare for the war they knew was coming. They started to craft shivs from toothbrushes and combs, and store metal bars and other blunt objects under their pillows. Their visitors buried machetes in their belongings or bribed the guards to let them pass with weapons.

The attack came on a quiet day. Rust from the rebar floated down to the cement floor. The mara looked up. A group of 18th Street and La Raza were making their way over the walls, machetes and Molotov cocktails in hand.

¡Nos van a matar! They're going to kill us! they screamed as the fireballs fell around them, starting a small blaze.

The mara fled to the bathroom, dunked their shirts in the toilet, and draped them over their shoulders to protect themselves from the rising heat.

Nos van a matar! they repeated.

The guards, slow to react at first, eventually started pushing La Raza and the 18th Street back into their section. They smothered the fire. The mara survived.

3.

Norman's next major riot was in Apanteos prison near the Guatemala border. By then, Norman had cycled through five prisons. In Usulatán in the eastern part the country, he had no visitors, since his family lived far west. When an earthquake partially destroyed the prison Norman was transferred yet again, this time to San Miguel, where he survived a second earthquake.

Still at San Miguel a month later, Norman was in a hallway

between a bank of telephones and the library when an 18th Street member called La Muerte, lunged at him with a shiv. Norman leaned back, and took the blow to the shoulder. Blood flew in every direction in the melee that followed. Again, he survived, at which point officials transferred him back to Apanteos where he'd begun his time in prison in 1999.

It had been almost five years. By then, the mara had accumulated numbers in Apanteos and were conscious they could force the government's hand using violence. It was a lesson they would employ effectively again during later confrontations with the state. In the meantime in Apanteos, as Norman told me, "It rioted." This time, two prisoners died and forty-nine others were injured.

In response, prison officials separated the mara from the general population. There he met a slew of longtime gang members, most of whom had been deported from the US: Crook from Hollywood. Cola from Western. Skinny from Stoners. Flaco from Francis. Some of them he already knew, like El Diablito from Hollywood, and his clique-mate and partner in crime Malvado.

These were the future leaders of the gang, and they began to hold regular discussions, or mirins as they called them. Norman said these meetings centered on one thing: creating order. Pick up after yourself and your area. Follow an exercise regimen. No theft. No rape. Respect visitors. The gang had inherited some of these rules from the Mexican Mafia but now it was time to live them. Infractions would lead to punishments—beatings in thirteen-second intervals, another Mexican Mafia hand-me-down.

"The gang," Norman told me, "was now correcting itself."

The gang ruled by committee. They called it *la ranfla*. *Ranfla* in Spanish means small circle or wheel. It was also slang for lowrider, a remnant of their Los Angeles's gang forbearers' obsession with cars. The ranfla would soon become the pillar of their organization in El Salvador, both inside and outside of prison.

They designated an intermediary who took their messages outside of the prison walls and began to enforce their will. When someone disobeyed, there were consequences. Punishments were swift, certain and severe. Gang members died, and the self-correction continued.

The MS-13 also started to better organize their criminal economy. They pooled resources to buy marijuana and sell it inside the prison. Then they got others outside of the gang to do it for them. One prisoner at the time testified that Norman "forced him to 'move' drugs" from the visiting area to the cellbock. The prisoner did not immediately tell the authorities because, he said, it was "prohibited by the laws of the MS," and that anyone who did talk to the guards risked being "beaten" by the mara.

Norman was prosecuted after a guard found "two, transparent plastic bags, closed with yellow string...with some kind of vegetable material," in his bed. That "vegetable material," forensic investigators later concluded, was 53.7 grams of marijuana, worth about $61 inside the prison at the time. But the case fell apart because the guards could not determine whose bed was whose. There were, the judges noted in their decision, thirty-five beds and fifty-five prisoners in that area of the prison.

It was a fitting way for the case to end—the state's neglect was not only hurting its ability to prosecute mara crimes, it was opening the door for a gang takeover. The mara used the drug money to buy mattresses, toothpaste, soap, toilet paper and other items for those who were not getting any visitors, had no family or whose family was too far away to travel and see them. In short, the prison community was becoming the strongest mara community of them all.

4.

At some point in late 2001, an MS-13 nicknamed the Superabuela de Arza took a Siemens C45 cellular phone, wrapped it tightly in plastic, lubed it generously and slid it into his anus. He knew prison contraband could enter through many channels. Mail carriers could bundle items into parcels, family visitors or girlfriends could stash contraband in gifts, or corrupt guards could smuggle items in their bags. The Superabuela de Arza was using his "prison wallet." Other visitors snuck in a charger, which had been broken into smaller pieces. On New Year's Eve, 2001, Norman called his family from the MS-13's first jailhouse cell phone to wish them *un feliz y próspero año*.

The Siemens, and the many others that followed, changed the gang forever. Meetings now happened via conference call, and the ranfla spread to other prisons, especially after authorities transferred some of the leaders. The phone also gave them access to the street-level leaders. Soon, they started a *ranfla en la libre*, a leadership structure on the outside to implement and enforce more new rules: no long hair and no crack cocaine. Some on the outside disobeyed. But the ranfla remained calm, patient. Like their patrons in the Mexican Mafia, they understood that if they controlled the penitentiary system, they controlled the gang.

Sooner or later, you will land here, the jailed leaders told the dissidents on the street.

To be sure, by the mid-2000s, the government was rounding up hundreds of alleged gang members under the guise of a new draconian antigang law that was modeled, in part, after Los Angeles's own laws from the late 1980s. The policy, which was known as Mano Dura, or Iron Fist, had such a wide and ill-defined purview that the courts declared it unconstitutional. The next year, politicians passed a law they dubbed Súper Mano Dura.

Following its implementation, the prison population in El Salvador increased faster than almost anywhere else in the world. Between 2002 and 2010, the number of prisoners in El Salvador more than doubled from eleven thousand to twenty-four thousand. By 2010, about eight thousand of those were suspected gang members, picked up for now-codified violations such as "marking the body with a tattoo" or "meeting frequently." The law sanctioned identifiable crimes such as recruiting, fights and extortion, but there were an equal number of vaguely defined crimes such as "association," and making a "scandal" in a public place. Penalties were stiff: just being declared a member of a gang, for example, could land someone in prison for six years.

Another huge chunk of prisoners were in pretrial detention, housed in overcrowded temporary holding facilities called *bartolinas*. Many of them would stay for months awaiting movement on their cases. Some were kept so long they had to be transferred to other, more permanent prisons. By 2010, prisons were at 250 percent capacity.

The conditions in both the prisons and the bartolinas were subhuman. In the bartolinas, they crammed dozens of inmates into cages the size of a living room. There, they took turns sleeping, sitting and standing, just to keep their blood circulating. They got their basic provisions mostly from their relatives. But when family was far away, it was the gang that filled in the gaps, providing clothes, blankets and a safe place to rest. The prisoners survived inside because of the gang, and its network. And in spite of the state.

As more mara were incarcerated, the ranfla gained power. In reaction, the government converted military barracks into temporary holding facilities and refashioned old schools into makeshift bartolinas. It doubled and tripled capacity in its already established prisons like Apanteos and Mariona, where the population increases would lead to more violence.

In August 2004, a fight in Mariona between the 18th Street members and the remnants of La Raza left thirty-four dead and dozens more injured, most of them members of La Raza. The massacre in Mariona pushed the government to be more proactive, transferring a thousand 18th Street members to their own prisons. To avoid a similar explosion in Apanteos, the government moved seven hundred MS-13 members to Quetzaltepeque and Ciudad Barrios, a juvenile hall it had converted into an adult prison. Barrios, as they called it, would soon become the MS-13 headquarters.

The moves allowed the mara to add yet another ranfla to the penitentiary system and expand its reach. The government was unwittingly helping the MS-13 build an army.

The mass incarceration of the mara also changed the gang's financial needs. More jailed members meant more expenses. In addition to provisions, incarcerated gang members had to figure out a way to provide for their families on the outside. They needed legal help and money to bribe guards and judges. And they needed money for extras: Christmas and Easter, funerals and, of course, parties.

Some of the first to suffer from the MS-13's pressing new financial needs were the bus companies. In the early days of the gang, the mara asked for "contributions." Then they began to collect a toll from buses when they crossed into their territory. At times they also exacted what they called a "one-time" sum of a few hundred dollars, especially during the holidays.

Eventually the gangs started demanding a weekly or monthly sum. They calculated the fee based on the number of buses or the number of passengers on a given line. They would install counters along the routes to confirm the numbers, and when they didn't add up or the payments were late, the gang attacked. The easiest targets were the bus drivers themselves and their assistants. The gang killed dozens.

The MS-13 eventually became more entrepreneurial, more Mafia in nature, demanding the bus companies write them—or third parties—into the paperwork as owners. The companies soon began to organize their business around these payments. Some would employ a third party to collect and hand over the money. Bus companies often had to pay several gangs. The mara were redrawing the country's map, one business at a time.

The gang channeled payments through a new MS-13 system. Not long after they started the ranfla, the mara created what they called programs. In the mara hierarchy, the program would answer to the ranfla, but it would have jurisdiction over the cliques in its areas of influence. The payments now moved from the homies to the clique leaders to the program leaders to the ranfla. They also divided the country into four territories: the East, the West, the Midwest, and the center. More than a street gang, the MS-13 was starting to look like an insurgency.

By one estimate, gang extortion increased fourteen times over between 2003 and 2009, and by 2010, authorities estimated that gang leaders inside prison ordered 78 percent of these extortions. Extortion also established a reliable food chain where everyone from gang leaders to gang members' families to corrupt officials was taking a cut. Some bus company owners also took advantage, employing mara to scare their rivals into selling their buses. The mara was becoming a criminal enterprise, but they were far from the only ones benefitting.

5.

In late 2008, Salvadoran authorities pulled Norman and several others from their cells and handcuffed their ankles and wrists. They shoved them in a van and wrapped their chains around a bar at the base, which forced all of them to bend over during the bumpy journey to what was to be their new home: the maximum-security prison in Zacatecoluca.

The prison was notorious. Salvadorans called it Zacatraz, an homage to San Francisco, California's most famous and shuttered maximum-security prison, Alcatraz. Zacatraz opened in 2003. During its first few years, the government filled it with the most dangerous inmates, including drug traffickers. But beginning in 2007, gang members began to arrive. Quickly, they came to occupy two-thirds of the prison. Still, their influence was muted, at least for a while.

Zacatraz was, in many ways, the result of a desperate government ploy to corral the gangs. Modeled after US maximum-security prisons, Zacatraz limited human contact as much as possible. Aside from short stints to shower and eat, inmates were confined to their cells twenty-three hours a day. Prisoners were allowed outside recreation only three times a week. Visits were every other week and limited to twenty-five minutes through a thick glass window. There were no conjugal visits in Zacatraz, and no newspapers or magazines—only books that prison authorities had to preapprove.

The Zacatraz guards were El Salvador's most committed, most feared. Norman said they established a brutal regime. When Norman arrived, for example, the guards stripped him and the other new inmates to their boxers and sent them down a corridor where more guards awaited. To get through the gauntlet, they remained hunched over, forced to inch forward on their knees, while the guards beat them with their wooden batons. In the back. The ankles. The ribs. The thighs. The arms. The testicles.

"It doesn't matter if you scream for your mother, father, aunt, uncle," Norman told me. "No one escapes that [beating]."

To avoid problems with family members, human rights groups or foreign inspections teams, the guards would refrain from striking the face. If they did accidently hit you in the face, Norman said, they would just prohibit your family from coming for a month until you healed.

You're in maximum security now, they yelled at Norman while they beat him that first day. Norman's testicles are still damaged from that beating, he says. And he told me that when he closes his eyes, he can still feel the blows.

"In El Salvador, when they want to fuck you, they fuck you," he said.

Once in Zacatraz, Norman tried to establish a routine. He says he would get up at 5:00 a.m. and shower. Then he would return to the cell and read the Bible for a couple of hours. When I asked him what part of the Bible, he hesitated. Psalm 51, he finally said, before adding that he also read Psalm 3, "The one that says, 'If you want to change your life...'"

After reading, he would eat breakfast, then rest. The worst part of Zacatraz was the heat, Norman said. He was on the first floor, which he said was bearable. The second floor was an *infierno*, a "fiery hell." Norman spent most of his time sweating, thinking about sweating, getting rid of sweat, trying not to touch the sweat of others. When you have few distractions, anything can become an obsession.

Around 12:00 p.m., the inmates would get lunch. Rice and beans, normally. Then Norman said he would read some more. When he was first in prison, Norman took lots of courses. His judicial records are full of honorary diplomas and recognitions from local schools and organizations. But there were no programs in Zacatraz, so he settled for novels. Paulo Coelho's *The Alchemist* and *Eleven Minutes* got passed around from sector to sector. Vampire books, Stephen King's lurid tales, and haunting stories like one about demonic possession, were also popular.

Come midafternoon, Norman would exercise for about two hours. Push-ups. Abdominals. Burpees. Dinner was at 4:00 or 4:30. After more quiet time, the guards would wake everyone at 8:00 to ensure they were tired by lights out at 10:00. At that point, the prison would go silent.

"The majority go crazy," Norman told me.

One guy, who Norman said had been convicted of numerous rapes, simply stopped moving from the waist down. For his part, Norman was barely holding it together. On the good days, he dreamed about what his life would be like if he were a doctor. On the bad days, he imagined his wife, Carla, with another man.

6.

By 2010, Norman's marriage was falling apart. While he was at the other prisons, his wife, Carla, had given birth to another girl. He was a leader in the gang, so there was money coming in—from extortion and petty drug dealing—which he was able to pass to his family. With the funds, Carla set up a spot selling vegetables and fruit at the central market in their home town.

But it was still tough, and Norman's move to Zacatraz had put an extra strain on his relationship with his entire family. His mother could make the trips only a few times a year. One time, she brought Laura, Norman's older sister—the one who'd been his surrogate mother—while she was visiting from the United States. When he saw her on the other side of the Plexiglas, he broke down crying. "*Perdóname,* Ruquita," he said, sobbing and using his longtime diminutive for her. *"Perdóname."*

Norman could only visit with Carla for those sparse twenty-five-minute stints, once every two weeks. The visits almost made things worse. One day, when she went to see him, he was tired and depressed. She was exhausted as well. They fought. She left the room. Norman thought she would come back and waited by the thick Plexiglas while others continued talking to their visitors.

There were twelve visiting booths in Zacatraz. It was a tight, closely guarded space, and one guard noticed Carla was gone. He told Norman to get up, but Norman refused.

"It's not over yet, Charlie," he told him, using the inmates' moniker for the guards.

"Get up," the guard said. "The visit is over."

"It's not over yet, Charlie," Norman repeated.

The guard pulled Norman from his chair. Norman wrestled away from him, then punched the guard square in the face.

Several guards pounced on Norman, pounding him with their fists, elbows and batons, and hitting him with pepper spray, but he kept resisting. One of the prisoners jumped in to help him. The rest backed away, cowering into a corner to avoid the fray. They knew what was next. The anti-riot unit arrived shortly thereafter, pulled out a fire hose, and sprayed the two prisoners into submission.

Prison authorities placed Norman in solitary confinement. The cell was tiny, about eight by ten feet, Norman said. There was a bed on one side and a toilet and a shower pipe on the other. When they shut the door, the room went dark, except for a small sliver of light that broke through a crack in the ceiling.

No one could visit with him. No one could talk to him. He was not allowed fresh air or exercise. He had no idea how long he would be in solitary. There he sat, in the dark, for weeks.

Pretty soon, Norman can't remember when, he started hearing voices.

"Estás solo, va?" the voice said.

"Yes," he answered. "I'm alone."

"Nadie te quiere. Nadie está con vos."

"Nope," he said. "No one loves me. No one is with me."

He thought of Carla. Nearly eleven years she had stayed with him, but Zacatraz had bent their relationship to a breaking point. He was convinced she'd found another man.

"Tu mujer ya debe tener otro," the voice chided.

It was not easy. Another mara who'd been sent to Zacatraz had recently hanged himself. Now, Norman considered the same. Above him, a large barrel full of water rested on a pair of metal bars that ran parallel from one wall to the other. As the voice in his head cajoled him, he looked at the bars.

"Do you think they can hold you?" the voice asked him.

Norman stood on the toilet and grabbed the two bars holding the barrel. He did some pull-ups, then jumped down.

"Yep. It held," the voice said.

"Why not just kill yourself?"

Norman thought of his wife. He thought of his kids. He

thought of his mother, his poor mother. She would suffer, if he killed himself. But most of all, he thought of Carla.

"I love my wife," he would tell me later, as he recalled his bouts with depression and thoughts of committing suicide. "It's a love that I don't even understand."

Most of the gang leaders in Zacatraz felt the same longing for their relatives. In their hierarchy of needs, keeping the family in good arrears was near the top. They had also lost contact with the gang on the streets. They were beaten, isolated, cut off from the cliques, cut off from funds, cut off from their families.

There was only one solution: they had to escape from Zacatraz.

PART III

GETTING OUT (2010–2019)

10

THE GANG TRUCE

1.

THE FIRST TIME LUIS AGUILAR HEARD ABOUT THE government plan to de-escalate gang violence in El Salvador was in February 2012. It was good timing. Luis had been working in a violence-stricken village west of San Salvador known as Lourdes, where a US-funded program had sent officials to help local police stem the rising homicides.

The program in Lourdes focused on disrupting the criminal patterns of street gangs by gathering intelligence and deploying patrols strategically. As Luis knew, the most effective police forces excelled at operating in small spaces at specific times. The US had financed and trained these "intelligence-guided" precincts throughout Central America. Unfortunately, the approach did not stick. While the police were willing to experiment (especially if it included new technology, vehicles and other resources), few programs lasted long enough to exact institutional change.

Still, Luis liked intelligence-based programs, so in February, when his ex-boss from the intelligence division, Juan Roberto Castillo, said he wanted to talk to him about an "intelligence project," Luis was immediately intrigued. The idea, Castillo told him, was to reduce violence and dismantle "the gang structure." Homicides had gone from eight per day in 2004, to twelve per day in 2011. Beyond extorting buses, the gangs were now extorting food and beverage distribution trucks, taxis, small shop owners and street venders. In areas like Lourdes the battles had become so fierce that first graders were not allowed to cross gang lines to get to school. The government, in other words, was losing ground. It was time, Castillo said, for a radically different approach.

Luis agreed. Like most police, he'd once believed in Mano Dura. But somewhere along the way, he'd changed his mind—it wasn't an epiphany but a slow realization, a sense that trying to physically overpower the enemy was useless, especially when the enemy was an amorphous, slippery, expansive group with a remarkable survival instinct.

The strategy would become known as *la tregua*, "the truce." In its most ambitious form, the truce was a means by which gangs would "demobilize" and "reenter society," similar to the guerrillas following the civil war. But the radical social program would have to start by establishing a ceasefire between the gangs—interrupting violence and breaking the chains of retribution that had given the country one of the highest homicide rates in the world.

After Castillo explained the idea, Luis glanced at his boss, his eyes widening. Luis doesn't get excited as much as he gets intrigued. When he talks, his mouth barely opens and the rest of his face betrays no emotion. It's something between stoicism and resignation, a professional hazard that came from years of fighting gangs on the streets and dodging political bullets inside his own precinct offices.

2.

The 1992 peace agreement between the government and the FMLN guerrillas called for the formation of a new police force. To ensure that it was balanced, the agreement allotted 20 percent of the police to ex-military and 20 percent to ex-guerrillas. The other 60 percent was open to the public. The quotas were meant to bring together once-warring factions under a shared vision for the future. In reality, the groups clashed, fomenting a bifurcated system that has been nearly impossible to dismantle.

Luis always felt sandwiched between these two rivals. Inspired by television dramas like *Starsky & Hutch*, he'd joined the police right out of high school at the tail end of the war and quickly rose through the ranks to detective. When the war ended, he had to leave the force and reapply with the public. Luis didn't mind. He believed in the idea that the new police could unite army soldiers and rebel fighters, and he was quickly reincorporated into the police. But almost immediately, he could see the blocs taking form: ex-military on one side, ex-guerrillas on the other. Luis says he tried to put his head down and get his career back on track, but he would always find himself between these two forces. "I'm not a politician," he told me several times. "I'm a technocrat."

While serving as detective, Luis earned his law degree and became a certified notary. He was quietly tenacious and never raised his voice. He contemplated—with his expressionless face, pursed lips and sleepy stare—then acted, boldly, without remorse. This approach would win him accolades that he would display in his house. Police who do what Luis do cannot second guess. "I'm not known as soft, but I'm also not arbitrary," he told me.

Without knowing it, Luis was preparing for his eventual work in the intelligence division. In the 1990s, the force's intelligence work was rudimentary at best: no crime statistics, sophisticated maps, strategic deployment plans or computer-generated data.

As postwar violence skyrocketed, the new police—fractured, undeveloped and under-resourced—were in no position to anticipate the rise of the MS-13, even when the mara started outfitting small metal pipes with firing pins to expel shrapnel at rivals; or when they switched from riding bicycles to motorcycles; or when they started systematically collecting renta from the buses.

"We didn't have any interest in them," Luis said of the gang. "Back then, we went after crimes, not groups."

Salvadoran police forces took cues from the United States, which had seemingly arrested its way out of a homicide problem. Politicians like New York City mayor Rudolf Giuliani—who would later do consulting work in El Salvador and other, violence-racked Central American nations—were touting their "broken windows" strategy, in which police cracked down on minor infractions to prevent bigger crimes. Luis initially supported this position.

"Our thought was that when you put them in prison, they're going to stop committing crimes," he told me.

Instead, as Súper Mano Dura led to more arrests, he began to see the opposite. In 2004, Luis joined the prison intelligence unit and began to speak regularly with the gang members. He realized they were reorganizing, rethinking their mission. Prison was brutal, but it also presented opportunities for those who sought power. The incarcerated gang members were often the ones who best intuited the politics of gang life and the natural human hierarchy of basic needs.

"I always thought the gangs were bad," he said to me, his cheeks sagging under the weight of two decades working on the front lines. "But the police strategy to fight them had contributed to their rise."

3.

The MS-13's first political envoy in El Salvador was Dany Balmore Romero García. Alias Dany Boy or El Poeta, Romero had joined the MS-13 in El Salvador in the early 1990s as the first wave of deportees arrived en masse. He was arrested and convicted of murder in 1995, and by the early 2000s, he'd become an activist for prison reform.

Romero's enthusiasm for social rehabilitation, poetry and work programs endeared him both to outsiders and his fellow inmates. He walked a fine line, remaining a committed member of el barrio, loyal to his mara, and becoming a human rights advocate, a soldier for demobilization and the reintegration of gang members into society.

After authorities released him from prison in February 2008, Romero formed OPERA. OPERA was a Spanish acronym that stood for Optimism, Peace, Hope, Renewal and Harmony. Romero made connections with local and international organizations focused on prison reform, at-risk youth, and human rights and put them in dialogue with imprisoned gang leaders. The impact was immediate.

In February 2009, both the MS-13 and the 18th Street led a protest inside eleven Salvadoran prisons and juvenile detention centers. Simultaneously, civil society organizations held rallies, and at one point even occupied San Salvador's downtown cathedral. In a joint press release, the prisoners called it, "a peaceful strike of civil disobedience against the penitentiary regime."

A month later, the FMLN, the guerrilla group that had converted into a political party after the war, won the presidential palace. The party's candidate, Mauricio Funes, was an open-minded journalist, closer to the political center than the left. Civil disobedience inside the prison had subsided, but the Funes administration kept talking to the gangs.

Romero stood at the center of these talks, shuttling messages between the gang's leadership in Zacatraz, the maximum-security prison where the gang leaders were, and the government. He was not alone. Other local and international NGOs played important roles. Catholic priests and evangelical pastors pushed for dialogue as well. One of them, Father Antonio Rodríguez, or Padre Toño, as he was affectionately known, had established a rehabilitation center for gang members in the embattled Mejicanos municipality just outside of San Salvador.

Toño—a fair-skinned Spaniard with soft features and an inviting manner—was a controversial figure in his own right, not least because of his openly charitable view of the gangs. There was "no line between the victims and the victimizers," he told me when we met.

"There is not violence because there are gangs," he added. "There are gangs because there is violence."

Many would disagree, especially after June 20, 2010, when a breakaway faction of the 18th Street known as the Revolucionarios burned a bus in the Mejicanos area, just a few blocks from Padre Toño's parish, killing at least fourteen people. Some of the victims were shot as they tried to escape. Three of the dead were children. A few blocks away, the gang stopped another bus and sprayed it with automatic gunfire, killing at least two more.

In response, the Funes administration supported an updated Mano Dura policy. The gangs protested, first via private channels then in a coordinated national transport strike in September 2010. By then, the gangs had a firm grip on the bus companies. The strike paralyzed as much as 80 percent of the country's transport system and cost El Salvador an estimated $24 million.

"We are ready to make a commitment to society, so that together we can create a better country," Padre Toño read from a joint statement issued by imprisoned gang leaders.

4.

A little more than a year and a half later, Juan Roberto Castillo called on Luis to help him with his "intelligence project." The meeting led to another high-level encounter, this time with the head of the penitentiary system, Nelson Rauda, and the security minister, General David Munguía Payés.

Munguía Payés was a powerful figure in El Salvador. A career military officer, he was almost always seen in public in a dark olive camouflage uniform and rimless glasses. He liked to use charts to explain things. He was not so much strategic as methodical. When I met him I was struck by his gentle demeanor. He reminded me of a math professor.

In the early 2000s, as part of a military protest, he'd joined a fledgling political party. Among the party's leaders was the former guerrilla, Raúl Mijango, and the two began a strange relationship that would eventually lead to the gang truce.

Mijango was the same rebel who'd operated in Morazán in the early years of the war, carrying the AK-47 that Fidel Castro had given him during his training in Cuba. In fact, the two had met on the battlefield some twenty years prior, a few miles from where the massacre at El Mozote occurred. Mijango had led an ambush on Munguía Payés's battalion, killing thirty.

After the war, Mijango became a congressman for the FMLN, only to be expelled following a power struggle with the party's more orthodox, Marxist-Leninist leadership. Others left the party as well, including Joaquín Villalobos, the one-time insurgent commander who'd vexed the army in Morazán. It was around this time, Mijango and Munguía Payés formally met.

Their political party eventually failed and Munguía Payés reintegrated in the military, but Mijango floundered. His fledgling business ventures flopped, and in 2009, he was arrested and charged with selling stolen propane gas cylinders. Among the items confiscated from his house that day was the infamous AK-47. In both instances he had plausible deniability—how could he know the cylinders were stolen? And the AK-47? they asked. *Nostalgia*, he replied.

Mijango always operated in the gray areas. As a longtime lawyer and friend of his told me, Mijango lived by the legal aphorism that, "What the law does not prohibit, it allows." In the holding cell after his arrest, he connected with a number of gang members. As a former enemy of the state, he felt he understood them.

The charges against Mijango were eventually dropped, but he found himself without a party or a business. Over the the years, he'd gained weight, growing a belly to match his barrel chest, bulging cheeks and wispy Fu Manchu. He drove the streets of San Salvador in his beat-up car doing odd jobs. In between, he wrote books—a semifictional account of a former guerrilla commander in postwar El Salvador, and a passionate plea to end poverty *(Goddam Poverty)* among them—until he reconnected with his unlikely friend, Munguía Payés, who had become the security minister. They talked, and Munguía Payés gave him some work as a security consultant.

Mijango dove into the job, telling Munguía Payés about his talks with the gang members and his ideas about how to mitigate the gangs' growing influence. The two men saw an opportunity, for themselves and for the country. If they could curb gang violence, they could win El Salvador, they thought. But to do so, they had to lower homicides. In the first two months of 2012, El Salvador had about fourteen homicides a day, two more than the 2011 average.

Under the auspices of the security ministry, Mijango began meeting with gang leaders who seemed interested in the idea of lowering violence but wanted something in return: they needed out of Zacatraz. Their access to amenities, including cell phones, was severely restricted in the maximum-security prison, and they'd lost control of their rank and file. Some, like Norman, felt they were losing their families as well.

By February 2012, a negotiating team comprised of Mijango, Castillo, and Catholic Bishop Fabio Colindres, had taken shape. Although he did not have the official approval of the Church, Colindres's religious affiliation could help bring hard-line businessmen and other political stalwarts into the process. Short but with a tight haircut and a thick body, Colindres was the military chaplain, administering to soldiers and their families in the barracks' exhaust-stained chapel in San Salvador.

In early March, the gang leaders, sensing a moment, reiterated their commitment to the truce, provided they could be transferred from Zacatraz. When the negotiating team wavered on the idea of a mass transfer, gang leaders seized on one of the government's greatest vulnerabilities: they threatened to upend the municipal elections with coordinated attacks. The government relented, and on March 12, 2012, under the cover of darkness, thirty gang leaders moved from Zacatraz to medium-security prisons. The truce had begun.

5.

The goal of the truce—to mitigate gang violence and crime—was laudable. And in that regard, it started well: homicides dropped by half almost overnight.

Yet the idea of negotiating with gang leaders was unpalatable to many. Although the security ministry fostered the truce,

President Funes never officially sanctioned it, and the Salvadoran legislature never established a legal framework. No one acknowledged Mijango or his role. The ministry channeled truce leaders' salaries through the penitentiary system, sometimes earmarking them as "workshops"—anything to distance Funes from the work at hand.

Munguía Payés carefully chose his words when speaking about the truce, even in private meetings. During Luis's first meeting with him, Munguía Payés confirmed that "the president knows about this," but said little more. In an interview with me, Munguía Payés was even more opaque: the government played "no role" in the truce, he said; it only "facilitated" the contacts between the gangs.

After the transfer, other quid pro quo followed, but little would be made public about these overtures, some of which may have included—or not, depending upon who you ask—bringing plasma screen TVs into prisons; giving the gangs control over the commissaries; smuggling hundreds of cell phones into cells in Pollo Campero boxes; providing gang leaders with monthly salaries; opening the penitentiary doors to prostitutes, liquor, marijuana and other party favors.

Behind the scenes, Mijango, Colindres and Castillo scrambled to provide some structure to the process. In a small office in the San Benito neighborhood of San Salvador they formed a roundtable group they called *la mesa*. Meanwhile, Luis and others established a support team, which Luis operated from the headquarters of the penitentiary system.

The biggest problem was keeping the violence to a minimum. While the truce was packaged as an armistice, it was really something more akin to violence interruption or what is referred to as street outreach. Street outreach works when people close to the gangs can interrupt the deadly chains of retribution by intervening at critical junctures, often before a potential murder or right after one.

In the United States, street outreach has worked to a degree, most notably in Chicago, New York and Los Angeles. But it has also failed. If interrupters aren't careful, their interventions can reinforce gang cohesion, especially if they approach the intervention from the top down via the leaders. What's more, critics say the chains of violent retribution between the gangs are never broken, only delayed.

La mesa and Luis's support team implemented a complex intervention strategy to quell potential conflicts. The support team sent daily homicide and intelligence reports to la mesa, who would address hot spots and advise on arrests.

"If they were going to do something, we could hit them before," Luis explained to me, referring to the troublemakers who might want to disrupt the truce.

In some instances la mesa would pass the hot spot reports directly to imprisoned gang leaders, who would then call their leaders on the street and issue a corrective, hopefully stopping violence before it happened.

But this exchange of information often only led to more violence. After one faction of the 18th Street killed some relatives of another faction, for instance, the police called la mesa. La mesa passed this information to the gang leaders. They talked and came to a resolution: the gang who'd committed the murders had to hand over the three perpetrators. Their bodies were found the next day strewn along a highway on the outskirts of San Salvador. This was not an isolated incident. In another case, the MS-13 executed five who'd disobeyed orders.

"We had to decide," a member of Mijango's team told me later. "Do we use violence to stop the violence? There was no choice."

Luis insisted to me that he never knew of any deaths as a result of the information he and his support team passed to la mesa. But he understood the implication. The truce was crossing the Rubicon.

6.

There are many reasons gang truces fail. Gangs are diffuse in nature. They suffer from frequent infighting and localized intra-gang battles that make it hard to deescalate conflict. Negotiations are also anathema to the gangs' ethos. Gangs need conflict to create and fortify their identity. Leaders who do participate expose themselves to huge risks. Talking peace is a tacit admission of weakness in gang culture. When leaders talk peace, rivals may suddenly challenge their territorial integrity and seize their revenue streams. It is, in other words, a perilous path.

Norman slipped into this vacuum when he was released from prison in the summer of 2012. He was respected, a leader. He'd even witnessed the beginnings of the truce inside Zacatraz. But once he was out of prison, the gang started to lose meaning and his real family became his focus. He helped his wife sell farm goods and prepared food at the local market and visited his mother more frequently. It would be a long road to redemption. His wife was despondent, distant. His eldest daughter was drawn to gang life, dating an MS-13 wannabe. Norman didn't really know any of his children. His daughters looked at him and said "Dad," but he didn't yet understand what that meant.

Norman also felt vulnerable. He had accumulated so many enemies: police, rival gang members, rival criminal groups, his victims and their families. Since the truce homicides had fallen to six per day. But Norman's mara friends reminded him of the dangers. The 18th Street still controlled other parts of the town and not even the truce could delay some vendettas.

What are you doing? they asked him when they saw him at the market helping his wife. *You're nuts. They're going to kill you.*

The irony, of course, was that it was Norman's own gang that represented the greatest threat to him. Norman was at a stage in his gang career where the stakes were higher. Norman carried valuable information about the mara, and the authorities had already tried to convert him into an informant in Zacatraz. If he asked to leave now, he would get killed by his own gang, regardless of his true motivations and promises to keep his mouth shut.

The MS-13 was also locked in a power struggle over money. Inside and outside, gang leaders began collecting cash to continue the truce. How much was not clear, but only a few enjoyed the spoils. At the top was the ranfla, the national leadership council headed by El Diablito. The ranfla shared the money with close relatives and associates, some of whom were gang leaders on the outside, the so-called *ranfla en la libre*. Fancy cars. New apartments. Top-shelf liquor.

By 2012, an entrepreneurial wing of the ranfla led by El Diablito was sending emissaries to Honduras and Mexico to explore relationships with drug trafficking organizations. Like Comandari, El Diablito understood the potential of the MS-13—its tentacles stretching into lucrative US drug markets like Los Angeles and New York.

Also like Comandari, El Diablito faced resistance, in part because of the secrecy surrounding trafficking contacts, meetings and negotiations, and in part because of the skewed revenue sharing. Rank-and-file gang members could see the riches at the leadership level, but the spoils never seemed to trickle down. The meetings remained centered on the truce, but mid-level leaders and the soldiers were getting restless.

Among the insurgents was Walter Antonio Carrillo Alfaro, alias Chory (the bastardized version of Shorty). Chory was part of the Fulton clique, beaten in on the streets of San Fernando Valley in Los Angeles and reared by mara like Ernesto Deras, the Salvadoran soldier who'd become a gang leader. After being deported, Chory had helped set up a formidable Fulton presence in various parts of El Salvador. In prison he'd also suffered through the dark days when MS-13 members were beaten by Bruno and his soldiers in La Raza.

Chory—who with his shaved head, intense brown eyes and bulging muscles had an intimidating presence—helped whip the gang into a disciplined, regional force. He'd fought in the prison riots and shown ingenuity and leadership. It was Chory, for example, who had arranged a hit on a guard who routinely beat Norman and the other mara at Apanteos in those early years. He was also part of the talks to form the original ranfla in the mid-2000s.

In other words, Chory had respect. And if Chory was saying the ranfla was disrespecting el barrio, then the ranfla had a problem.

7.

Shortly after he was released in 2012, Norman got a call from the ranfla. They had a job for him. He knew, instinctively, that they were testing his loyalty, ensuring the gang member they all knew as El Loco was still committed to the gang. The target was named Peligro (Danger). On the phone, the ranfla listed Peligro's alleged transgressions: he was stealing in the name of the gang; he had raped, killed and buried girls in unmarked graves. In sum, he was disrespecting el barrio.

At the time, Norman's clique was reconstituting itself. Norman's partner in crime, Malvado, had also been released. Like Norman, Malvado had been in prison for more than a decade and had helped establish the MS-13 inside the penitentiary system. He was a member of the Federation, a sort of board of directors of the gang outside of prison. Unlike Norman, Malvado was still firmly in the gang's grip. In Norman he saw a partner; he also saw a rival.

The tension between Malvado and Norman was normal in the gang. MS-13 cliques rotate personnel on a near constant basis. Gang members are arrested. They are killed. They move. They drift outside of the gang's orbit. The result is near endless instability. Tests are the only way to confirm if someone is committed. Peligro was a test.

"It was time to show what we could give. I mean, we had to kill that dude," Norman said.

The gang also suspected Peligro was an informant. According to a government indictment released later, he had been talking about showing authorities where some bodies were buried. "He didn't want to be in the gang anymore," the government document said. It was Peligro's stepfather, Abuelo (Grandfather), who told the gang he might be snitching. Abuelo himself was a recently released prisoner. Anxious to reaffirm his loyalty to the MS-13, he told Malvado and other clique members about Peligro's slide toward the police. It was all the information the clique needed. Peligro would have to die.

According to the indictment, the gang gave Abuelo a gun, so he could kill his stepson. It wouldn't be easy. The gang was family; so was Peligro. Days passed, and nothing happened. The clique began to whisper amongst themselves, wondering if Abuelo could do it. Peligro remained in the area. Questions about Abuelo's commitment followed, and his clock started to expire alongside his stepson's.

It was around this time that Norman says the gang contacted him. As it is throughout this story, there are significant differences between the way Norman portrays his actions and how prosecutors describe them. Norman says he was a reluctant soldier, dragged into a scheme that had nothing to do with him at a time when he was trying to distance himself from the MS-13. The government says he volunteered for it, alongside two others: Chivo (Goat) and Flaco (Skinny). Chivo was also recently out of prison, eager to show his commitment to the mara.

So it was that in early October 2012, El Loco, Chivo and Flaco went to kill Peligro. If this sounds like a children's story, it's because these life-and-death decisions inside the MS-13 come together like twisted fairy tales—full of playful names, symbolic gestures, colorful villains and unsuspecting victims. In this regard, testimony recovered by the state and what Norman told me line up.

El Loco, Flaco and Chivo made their way to Peligro's house, a rickety structure in the heart of the town. The area where Norman had grown up was by then inundated with gang members. The newest members had ditched the facial tattoos and the cholo garb to escape scrutiny from law enforcement, but they remained disaffected and idle.

On the way to the house, Chivo called Peligro. He told him to come outside, that he was going to give him twenty dollars. It's not clear what the twenty was for, but by then two things would have been clear to Peligro. First, it was a decent amount of money in the gang world—twenty dollars was about a week's wages for a lookout in El Salvador. Second, the mara probably wanted to kill him. Small enticements—marijuana and alcohol, a party with girls, cash or all three—were often used as traps.

What happened next is not entirely clear. Prosecutors say all three—Chivo, Flaco and El Loco—shot at Peligro when he emerged from his home. But Norman says it was just Chivo who fired his weapon, and that Peligro took off running toward Norman, while Chivo kept shooting, hitting Peligro in the chest and the wrist. Norman froze, he told me later, while Peligro, bleeding and slumped to one side, ran past him.

"I didn't have the heart to kill him," he told me.

Why? I asked.

"I didn't feel it," he said. "I'm old. I couldn't even try."

Peligro got away.

11

GOD AND THE BEAST

1.

AS I RODE WITH ERNESTO DERAS TO HIS OFFICE, his telephone rumbled on the console between us. He picked it up and kept driving, one hand on the wheel as he thumbed through the message. Ernesto, who was better known for years as Satán, had committed a lot of crimes. These days, his most serious offense may be texting while driving through the wide palm-laden boulevards of North Hollywood. The source of the text was unclear.

"Could be a homeboy," he said, as he began texting back, never leaving his lane. The two exchanged messages for a few lights, until Ernesto declared, "*Es un* homeboy."

Ernesto—whose long hair and thin face had given way to a bald head and round cheeks—had eased out of gang life and was now working in Communities in Schools, a gang intervention program in the San Fernando Valley funded by the city government. The program head was Blinky Rodriguez, the same kickboxer who'd fostered truces in the area in the mid-1990s.

About a half hour after they started chatting via Facebook, Ernesto pulled into a strip mall to wait for the homeboy. As we sat in front of a donut shop, he reminisced. The mall was the site of an historic melee in the early 1990s, which left him with a busted lip and a cracked head. The former Salvadoran soldier smiled at the memory. Five minutes later, an MS-13 named Andrés appeared.[15] The two greeted each other quietly. Andrés got into the car, and we continued driving to Ernesto's office.

Andrés was big for a Salvadoran, around five ten, one hundred eighty pounds. He had gentle, youthful features that belied his twenty-four years. His last name was tattooed across his right forearm, and three tiny dots were inked on his left cheek, just below the eye. The dots signify the three places where gang members believe they will inevitably go: the hospital, prison and the cemetery. He wore a Cleveland Cavaliers hat and was clean-shaven. Unless you were an expert in tattoos, you couldn't tell he was a gang member. He was working part-time on a construction site, he told me. And that afternoon, he was going to help a friend install security cameras. He wasn't trained for either job, but that didn't matter.

Andrés was a law enforcement nightmare. He'd already cycled through the entire system—arrested, jailed and deported, and now he'd returned. Local and federal officers search for these types of gang members. Because of their unstable lives, they are the most likely to fall back into hard-core gang life. Ernesto looked for these types of gang members too—to help them leave the gang, he said.

We arrived at a one-story brick building. Ernesto brought Andrés into his office. Ernesto's cubicle was covered with photos of murdered mara, and he spent the first ten minutes talking

---

15 For security reasons, his name has been changed.

Andrés through the dead, photo by photo. Chato. Hyper. Pantera. Raven. Smokey. "No mothers crying and no babies dying," read a sign above the pictures.

Ernesto also had a photo of Donald Garcia and copies of his book, *Big D: Victorious Through God's Grace*, lined up neatly on his desk. He pointed to the cover: boxing gloves hang from a giant *D*, the entrance of a jail shimmering in the background.

"He had two or three murders hanging over him," he told Andrés.

Ernesto then launched into the story about how he met Big D and Blinky during the days of the Mexican Mafia–inspired gang truces in the mid-1990s; how he wore his "Fuck Everybody" skullcap to the meeting, and how he nearly got in a fight before they all stopped at Blinky's behest and prayed.

"If you want respect, you have to give respect back," Ernesto told him.

Andrés nodded, a blank look on his face.

The spiel was part threat, part male ritual. Dead homies. Prison. Murder. Technically, it was a gang intervention strategy. Practically, it was a scare seminar.

Andrés listened. He seemed marginally interested, especially when the subject turned to the possibility of Ernesto helping him get work. As they talked, it was clear that employment was his biggest concern. Ernesto likes to say that gang members are "one job away" from leaving, but most gang members also need a lot of community support to pull them through to the other side. Even then, many remain in the middle—"fifty-fifty" as it's sometimes called.

Andrés had a three-year-old daughter. She was born not long after police tailed him and his girlfriend into a local Target and arrested them. His girlfriend was carrying crystal meth and got hit with a drug charge. She served eight months, then was deported to El Salvador. He was carrying an unregistered weapon and got two years. On the day he was released, customs officials were waiting and brought him to an immigration center. A few days later, they packed him into a plane and flew him to El Salvador.

"I'm trying to get out," he told me softly. "I have another reason to live."

His daughter had been placed in a foster home. Andrés had seen her twice since he'd returned, but he didn't think she recognized him.

We got back in the car to take him to meet his friend, the one installing security cameras. Along the way, Ernesto talked to him about his parenting duties and gave him advice about how he should approach his daughter after not seeing her for so long. He also suggested that Andrés could move to another state, *"un estado calmado."* Andrés resisted, saying that he'd tried Las Vegas, but there was no work.

Andrés told Ernesto he was planning to reunite with his girlfriend; that she was in Guadalajara, making her way back into the United States.

Are you going to leave the gang? I finally asked him, point blank.

"You can't leave," he replied quietly.

He looked away.

2.

Broadly speaking, there are three types of gang prevention strategies: primary prevention targets populations who are at risk because of the gang activity in their neighborhoods or schools; secondary prevention is aimed at high-risk youth and gang wannabes; tertiary prevention targets committed gang members, usually with criminal records.

These strategies involve families, schools, churches and other nongovernmental organizations. They create safe spaces to demobilize gang members and early intervention programs to divert kids before they develop rap sheets. They connect at-risk youth to sports teams and psychologists. The best programs offer tailored intervention strategies that include programs for the entire family.

These programs are woefully underfunded and politically unpalatable. Even the most hopeful gang interventionists will tell you they are part of the solution, not *the* solution. Law enforcement agencies are especially skeptical. When I spoke to police about the programs, most were dismissive. They say there's no way out of the gangs, especially the MS-13. Some officers were especially disdainful of ex-gang members who participated in or, worse yet, ran these programs.

These were the same officials who had prosecuted Alex Sanchez, the former MS-13 leader who ran tertiary-prevention programs at Homies Unidos in Los Angeles. After the case against him fell apart, their ire only increased. To them, his wiretapped expression "we go to war" and "face the consequences" were proof that he ordered the murder of his former protégé, Walter Lacinos, in El Salvador.

The Alex Sanchez case ultimately fell apart because of a parallel murder plot of another gang intervention specialist. Ernesto Miranda, aka Smokey, had joined the gang in Los Angeles, been arrested, jailed and deported, then started working countergang programs. He and Alex were friends, and Alex had sent Smokey to pick up Lacinos when he'd arrived at the San Salvador airport following his deportation in 2006. A week after Alex and Lacinos traded barbs on the telephone, however, Lacinos shot and killed Smokey. Alex said it was part of Lacinos's revenge against him.

"Smokey was as close as he could get to [killing] me," Alex told me.

Smokey's murder set into motion an internal gang investigation. A week later, Zombie shot and killed Lacinos. Prosecutors thought this Zombie was the same Zombie who Alex told on the phone, "we go to war." But in fact, the Zombie who killed Lacinos was a different Zombie. There were, in effect, *two* Zombies. Such was the complex world of intragang warfare and part of why the case against Alex Sanchez took years to sort through before prosecutors finally dropped it.

Yet the belief Alex had a double life persisted. When I last spoke to him, LAPD Detective Frank Flores was still smarting about the case. He said Alex and others had used Homies Unidos as a kind of counterintelligence unit, gathering information on other gangs via their intervention programs and collecting intel on police operations during meetings at precinct houses. Frank claimed Alex and others had also staged gang meetings on street corners—in violation of gang injunctions—so they could lure police to the scene, then photograph them stopping and frisking the youth to add to their complaints for harassment. And he said Alex helped active gang members escape prosecution and deportation. He saw the decision to drop the case as a political, not a legal one, since the question of which Zombie killed Lacinos was, in his mind, irrelevant. He still held out hope a marero would one day walk into his office and flip on Alex.

"There's always that chance someone will step forward," he said. "A lot of time has passed, but you never know."

Police had arrested several other ex-gang members who'd become tertiary-prevention specialists. A year before Alex was charged, an 18th Street gang member plead guilty to using a gang prevention program to camouflage his gunrunning activities in Los Angeles. A year prior to that plea, a Pacoima gang member who was working in Communities in Schools was stopped with methamphetamine in his car.

Another of Ernesto Deras's colleagues, who'd come from the MS-13, was later charged with murder. Ernesto himself said he suspected that he was under investigation as well, and when I asked investigators about him, they snorted, as if to suggest that I was naive to think he was dedicating his life to gang prevention.

Homies Unidos had problems beyond Alex. In El Salvador, the original founders were killed in a shootout with other gang members as part of a power struggle. The one who picked up the pieces and tried to start anew was also killed. In Long Island, an MS-13 who wanted to establish a Homies Unidos branch openly refused to renounce the mara and was later arrested and deported.

All these cases were spread out over years and were not necessarily representative, but for the most cynical observers, they tended to reinforce the worst stereotype: there was no such thing as an ex-gang member.

3.

One of Ernesto's clients called himself Little Danger. He was eighteen, about to turn nineteen. He had a baby face and an endearing smile. He was wearing a black long-sleeved shirt, gray-and-black cargo shorts, and a black Los Angeles Rams baseball hat the day I met him. His shoes were black Nikes that were not, he emphasized, Cortez. Cortez was long the mara shoe of choice but had become a dog whistle for authorities. His mom wanted him to wear "skinny jeans" that morning, he told me. But he'd opted for this more subtle gang uniform.

Little Danger, who asked me not to use his real name, was originally from Santa Ana, El Salvador, Ernesto's home state. He'd come a few years earlier with the rush of children that had flooded the US. His mom thought she was getting him out of the gang's purview by sending him to live with his grandparents in the Valley. It was both sad and ironic: the Fulton beat him into the clique about a year after he'd moved there.

Little Danger was obsessed with the 18th Street. His father, he told me, was killed by an 18th Street member in El Salvador when Little Danger was three years old. He found out when he was eleven, at which point he drifted toward the MS-13. His older cousin was a respected member of the local clique. That cousin had a growing family and was starting to go to church, inching toward becoming a retiree—*calmado*, as they say. But that connection gave Little Danger an entry point to become a paro, "a lookout."

"You're young," one of them said to him. "Just kick it with us."

Paros have committed to the gang, but they are not yet members. It is the beginning of an education that can take years to complete in El Salvador. And it is the last chance any secondary prevention program has to reach someone like Little Danger. But in El Salvador, there are few programs like this.

Little Danger discovered his father's killer was a man who had fled to the United States. So he targeted the man's family, extorting the mother for $25 a week. The gang, he said blithely, also murdered his father's killer's two brothers.

"I didn't do anything bad with his mom," he insisted. "The gang wouldn't let me. Unless the old lady would snitch on me."

Still, Little Danger felt like he was getting a little revenge: "He [his father's assassin] knew I was collecting renta from his mom."

By the time he was thirteen, Little Danger says he was a chequeo, a more advanced stage of gang school. Chequeos have more serious duties that can include killing for the gang. Murder is part of the mara's way of testing their recruits for loyalty and commitment. It's also what gets many stuck for good: once you have taken part, collectively, in a serious crime, you are equal parts perpetrator and witness. If you leave, you are a liability for anyone who is still on the inside.

In El Salvador, you have to murder someone to gain entry to the mara. In the US, you do not. The difference can change the internal dynamic of a clique. Salvadoran initiates like Little Danger leverage the perception they've gone through a tougher initiation to gain more respect and move up the gang ladder faster when they come to places like Los Angeles.

It was when he became a chequeo that his mom started getting really worried. She would see him posting up with a machete, and she noticed he was smoking a lot of marijuana, so she decided to send him to the United States.

"I hope there are no gangs up there," she told him.

Little Danger played dumb. In the US he could finally exact his revenge.

"I don't think there are any gangs there," he responded.

By the time Little Danger got to his grandparents, his father's assassin was dead. His primary motivation to join the mara was gone, but Little Danger said his resolve to kill anyone in the 18th Street was not. His animosity, he came to realize, had shaped his life.

What did you tell the gang when they asked why you wanted to join? I asked him.

"Because I like it. I like gangbangers. The MS," he said. "Other people. I don't even like how they talk, you know. I just want to like, kill, you know. Straight up."

You just felt like you wanted to hurt somebody?

"Yeah."

Why do you think you felt like that?

"Because they didn't let me get to know my father."

4.

In gang life there are periods of intense involvement, and degrees of responsibility that tend to dissipate with age or competing family obligations. After a few years, most want to quit. In an academic survey of more than 1,100 gang members from various factions in El Salvador's prisons—half of which were members of the MS-13—68 percent said they wanted to leave. Many of these were leaders. Of the gangs surveyed, however, the MS-13 was considered the hardest to leave. And those who did want to leave saw only one way out: the evangelical church.

In his treatment of this topic, sociologist Robert Brenneman notes "the structural similarities between evangelical congregations and gang cells," including the "bright boundaries between members and nonmembers" and their highly regimented social rhythms. Both are, in other words, places where people find an alternative family. The church can also come to dominate your life in the same way a gang can. In some evangelical churches worshipers gather nearly every night and throughout the weekends. Some members address each other as brother and sister, Brenneman observes, and like gangs, they are expected to look out for one another, providing jobs, shelter, childcare, and food when needed. In addition, churches are highly patriarchal, mimicking another central aspect of gang life. For gang members, the regimen works.

Ernesto Deras says his own departure was facilitated by the church. It was 1997, and he was eating in a restaurant with some mara. A former gang leader who was going to church showed up at the restaurant and asked them if they wanted to go pray with him. They laughed, but he persisted.

"Vamos Satán," the former mara said. "There's food."

"And are there *jainas*?" Ernesto asked.

"There are lots of girls," he replied. "Let's go, man. It'll give your head a break."

Ernesto and four others went with him. The church was crowded, so they squeezed into the plastic seats in the back row.

At the front of the room, the pastor began: "From the time of John the Baptist, the southern kingdom was full of violence, and only the bravest pushed back."

Satán laughed.

"Ese vato," he said softly. "Why doesn't he come out with us...? We're the bravest."

The others started to chuckle.

"The tough ones are the homeboys," he continued, emboldened by the others' snickers. "These guys are all cowards."

Ernesto left the church and had no intention of returning, but a few days later, when he found himself running from the police, he hid in the church and eluded them. A few days later, he happened on the church a third time, and again stepped inside—this time not for refuge but because he liked it. Later, he would tell me that it was the "environment"—a good energy—that drew him closer to religion.

He started to attend regularly. They had mass almost every night and on the weekends. One Sunday a woman preached. Ernesto doesn't remember what she said, but after the sermon, the congregants closed their eyes and began to pray. Some in the congregation cried out for help, and Ernesto says he felt something. He got up and began to walk toward the front of church where the woman was. There, he says he felt a powerful force that knocked him to his knees. Then he burst out crying—*"a llorar, a llorar, a llorar"*—and the only thing that came from his mouth was a plea for forgiveness.

"Perdón. Perdón. Perdón."

"I never cried," he told me later. "I'd been shot. I'd had broken bones. I was in jail. My mom couldn't even make me cry."

"But that day," he told me, "that day, I found out God existed."

Satán, in other words, had met Jesus.

When his fellow mara learned he was going to the church, they tried to distract him. They'd show up at services and attempt to lure him away, fabricating emergencies, fights, or promising him parties with girls. Jainas, they said, a plea that had usually worked with Ernesto—he would have thirteen kids by three different women by the time I met him.

But he stuck with it, and he was, in a manner of speaking, fortunate. The leader he had left in charge of the Fulton had been killed. Others with similar stature were deported. His clique was decimated, and it freed him.

"If they had been there, they would have dragged me back," he told me, referring to the other leaders. "But there was no one left who could control me, and so I was able to get more involved [in the church]."

After a while he felt confident enough to say it out loud to all his homeboys, even the new leadership. They all knew by then anyway.

"Is it true you're going to the church?" one of them asked him on the street one day.

"Simón," he replied, using the gang slang for "yes, man."

"Do it," the other said. "But do it for real. I'm not gonna do it, because I don't think I could stick with it, but you should do it and keep going."

Little by little, they left him alone. As Brenneman might say, homies became *hermanos*. Ernesto didn't go to mirin, he went to *misa*. Soon *la iglesia* replaced el barrio.

5.

On October 6, 2013, a Los Angeles–based MS-13 leader named José Juan Rodríguez Juárez, alias Dreamer, organized a conference call. He wanted to connect the MS-13 from one coast to the other. If the plan had a familiar ring to it, that was because Dreamer was a descendant of the same gang circles as Nelson Comandari, the imprisoned MS-13 leader whose failed efforts to turn the mara into a drug trafficking organization (DTO) had led to the secret testimony that helped build the case against Alex Sanchez. Comandari's whereabouts remained unknown, his statements to authorities sealed.

Dreamer's plan had emerged from a separate international drug trafficking scheme. A former Comandari lieutenant named Luis Vega, alias Lil' One, had helped the Mexican Mafia make connections to a Mexican DTO. The Mafia promised to distribute drugs through its vast Sureños network and offered to protect jailed drug traffickers. After operations began, Vega became the first MS-13 member to earn a spot in the Mexican Mafia's leadership, Los Señores. But in 2013, authorities arrested Vega and eleven others and dismantled their drug trafficking scheme.

A few months later, Dreamer was hoping to pick up the pieces from Vega's network. He got leaders from as far away as El Salvador and New Jersey on the phone. They called the project the National Program. In subsequent calls, Dreamer's lieutenants talked of corralling cliques in New Jersey, North Carolina, Virginia and Maryland, and folding them into a nationwide drug distribution network they hoped would eventually stretch to Spain. Dreamer "is the owner of all the United States," one of the program's operatives said in a wiretapped telephone call.

The Mafia liked the plan and would make Dreamer a Big Homie, the second MS-13 after Vega to reach that status. But by November 2013, the plan began to crumble when some East Coast cliques balked. Dreamer's lieutenants gave orders to beat up the offenders and, when that didn't work, to kill them. But by then, El Salvador leaders were also refusing to follow Dreamer's commands. And like Vega and Comandari before him, Dreamer became a prime government target. A month later, US authorities captured him.

Dreamer's arrest thwarted his drug trafficking scheme and also sent the MS-13 in Los Angeles into disarray. No one, it seemed, wanted to take the lead. Instead, the gang created a sort of board of directors. The lack of authority came at a bad time. The gang truce was shifting power south to El Salvador.

It was around this time that Little Danger came to Los Angeles. He and his generation of Salvadoran–born and bred gangbangers remained loyal to their roots and gave Salvadoran leaders a leg up in the States.

Do you like it? I asked Little Danger about the gang.

"Yeah," he said. "When I'm hurting people, I don't need to feel sad. I just laugh."

Why is that?

"Like you, let's say you play soccer, it's like fun. It's like a sport. Put it that way."

I looked at Ernesto, the one-time MS-13 leader who had become a gang-prevention specialist and who'd introduced me to Little Danger. His eyes widened and his mouth broke into a small smile. He and I had already discussed how the "new ones," the ones "from El Salvador" had a different mentality because the violence they'd seen and had committed inured them. One of Ernesto's clients had just been implicated in the machete killing of an 18th Street member on the edge of a public park. Other recent arrivals were connected to numerous killings along the East Coast.

Little Danger's story reflected this rising violence. Since he'd arrived in the US, he been kicked out of multiple schools. Wherever he went, he said, he recruited "the little ones" for the gang. He made a name for himself, which put him on the LAPD's radar. Eight arrests followed: assault, theft, weapons charges and more. When I met him, he'd just done a six-month stint in a camp for juvenile offenders.

Unable to secure steady work because of his parade of court appearances, Little Danger said he sometimes helped his grandfather, who did landscaping and gardening. His grandmother and mother cleaned houses. His mother had come to the US just a few months after him, and the four of them lived together in the Valley. She tried to kick him into shape, but "she got tired," he said. "She always tells me like, 'I love you. Think about what you're doing.'"

Like Andrés, Little Danger had a tattoo of three dots, only his was inked on the fleshy part of the top of his hand between the thumb and his forefinger. *"La vida loca,"* he said to me, smiling.

I asked him about his initiation.

"That was the day when I became a different person," he said.

Why did it make you a different person?

"Because, I can't..."

"Se metió a la bestia," Ernesto interjected.

"Because I can't get out no more," Little Danger added.

"You've been swallowed by the beast," Ernesto repeated.

"Pues sí."

Little Danger laughed.

6.

Every time Alex Sanchez picked up the phone, he spoke slowly, deliberately. When he went to meetings, he was mindful of who might be eavesdropping. When he did errands, he looked over his shoulder. One of the last times I saw him, he and his colleagues at Homies Unidos were preparing for their annual Central American Youth Leadership Conference at the local community college. The conference was the next day, and they were making a shopping list.

"Chairs, ropes, razors," one of them said, as another jotted down the items on a small piece of scrap paper.

"Don't write razors," Alex said, half joking. "Write box cutters. Otherwise the cops are going to stop us and say we're gonna kidnap and torture someone."

He may have been exaggerating only slightly. His detractors in law enforcement still believed Alex was the head of a "supergang."

"They are waiting to see if I trip up," Alex said.

However, Homies Unidos appeared strong, institutionalized even. Community organizations and the local college sponsored their event. Representatives of the District Attorney's Office, as well as members of churches and NGOs, set up booths. A Univision host played master of ceremonies, and Latino youth sat twenty-five rows deep under a tent half the size of a football field. Two teenagers danced to a cumbia between the seats before the conference launched with a series of speeches by activists and Homies Unidos reps.

"Que viva Alex Sanchez!" one speaker bellowed at the end of his short talk.

"QUE VIVA!" the teenagers shouted back.

But Alex never felt safe. And the conference was, in a strange way, a trigger. He saw his own journey reflected in the young folks in the audience, and as the conference got started, he offered a kind of rambling, condensed version of his own story.

"You came running from the violence there," he told them, referring to their war-torn homelands and speaking in their native Spanish. "And then you arrived here, and you had a culture shock. Different races. A different language. A different type of education. Parents who didn't know you because of all the time you've been separated. You felt like you'd entered into a haze. You felt abandoned... And then, your introduction to the United States was to be thrown in jail. How many of you were jailed when you arrived?"

He paused, as some in the audience tentatively raised their hands.

"That's your introduction."

Although Alex was finally removed from the MS-13 indictment in 2013, the judge gave prosecutors the right to revive charges against him, should they find more evidence. And aside from Frank, one of those who worked the case told me privately his office had continued to collect more information on Alex, but admitted that politically, it would be an uphill battle to charge him again.

In the years since Alex's indictment, Homies Unidos rebuilt its brand and recouped many of its sponsors, including the Los Angeles city government. It moved into a small office overlooking a rectangular courtyard and channeled resources toward tattoo removal, job training and art classes.

That was where I first met Alex. His brown Fu Manchu from the "Free Alex" days was now salt-and-pepper and drifted four inches below his chin. He was buried behind piles of paper and constantly distracted by emails and phone calls on his landline and cell.

"This is where it all happens," he said with a smile.

The office attracted a near constant flow of former gang members, some of whom had turned to religion to help them with their transition. While I was visiting I met one mara who had become a pastor. José Díaz worked in a factory by day and preached by night in his fledgling storefront, the Iglesia Pentacostal Fuego en la Zarza (Burning Bush Pentecostal Church). Although his church was in an 18th Street stronghold, he did not and could not hide his past: two tattooed horns poked from the top of his hairline.

"When I walk through my neighborhood, God makes me invisible," he told me when I asked him about the threat of other gangs.

Still, what's most striking about Homies Unidos is its secular feel. So much tertiary gang prevention occurs in religious settings, but Homies Unidos was relatively free of God talk, if not exhibiting outright hostility toward the church. Alex and another former gang member who worked with him, for example, said they do not believe in organized religion.

"To me, the church looks exactly like the gang," Alex said. "It makes you blind."

The closest Alex came to a spiritual awakening was during a weekend at a sweat lodge some years after he'd left the gang. There, as the embers raged and the tent heated up, he saw the image of his mentor, Rata, the same mara who'd been killed in the late 1980s by the Fedora.

What did he say to you? I asked.

"'You're doing good,'" Alex said.

12

THE NEW WAR

1.

IN LATE 2012, A REPRESENTATIVE OF THE ARROCera San Francisco called Raúl Mijango at his office in the San Benito neighborhood of San Salvador. Arrocera was a food production and distribution company run by a prominent Salvadoran family. A few years prior, the gangs had begun to target the company's trucks when they entered their territory.

The extortion system was a mess. Individual cliques, not the central gang leadership, managed the collection, exacting payments on a neighborhood-by-neighborhood basis: $20 here, $175 there, $100 elsewhere. It added up. By 2010, cliques from the three major gangs—MS-13, 18th Street Sureños, and 18th Street Revolucionarios—were collecting roughly $15,000 per month from the company. The costs were not just monetary. Miscommunication and theft within the gang were common, but when company representatives claimed to have paid the renta and the leaders had not received it, there was no recourse. These misunderstandings led to violence: the gangs killed drivers and destroyed trucks. The company was suffocating, and so they called Mijango.

By then the truce was underway. It was not exactly clear what it was or who was behind it, but homicides had been halved, and the private sector thought that if la mesa could help lower murder rates, it could also help with extortion.

The irony, Mijango thought. Most of the country's elites had taken strong positions against the truce, and the president continued to keep his distance, so he could maintain some semblance of plausible deniability should the situation reverse and homicides spike again. But the gangs had spread to nearly every corner of the country. They were the reason behind every large line item in the security budget. They impacted businesses, religious organizations, educational facilities and transport systems. And they were driving migration to the United States and elsewhere.

The MS-13 had also become a de facto political actor. They were not leftist insurgents, and they didn't have a political message or platform, but they had political capital, and politicians would soon be seeking their support for election. Their mere existence was a reminder that something in the system was broken. Yet "brokering across the gap between the state and the street," as James Cockayne wrote in his book on organized crime and politics, was messy, chaotic, dangerous, violent and very often criminal.

Negotiating with gangs came with steep risks. Giving them a platform, imbuing them with political, social and economic capital, and providing them with an avenue to possibly skirt justice was understandably hard for people to accept. Even worse, such negotiations could strengthen the gangs' brand. The biggest challenge of the gang truce—of any negotiation with gangs—was dealing with the problem without legitimizing the group.

As it was with the Mexican Mafia in Los Angeles in the early 1990s, there were indications that the gangs, in particular the MS-13, were using the truce as a means to expand their criminal portfolio. Rumor had it the cliques were "disappearing" their victims to account for the dip in homicides. For every critique, Mijango and his team had an answer. According to data from the police, the number of reports for the disappeared did not significantly change during the truce, making that claim implausible, they said. Stories about a criminal expansion, they claimed, were simply not true.

"In seventy-two hours, that little agreement did something that this country hadn't been able to do in twenty years, which was to stop the spiral of violence and reduce it significantly," Mijango would tell me years later.

The next step, Mijango said, was to tackle the problem of extortion. That was when he got the call from the Arrocera. They weren't the only company that had requested la mesa's help with extortion, but they were one of the most open to using Mijango's influence with the gangs. Mijango arranged the first meetings between an intermediary of Arrocera and the gangs in late 2012. The gang leaders negotiated via telephone from prison.

Eventually, Mijango brokered a new deal: instead of $15,000 per month, the gangs agreed to take $6,000 in what a later indictment in the case described as "pre-cooked rice, beans, [cooking] oil, pampers and other goods." What's more, the company channeled the payments directly to the leaders, who ensured the trucks and company drivers did not have to pay clique by clique as they traversed different neighborhoods.

For the gangs and the company, it was a deranged win-win. The company paid less and had less exposure. The gangs received less but could sell the products for a greater profit in the markets where they controlled food stalls. Mijango also ensured the company would provide receipts to the gangs' emissaries and thereby deflect any police who might stop them en route to the markets. According to one negotiator I spoke with, the idea was that the gangs would stop the extortion once they gained a foothold in the market.

It was a decidedly imperfect solution, and in that way a near ideal metaphor for the gang truce itself. Mijango later admitted as much to me. He took a chance, he said, because he saw no other way. Throughout history, criminal actors have been convinced, cajoled or forced into proper society, into political discourse and economic systems. It's a messy process not unlike Boss Tweed's work in the Five Points of New York City in the 1850s. But in El Salvador in 2013, the space for nuanced solutions was closing quickly. And eventually, Mijango himself would feel the pinch.

2.

During the truce, MS-13 leaders presented an image of goodwill. They held news conferences with Mijango and the two factions of the 18th Street. They celebrated mass inside the prisons with Bishop Colindres. They gave interviews in which they accepted some of the blame. They also talked of poverty, oppression and repression. This was el barrio, the community of marginalized human beings who'd banded together because of circumstance.

But behind the curtains, they employed a duplicitous strategy. As part of the truce, authorities transferred MS-13 leaders to other prisons, where they quickly reasserted their command and revived their criminal economies. The gang established committees, or what they called *líneas*, to deal with various issues. The principal line dealt with homicides—bringing proposed green lights to the ranfla. The report line was responsible for consolidating information and providing a briefing to the principal line. The expansion line dealt with issues around territory. The investigation line was responsible for looking into violations of gang rules and regulations. The legal assistance line collected money for legal fees, recommended lawyers and connected with sympathetic religious organizations and NGOs.

The new divisions were supposed to streamline information and logistics, as well as consolidate the ranfla's hold on the rank and file. In some ways it worked. But the units were ultimately camouflage for the ranfla's unchecked power.

During one particularly revealing conference call in 2016, leaders discussed potential green light targets, mara and others who had violated the rules. Authorities wiretapped the call, and in the span of just over an hour, gang leaders sanctioned fourteen murders, about one every four minutes. It was due process, mara style.

The gang also established a council outside of prison called the Federation—a group of thirty or so leaders who would have "the last word." Norman's name was up for consideration, but following the botched attempt on Peligro, the ranfla was having doubts. Police had captured Chivo and Flaco right after they'd shot Peligro, and after recovering in the hospital, Peligro started working with authorities. The gang called corte to ask Norman a few questions. Norman would get more due process than most who confronted gang justice, but he still faced severe punishment.

"They're going to fuck you because you didn't want to shoot," a fellow mara told him. "For being a pussy!"

Norman understood. Part of him was resigned to his fate. He was done, or, at least, almost done. After his explanations faltered, they beat him badly for about three minutes, he told me. He suffered two broken ribs, he testified later, and he had to recover in the hospital.

Prosecutors tell a slightly different story. They say Norman wasn't a reluctant soldier but rather still actively working with the MS-13. They arrested him a month after the murder attempt on Peligro and sent him to a holding cell. His arrest angered

Malvado and the others in their clique who correctly presumed Peligro was talking to the police.

On a subsequent conference call, which prosecutors say Norman took part in from his holding cell, the clique's frustration was palpable. A message had to be sent. They couldn't get to Peligro, but they could get to Abuelo, Peligro's stepfather. After all, it was Abuelo who had failed to kill Peligro when he had the chance. In the gang's logic, this meant Abuelo also had to be punished.

The clique issued a green light for Abuelo and his lifelong girlfriend. Anyone who saw Abuelo or his girlfriend now had the obligation to kill them. Failure to do so would also result in repercussions and set off yet another chain of retribution. This was the gang in miniature—spiderwebs of violence spinning from the paranoid eggshell egos of men.

Specifically, the government claimed that it was Norman, from his jail cell, who argued that Abuelo and his girlfriend needed to die. When I asked him about this, Norman denied it. It hardly mattered. The reality was that Norman, even if he didn't think Abuelo or his girlfriend deserved to be murdered, couldn't have saved them. Inside the gang, the only people who are saved are the ones who are clever enough to attack first.

Word spread through the mara ecosystem, and in late December 2012, someone spotted Abuelo, his longtime girlfriend and her daughter riding a bus. The informant network passed the intel to a gang member named Demente (Demented), who contacted another gang member, Furia (Fury). Abuelo, his girlfriend and her daughter got off the bus around 5:30 in the afternoon and began walking toward a shopping corridor alongside a housing complex. Demente and Furia followed, and when the victims passed the entrance of the mini-mall, they opened fire. Abuelo tried to deflect them.

"*¿Qué pasa? ¡Cálmense!*" he reportedly said after the mara fired the first rounds.

But the mara kept shooting. Abuelo's girlfriend covered her ears and scrambled toward the shopping corridor, taking a bullet to the left hand. When the shooting stopped, she returned to find Abuelo and her daughter on the ground. The two died—the government report reads—the daughter at the scene and Abuelo at the entrance of the hospital.

At the hospital, a few gang members visited Abuelo's girlfriend. She could live, they told her, if she kept her mouth shut. She agreed, prosecutors claim, but asked they pay for her medical bills and medicine. The gang members gave her $300, and she did not breathe a word.

Peligro, meanwhile, repented. As it turns out, he hadn't seen Norman try to kill him. Shortly thereafter, Norman was released from prison again.

3.

The truce had opened a political door for the gangs, and they were taking advantage. They began interacting more regularly with major political players from both parties. A mayor from Ilopango, a municipality on the edge of San Salvador, was the first to declare himself ready to work with the gangs to reduce violence and integrate them into educational, social and economic programs. Mayors from eleven municipalities would eventually declare their regions "peace zones." These mayors also employed MS-13 members and their relatives, hiring them for cleaning services, public works projects and security.

But few trusted the process. Newscasts talked menacingly of the truce, and images of incarcerated gang members—sitting in neat rows, wearing matching shorts and T-shirts, and receiving mass from Bishop Colindres—evoked a criminal army. In addition, the truce remained an under-the-table negotiation. The president never formally recognized it, and Congress ignored it completely. In polls, Salvadorans consistently rejected the truce by five-to-one margins. And in May 2013, the Bishop's Conference—the Catholic Church's highest authority in El Salvador—issued a public rebuke of the secret armistice.

US officials were almost uniformly against the truce. Some in USAID saw the truce as a Hail Mary, perhaps the only way to escape the vicious cycle of gang violence and state repression. But most in the State Department and FBI saw it as an exercise in futility or worse—a dangerous means of granting the gangs legitimacy. To these detractors, the tradeoff—lower homicides, but empowered gangs—would be a long-term disaster for El Salvador and the United States.

Influential US gang watchers like Douglas Farah, the award-winning, former *Washington Post* journalist who had become a security consultant, warned that gang leaders "are beginning to understand that territorial control and cohesion make it possible for them to wring concessions from the state while preserving the essence of their criminal character." Farah's work circulated widely in US government circles, especially the Pentagon, which also began to express concern.

The assertions led to overblown policy decisions while the truce was in motion. In October 2012, for instance, the US Treasury Department announced the inclusion of the MS-13 on its list of high-value targets alongside more established transnational criminal organizations like the Mexico-based Zetas and the Japan-based Yakuza. The Treasury Department later placed six gang leaders on its Kingpin list. An FBI agent working in El Salvador at the time laughed when I asked him about the Treasury's move—the gangs had thousands not millions of dollars in their bank accounts. He told me their decision was part of a "pissing match" over US government resources; the MS-13 was "hot," he added.

But the gesture was politically substantial. Businesses and NGOs who were wary of the truce steered further away. US development and aid agencies could not intersect with the gang or with those working with the gang without a special waiver, thereby undermining potential soft approaches during the truce and thereafter.

Collectively, the resistance made the government's dance with the gangs untenable, and in May 2013, just a little over fourteen months after it had sanctioned the transfer of prisoners out of Zacatraz, the government found an excuse to remove General Munguía Payés from his post as security minister.

The new security minister developed a policy called National Pacification, which included the dismantling of Luis Aguilar's police intelligence unit. The policy also rescinded access to the prisons and prohibited communications between the gang leaders and Mijango's team. Padre Toño, the would-be spokesperson who'd lobbied hard against Mijango in the earlier negotiations, was reinstated.

The truce was not officially over, and authorities did not immediately transfer gang leaders back to Zacatraz. But while Padre Toño tried to pick up where Mijango had left off, any hope for lasting peace began to fade.

4.

In the months leading up to the 2014 presidential elections, both major political parties in El Salvador sent high-end emissaries to meet with gang leaders. The quid pro quo was relatively straightforward: political support from the gangs in return for money, protection and a possible revival of the truce.

In February 2014, the vice president of the right-wing ARENA party—the original architects of, among other things, the death squads of the 1980s, neoliberal policies of the 1990s and Mano Dura laws in the early 2000s—promised to close Zacatraz and reinstate the truce should they win the elections. Gang members taped the conversation and later leaked it to the press.

In another secretly filmed meeting inside a party headquarters, two high-end political operators from the FMLN offered gang leaders from the three factions ten million dollars in micro-credits, which they said they would channel through a "credit committee" made up of gang members or their relatives and associates. "The credit committee is you," an FMLN leader explained, making the corruption scheme as simple as a third-grade math lesson.

According to the testimony of one participant, the MS-13 leader Dany Balmore Romero García, aka Dany Boy, was in attendance at most of these political meetings. During the gang truce, Romero had further ingratiated himself with international youth prevention programs, sociologists and foreign ambassadors because of his laudable work with gang members. Romero would soon turn his efforts toward documenting alleged abuses by security forces.

Another attendee in some of these political meetings, according to the same testimony, was Marvin Adaly Quintanilla Ramos, aka Piwa. Piwa was a longtime member of the Criminal Gangsters clique in Ilopango but had begun posing as an evangelical preacher. By then, joining an evangelical church was a known way out of the gang. Piwa was a good actor and a charismatic leader who'd been certified by a national network of pastors in El Salvador. He was clean-shaven, with short hair, and wore sport casual attire, which served to downplay his importance.

Prosecutors say the ranfla named Piwa and Malvado as heads of the Federation, the MS-13's governing body outside of prison. Piwa handled the gang's car businesses and managed the money, according to a government indictment. Investigators described him to me as the right-hand man of the MS-13's top leader, El Diablito. Malvado managed the gang's budding drug trafficking contacts. He held regular meetings with drug wholesalers at a local hotel in Sonsonate.

Throughout this period, gang leaders maintained hope that

whoever won the presidency would revive the truce. Mijango held similar hope. The truce wasn't just a business opportunity for the gangs, but for gang prevention specialists as well. Mijango and Padre Toño's rivalry endured, in part, over who might secure the expected windfall. The fight would get ugly as both Mijango and Toño tried to ingratiate themselves with the gangs. The government would eventually expel Toño for sneaking contraband into the prisons, among other charges.

Mijango would face even graver accusations. One gang leader claimed Mijango told the gang leaders that "sometimes it's necessary to put your foot on the accelerator" when it came to silencing dissidents.

Eventually, the witness said, the gangs decided to kill more people and determined the best victims would be "snitches within the community and people with accounts that needed settling." Homicides went up nearly 50 percent in the first few months of 2014.

The elections arrived amidst this tumult. The gangs strong-armed would-be rival party voters by taking away their IDs. They galvanized supporters, urging friends and relatives to vote with them. The political parties helped, facilitating voter registration cards and transportation. It was Tammany Hall, Salvadoran style.

The gangs split up their assistance. The MS-13 worked almost exclusively with the FMLN during the first round of the presidential elections and the runoff that followed. The 18th Street factions divided their efforts between the two parties. According to testimony taken by government investigators, the FMLN gave $250,000 to gang leaders for their services—one payment of $150,000 before the first round, and one payment of $100,000 before the runoff—while ARENA gave $100,000 to the gangs before the runoff.[16]

16 El Salvador's presidential elections automatically go to a second round if no one candidate tops 50 percent of the vote in the first round.

Norman remembers the controlled chaos of this time period. Prior to the elections, he said the MS-13 tore down advertisements for the opposition and told people they could not go to the rallies for ARENA. They also made sure ARENA could not hold rallies in MS-13–controlled territory. On election day, Norman told me they made the choice clear to the electorate. "If they didn't vote for the Front [FMLN], then they were going to get it," he said.

5.

While estimates of gang influence on voters vary widely, there is a strong argument that the MS-13 was the difference in the victory of the FMLN candidate, the former guerrilla leader Salvador Sánchez Cerén. Mijango reportedly said the gangs controlled between 60,000 and 70,000 votes; other estimates hovered closer to 500,000. On March 9, 2014, after nearly three million ballots had been cast during the runoff, Sánchez Cerén won by a mere 6,364 votes.

The FMLN's interactions with the mara gave it more than an electoral triumph—it gave them intelligence. A participant in the gang truce told me that during the elections, the party got a deep look at the mara's operations. To be sure, during the campaign the FMLN gained a detailed understanding of the areas where the MS-13 was strongest, as well as who its political and military leaders were and where they operated. The MS-13's support would eventually be weaponized against it. The political party created by former insurgents had never stopped thinking like guerrillas.

What's more, the FMLN broke the promises they made behind closed doors. There were no microcredits for gang leaders. Instead, some of those who attended the secret meetings got killed; others were arrested. The gangs' recourse was murder. At least part of the money given to the gangs by the political parties had gone toward purchasing weapons. Homicides rose again.

Norman said he was trying to get away from the mara during this tumultuous time—working with his wife at the market and visiting with his mother. But according to court documents, he was an active participant in this new phase of war. In 2014, the documents say, he was part of the small committee in his gang that decided to kill three members of the clique they believed were talking to the police. They had one member dig three graves, then called two of them for a meeting where they strangled one and stuck the other one with a knife in the neck. The third would-be victim escaped their grasp and became an informant.

Court documents also claimed that Norman and eight others decided to kill a fellow gang member for stealing without authorization. During the meeting, the mara decided Norman would coordinate the murder because the gang member lived in his zone. Norman reportedly agreed and said he would send two others—El Niño (Kid) and Chicle (Bubble Gum)—who posted outside the victim's house until he slipped out to smoke marijuana just minutes before midnight. A few minutes later, Norman reportedly called his fellow leaders with the news. The victim lay dead from gunshot wounds on the street.

There were impromptu kills as well, of the type the truce had successfully quelled. In October 2014, Norman was at a repair shop getting his motorcycle fixed when he saw a rival gang member. In calls to Malvado and two others he claimed the rival had "insulted" him and insinuated the man was armed. During the call, he reportedly asked for a luz verde, and after getting it, he called another gang member who arrived with two weapons. The court documents say Norman and the other gang member shot and killed the man and left the scene, abandoning Norman's motorcycle in the process.

In all, authorities would charge Norman with five homicides, one attempted murder, kidnapping, forming an illegal group and terrorism. When I confronted him about these multiple accusations, Norman said gang informants had made them up, so they could get better deals with prosecutors and better treatment from the police.

The conflict accelerated in January 2015, when President Sánchez Cerén declared an end to all gang negotiations. A month later he moved gang leaders back to Zacatraz. It was part of a mounted offensive, and by the middle of 2015, the fighting resembled the heated conflict of the 1980s that had left thousands dead.

The police took on the role the Salvadoran military had once played, sweeping into neighborhoods in search of suspected gang members and their collaborators. In some cases, they roughed them up, leaving them to stew in their own blood. In other cases, they took them to the police station where they tortured them for more information. In the worst cases, they lined them up and shot them at point blank range.

The parallels between the war on gangs and the civil war were eerie. In a case that exemplified the excessive force employed by law enforcement, a unit known as the Special Reaction Police (Grupo de Reacción Policial) executed eight suspected MS-13 on a farm. A subsequent investigation by the local news group *El Faro* revealed that many of the victims were not gang members but farmhands and their family members.

In a later report, *El Faro* found that between January 2015 and August 2016, the police had killed 693 suspected gang members. For every officer or soldier injured, three suspected gang members were killed in what authorities called "confrontations," an extremely high kill rate in any conflict.

The gangs responded, organizing a handful of ambushes of police caravans. Suspected gang members set off a series of crude improvised explosive devices, one of which detonated outside a prosecutor's office. They obtained M60 rifles and grenades. Prosecutors said Piwa also collected money—upward of $600,000—to purchase assault rifles. He reportedly called for each of the cliques to give the Federation their most experienced fighter, so he could form an MS-13 Special Forces.

But mostly the gangs did what they do best: they waited until the police were off-duty then ambushed them individually. Many rank-and-file police officers lived in the same neighborhoods as the gangs. In 2015, the gangs murdered over sixty police and a handful of soldiers.

By year's end, El Salvador was the most violent country on the planet not at war.

6.

At the same time the MS-13 and the government were fighting this new war, the mara was exploding in an unprecedented internal conflict. Chory, the Fulton member and Norman's one-time prison companion, had launched a full-scale rebellion against the ranfla from his prison cell in Izalco. In meetings, he complained openly about the proceeds from the truce, political pacts with the country's main parties and the secret negotiations with drug traffickers. "That's bullshit that they are hanging with narcos and not telling any of the others," he said in one meeting.

Chory targeted his ire at Piwa and El Diablito, since he suspected they had made millions of dollars in their dealings but had not shared the proceeds with el barrio. Chory also questioned the ranfla's strategy of fighting the government head-on. Not only were they not sharing money, they were also using the rank and file to fight their battles. The argument resonated, and by mid-2015, Chory had recruited as many as fourteen cliques to his movement, which he'd named the MS Revolucionarios.

The internal rifts tore apart Norman's clique as well as his family. On one side was Norman, who saw El Diablito and Piwa as underhanded and devious. On the other side was his longtime companion Malvado, his brother Rodrigo and his half brother, all three of whom remained loyal to El Diablito.

Chory made his defiance public on December 21, 2015, when his Fulton clique ransacked and burned one of Piwa's car dealerships just outside of San Salvador. The fire was the excuse Piwa needed to extinguish the MS Revolutionarios. Prosecutors say Piwa called the ranfla, who issued a green light. The ranfla then obtained a schedule of court appearances and coordinated with Piwa and their lawyers so that two gang members—one from Zacatraz, who would carry the message, and one from the prison in Izalco, who would receive it—were at the same court on the same day.

The message from the ranfla to kill Chory and his bodyguards made it into Izalco just days after Chory and his Fulton clique had burned Piwa's dealership. The ambush itself took place on January 6, 2016. The plan relied on speed and overwhelming force. Within minutes Chory and two of his bodyguards were dead, killed in a bloody, machete-laden assault inside the prison.

In the days that followed the mara killed other members of the rebellion, as well as Chory's longtime girlfriend. Prosecutors say Piwa and the ranfla then reorganized the leadership structure inside and outside of the prisons. Fulton and other rebellious groups were pushed aside. In an act of extreme contrition, some Fulton leaders later paid Piwa $40,000 for his car dealership losses.

7.

In September 2015, Norman's wife had a son. It was a difficult birth. She had to stay in the hospital for a few days, and the boy was released into Norman's care. By then, Norman had three daughters, but when he saw his son, he melted.

"That changed my life," he would tell me later. "I mean, it was a complete turn. It was unbelievable. The love. I felt love."

He was also petrified. With his three daughters, one of whom had a child herself, they went to the pharmacy. Norman grabbed a baby bottle. *"No, papi,"* his eldest daughter told him, picking up a different size.

After buying the correct baby bottle, plus baby formula, diapers and wipes, they went to the house. Norman was not the caregiver, but for the first time he was there, with his own child. He looked at his son. It was as if he was seeing for the first time the fragility of the human species, understanding its vulnerability, feeling its defenselessness.

"It's fucked up. All that shit you deal with in the gang," he told me, as he thought about his tiny, infant son. "I couldn't imagine him getting beaten in, working as a lookout."

The birth of his son solidified Norman's resolve to leave the gang. For months he went into hiding, and for a while it worked. He was able to turn his attention to his family, and start to rebuild what he had lost all those years in prison. But it didn't last. It couldn't last. The gang doesn't go away when you ignore it.

Besides, they had other plans for him. In July 2016, the MS-13's street leadership was upended when the government arrested dozens of gang members, including Piwa, Malvado and Dany Boy Romero. The arrest of Dany Boy—the original intermediary of the gang truce who had won the support of foreign embassies and nongovernmental organizations alike—sent his diplomatic and civil society allies scrambling. Like the case against Alex Sanchez in Los Angeles, Dany Boy's supporters immediately came to his defense. Unlike the Sanchez case, they soon disappeared.

This was in part due to the wide-ranging indictment of the MS-13 leaked after the arrests. Prosecutors deemed the case *Jaque*, as in "checkmate." The 1,355-page document was part raw intelligence, part indictment and part political manifesto. It contained descriptions of criminal acts and diagrams of the gang structure. It described stakeouts and intercepted phone conversations. Most importantly, it positioned the gang as a sophisticated criminal enterprise with members like Dany Boy playing a duplicitous double game.

With the leadership in disarray, the MS-13 moved again to reorganize. It was during this time they called Norman. It was bad timing. He'd remained focused on his family and had started going to church. But some of the most experienced leaders of the MS-13 were now in prison. Others were cooperating with authorities. With the street ranks depleted and morale slipping, the MS-13 had a request for Norman: become part of the Federation.

"The word is that they're going to move you up to the R," a fellow gang member told him, referring to the ranfla on the streets.

When the call came, Norman demurred. He said he was busy. They called him again, and this time asked him if he would train with the MS-13's nascent Special Forces. He told them his boy was sick. They called him a third time. He made yet another excuse. In the end, he could not say no. But he also didn't say yes.

8.

It was Norman's half brother who was tasked with organizing the plan to kill him. The two had grown up together. Their families had joined forces when Norman's father returned to his mother.

In the gang, though, they were rivals. Norman's half brother was a candidate for the Federation. After Norman dodged the invitation to join the leadership a third time, a gang member close to his half brother asked to meet. Norman knew what that meant, and so he called his eldest daughter and asked her to take him to the meeting. He needed a witness, someone to know where he was going to be murdered.

"What's wrong?" she asked him when they met and he mounted the scooter she was driving.

"Nada," he responded.

But as he got off the scooter at the appointed place, he gave her a message: "If something happens to me, come to this house because this is where I'll be buried."

His daughter rode off, and Norman approached the house. A marero was waiting at the door. The small living room led to a patio in the back where he could see three others, including the one who'd called him. Two held baseball bats, one had an ice pick.

Norman stalled. He took out his phone, dialed his wife and started to talk. The mara began complaining to him, asking where he'd been, why he'd been hiding from them. But he ignored them, kept speaking with his wife.

He circled back to the living room then to the patio, where he leaned against the wall, still talking, telling his wife where he was and who he was with, so the gang would know that someone else knew. One of the mara tried to nudge him from the wall, so he could hit him with the bat. The one who'd called him to the meeting just stood silently, watching at a distance.

That's when Norman noticed El Niño, the youngest among them and the one who'd worked with Norman in the past. He was crying. He didn't want to kill Norman. But the others were getting frustrated at his stall tactics.

"Stop talking," one of them said. "I want to talk to you."

"Let's just do it with the silencer," another said, turning to the one who'd called Norman.

Still leaning against the wall talking on the phone, Norman reached toward his belt area and began to play around with his shirt, pretending he had some sort of weapon beneath it. He didn't.

"Let me talk to my mom," he said to his wife, not wanting to get off the phone and reminding the mara of just how intimate this encounter was.

At some point, the mara got frustrated and worried. They did the math. His daughter had dropped him off, and the mara who was at the door when he arrived told the others that Norman's daughter had seen him. His wife and mother also knew where he was and who he was with. Norman was making it too public and too familiar.

"No se hace ahora," the mara who'd called him said suddenly. "It will have to be another day."

As Norman left the house, he saw his half brother outside.

"What's the problem?" his half brother asked the others who were standing at the door. "Today it was supposed to happen."

Norman kept walking.

13

NOTHING TO HIDE

1.

CRISTIAN MERCADO RAMÍREZ WAS ASLEEP WHEN agents from Immigration and Customs Enforcement (ICE) arrived at his house in Huntington Station, a mixed-income hamlet tucked into the northwest corner of Suffolk County, Long Island. It was just after 4:00 p.m., on a warm September day in 2017. Cristian had been laying spackle and painting the walls of a basement not far from the multifamily home he shared with his mother, Rosa, his two older brothers and a family from Guatemala. His mom was cooking chicken for him, his favorite. She liked to spoil Cristian, and he knew how to take advantage of being the youngest. He'd come home, taken a shower and climbed into bed.

As the smell of dinner floated through the house, ICE agents knocked. Cristian's mother opened the door, and the agents asked for Cristian by name. His mother, already trembling, called to him, and after a few basic questions, the ICE agents said they needed to take Cristian to their office in a neighboring town. Rosa asked if she could go with him, but the ICE agents said only Cristian could go. Besides, *it was routine*, they told her.

Cristian was startled but not yet afraid. While he'd entered the country illegally in December 2013, he was a minor with a special immigration status that gave him some measure of "relief" from deportation. He had no police record, no run-ins with authorities in the nearly four years he'd been in Long Island.

"El que nada debe nada teme," Cristian told his mother. He who has nothing to hide has nothing to fear.

Rosa suspected otherwise. Over two hundred thousand Salvadorans live in Long Island, but the community is tight-knit, and ICE activity had prompted a wave of text messages and frantic phone calls.

Cristian's detention, as it turned out, was part of an area-wide sweep called Operation Matador. It was the latest phase of the fight against gangs in the United States. What had started in the 1980s with gang injunctions and police operations with INS in Los Angeles had morphed into a national, broad-sweeping anti-immigration effort. The logic was understandable: the gangs had continued to spread. Violence by the MS-13, in Suffolk County in particular, was spiking. But Matador—and other operations like it—suffered from the same problem the efforts in California did. Authorities had no clear criteria nor any way to test who was a gang member. ICE rounded up hundreds under this pretext, to the point where gang repression and immigration enforcement were now one and the same.

At the station, agents asked Cristian about his immigration status and his unauthorized entry into the United States. They probed his history in Long Island, his school record and his routines. They focused on specific details from his time at Huntington High School. They seemed particularly interested in

Cristian's clothing and his cell phone case. They were sure that the Joker, from the Batman series, pictured on the back of his phone meant something.

"It's just the Joker," Cristian said.

School officials had also told police that Cristian had "harassed" a school resource officer and liked to wear gang colors to school. They had a picture of him wearing a baseball jersey that read El Salvador and 503, the country's international telephone code, a possible gang symbol.

Finally, they asked about his "known associates." One of them, José Novoa Ulloa, had been arrested for assault and for smoking marijuana.

"You're in contact with José," one of the agents insisted.

Cristian said he knew Novoa only from school.

"A judge will determine that," one of the agents told him before they took him to a detention center.

Cristian cried, then called his mother: he would not be coming home for the chicken dinner.

2.

When I met him, Cristian had been in a detention center in Kearny, New Jersey, for six months. We talked in a small room with his lawyer by his side. He looked exhausted. His dark eyes were drained and sunken and his round, seventeen-year-old face sagged.

Cristian was what my mom might call "a string bean," his skinny forearms sprinkled with tattoos—homages to his mother, father and brothers; music symbols and Chinese letters signifying "love" and "peace." On his neck was written "family," and on the back of his left hand was the name of his niece. On a forearm, three different-sized doves took flight, which he told me symbolized his two brothers and him. His hair was tightly braided and fell to his shoulders. He wore an orange jumpsuit, and his skin beamed under the fluorescent light.

Cristian was part of an unprecedented wave of Unaccompanied Alien Children (UAC) who arrived in the US between 2012 and 2014. Alex Sanchez used to joke that he and his brother, Oscar, were some of the first UAC, dropped by an unknown couple in Skid Row who they never saw again. Alma was also part of an earlier wave of UAC. But Cristian's class of UAC was remarkable. In the two-year period in which he came, over 210,000 UAC arrived in the US. At its peak, in 2014, the number of UAC arriving was 17 times the number that had arrived in 2009, around the time that Alma landed stateside.

Most of these new UAC came from El Salvador, Honduras and Guatemala. They were fleeing gangs or reuniting with their parents, or both. They had little to lose. Their countries were buckling under gang- and drug-related violence, perpetually corrupt governance and impunity, poor schooling and ineffective health care. The three countries—collectively referred to as the Northern Triangle—had become the most homicidal region in the world. Experts asked themselves why the surge in minors arriving at the border had happened; I wondered why it hadn't happened sooner.

The Mercado Ramírez family came from the small village of El Congo, in the western state of Santa Ana. Cristian's earliest memories there are of helping out his dad, Antonio Domingo, on a farm the family managed for an absentee owner. In one family photo Cristian is sitting in a chair with his father crouched beside him. He is no more than five, but his tiny face is serious, and his long hair stands straight up as he stares intensely into the camera. His father has a mustache, dark and wavy hair, and is wearing leather boots. Cristian's family drew from the land as well, securing oranges, bananas and other fruits and vegetables to sell at the market in the capital, which goes by the same name as the state.

One morning, when Cristian was nine, his father, mother and grandfather went to the highway to catch a transport truck when, according to his mother Rosa, a "dark, dark brownish-green" sedan passed them on their side of the road. The car circled back, pulled over, and a man got out. Domingo was always armed, but he didn't have time to react. The assassin shot him twice in the back of the head, then twice more in the chest as he lay on the ground. Rosa let out a guttural scream, and as the man fled, she pulled Domingo's gun from his waistline and fired a few shots, but the assassin escaped.

Cristian blames his father's death on the gangs who by then ruled nearly every inch of El Congo and had thus become the catch-all for any suspicious death. Cristian also says the gangs killed his grandmother, who was knifed to death walking home from his family's house the year before his father was killed. But from the way Cristian and his mother described it to me, her death sounded more like common delinquents than gang members. And in both cases, no one was arrested or charged.

To compound his problems, Cristian's mother left shortly thereafter, making her way to Long Island. And the boys moved to another neighborhood in El Congo, where 18th Street members regularly encouraged them to hang out and smoke marijuana. When Cristian ignored them, the invitation turned into a warning.

"If you don't do it, no one will save you."

"Nadie te va a salvar." The words stuck with him.

At first, Cristian took the long way to school to avoid the gang. But soon, he avoided school altogether, opting instead to go to his aunt's house and help her family build their home. It combined the two things he loved most: work and family. He was their *chele*—their light-skinned nephew, a little gangly, a little awkward and always fidgeting. But the gang got more aggressive and started to look for him, his brothers and his cousins. His cousins would eventually join the 18th Street.

In Long Island, meanwhile, Cristian's mother worked the graveyard shift at a local movie theatre and cleaned houses on her days off. She sent money to the boys, eventually arranging for them to join her. Cristian's eldest brother went first, followed soon by the other two. As he and his brother crossed into the US on foot, border guards captured and separated them. His brother applied for asylum and was quickly released. Cristian was in custody for a few months before reuniting with his mother in Long Island. He would eventually get Special Immigrant Juvenile Status and become one of the nearly five thousand UAC resettled in Suffolk County during that two-year UAC surge.

3.

Salvadorans started to come to Long Island in sizeable numbers during the war in the 1980s. At first, they settled in Nassau County, in towns like Hempstead and Freeport, farming villages that had become commuter hubs and bustling suburbs with a tradition of absorbing immigrants. By the early 1990s, a steady flow from El Salvador, Los Angeles and the DMV had resettled on Long Island. The area—with its tight-knit, White, working-class heritage—corralled rather than embraced the new arrivals. And when there were problems like the type the MS-13 posed, authorities sent police and immigration officers, rather than social services and education funding.

A small group of resettled Salvadorans began setting up cliques. Initially, the MS-13 fought everyone: the Latin Kings and the Ñetas; the Bloods and the Crips. With the arrival of the Los Angeles–bred MS-13 members, the battles took on a more serious tone. Fists begat knives, which begat guns. Bodies fell and the gang proliferated.

Storied cliques like the Normandie Locos soon established a satellite presence in Long Island. But strong, locally born cliques also took root in Mineola, Long Beach, Uniondale, Roosevelt,

Hicksville, Freeport and Hempstead. In neighboring Suffolk County, in the towns of Brentwood, Central Islip and Huntington, the MS-13 also formed new cliques named after their areas, adding to the presence they already had in neighboring Queens. In 1998, the Nassau police claimed there were as many as six hundred MS-13 members in the area.

Still, the police feared another gang, Salvadorans With Pride (SWP), even more. The SWP had originally coalesced around workers' and immigrants' rights, in part because of the attacks day laborers suffered in the area. But they also opened their doors to street toughs, which led to a steady transformation from workers' rights organization to street gang.

"Starkly different perceptions allow the group to wear the two personas," *Newsday* wrote in 1998. "Depending on whom you talk to, SWP is either a nonviolent alternative to the gangs that have taken root in Nassau County the past five years, or another branch of them."

That same year, the MS-13 and the SWP broke into a bloody, drunken brawl at a party in Uniondale, along the Hempstead border. A few weeks later, the MS-13 shot and killed an SWP member in front of a church in Mineola. A regular tit-for-tat was soon underway. Local and federal authorities began to build RICO cases against the gangs.

In December 2000, authorities swept into six different towns and arrested eight members of the SWP, including one of its founders, and charged them with multiple crimes. The indictment didn't end the gang, but it hobbled it, and the MS-13 took advantage, throwing wave after wave of soldiers at the SWP and other rivals.

Authorities were ready, but the RICO indictments employed against the MS-13 only seemed to inspire more violence. For every Chusiado charged with attempted murder of an SWP member and assault with a .25 caliber Beretta, there was a Hueso (Bone), Scorpion, and Gigante (Giant), who were ready to kill. While Araña (Spider) faced trial for the murder of an SWP member, Angel, Snack, Fantasma (Ghost), Chofre, Speedy, Hunter and Anvil were conspiring to murder other rivals, and Flecha (Arrow) and Taz were killing yet another.

A decade later, the SWP was reeling, while other rivals were cowering. By then, the MS-13 was following a predictable pattern, especially along the East Coast. The mara could uproot other gangs, but its violence was also its undoing. Each spasm was met with an equally charged, prosecutorial response, and usually accompanied with new resources for law enforcement. Authorities would eventually send the top members of the gang to prison or deport them. Then the pattern would begin anew as the cliques rebuilt themselves, often filling their ranks with the vulnerable new arrivals.

In Long Island, the latest spasm occurred in 2016 and 2017, when the mara killed seventeen people in an eighteen-month span, accounting for a third of all murders in Suffolk County in that time period. In one notable case in April 2017, the gang ambushed five unsuspecting boys at a local soccer field, killing four of them for, as an indictment would read, "the purpose of gaining entrance to and maintaining and increasing position in the MS13." In another case, gang members had slashed and beaten their two female victims so brutally that the first police who saw the bodies of the girls thought they'd been run over by a car.

The murders generally coincided with a surge of UAC, and for those trying to conflate immigration with gangs, it was a gift. Hard-line officials like Suffolk County sheriff Vincent DeMarco, for example, falsely claimed that drug cartels were helping to smuggle UAC into the United States, and implied the gang and the cartels were behind the surge of kids.

"MS-13 has found the loophole," DeMarco said on Fox News.

The two events were in fact related but not because the MS-13 had found a loophole. As then Suffolk Police Commissioner Timothy Sini pointed out in testimony to Congress in May 2017, the UAC were a vulnerable population—displaced and traumatized, often without family. They were easy recruits.

"It is not entirely clear…the percentage of UACs who came into the United States as MS-13 gang members, were recruited while in federal custody or were preyed upon once they reached Suffolk," Sini said, steering away from the conspiracy theories of some of his Suffolk County law enforcement colleagues.

Still, there were some troubling statistics emerging from Long Island. Of 159 suspected MS-13 members in Suffolk County, Sini said 39 were UAC; and 7 of the 13 charged in the soccer field murders and the murder of the 2 females were also UAC. It was vintage MS-13—they were victims and victimizers, beasts and barrios.

4.

Much of the discussion that May 2017 day in Congress centered on something called "287(g) agreements." Under these agreements, DHS trains and deputizes local government officials—sheriffs, county executives and others—to act as immigration enforcement. The practice began in the mid-1990s, and became common after 9/11. But such latitude can damage communication between Latino communities and authorities. These are the same communities most impacted by gangs like the MS-13. In other words, the practice makes the most vulnerable even more vulnerable.

When it comes to 287(g) agreements and the MS-13, government leaders and security officials play both sides for their own political gain. Sini was a good example of this. I met Sini a few months after the soccer field murders. Well-dressed and clean-shaven, he is self-assured and thoughtful. He also projects strength and order.

Sini is a Democrat in a conservative county—President Trump won 52 percent of the Suffolk vote in 2016. In the MS-13, Sini recognized a threat, but he also saw a political opportunity. By the time he stood in front of Congress in May 2017, he was positioning himself to run for the District Attorney's Office. Under his direction, the county would help ICE round up suspected MS-13 members like Cristian. Sini was, in other words, perfecting the art of pandering to both sides.

"We believe that if we entered into a 287(g) agreement, that could compromise our mission in creating that environment and could hurt our ability to make cases and encourage witnesses and victims to come forward," he told Congress, explaining why his county had no such agreement. Then, in the same breath, he declared: "With that said, whenever we arrest a person for a crime, misdemeanor or felony, and that person is not here legally, we automatically notify the Department of Homeland Security."

The lack of consensus on how to deal with the gang came, in part, from the gang's own split personality. During and after the truce in El Salvador, communications picked up between gang leaders in El Salvador's prisons—the so-called ranfla—and MS-13 leaders in Honduras, Guatemala and the United States. The ranfla also sent emissaries to meet with leaders in the US to recharge the East Coast Program.

A Salvadoran police intelligence official told me that a half-dozen leaders had gone to the US at the behest and expense of the ranfla. In an interview in a jail in Virginia, one gang member told me that an emissary had called him out of retirement and pushed him back into gang activities, which was what had gotten him arrested. According to US authorities, this was also happening all along the East Coast and in parts of Texas. Taken alongside the arrival of UAC, the uptick in violence and the increased communication between various cliques, you could see why authorities at Suffolk County Sheriff's Office were alarmed. Many feared the MS-13 were developing into a powerful transnational criminal organization.

But the MS-13's efforts were just as haphazard and chaotic

as always. The East Coast Program, for example, oversaw several cliques which ostensibly reported to one single leader in Virginia. But individual cliques were operating outside the hierarchy, including the ones behind a good portion of the horrific violence in both Long Island and the DMV. Their crimes brought unwanted scrutiny to the gang and undermined the MS-13's more sophisticated criminal enterprises.

The case of Christian Alexander Sosa perhaps best typified the gang's weak, disorganized structure. Sosa arrived in the DMV and falsely claimed to be MS-13. The MS-13 cliques didn't notice for months, as Sosa moved up the ranks. His exploits and homemade YouTube rap videos earned him cachet and girlfriends.

When a local clique finally figured out the truth, they got a few women, including one of his ex-girlfriends, Damaris Reyes, to set a trap. Sosa escaped, then posted a song about it for his YouTube followers he titled "I'm Still Alive." Incensed, the gang had another woman lure him into another trap with a simple Facebook message, "Come sit with me." This time, they were successful, beating and stabbing him to death, then dragging his body into the Potomac River and tying it down with a rock.

The chains of retribution then reached Sosa's girlfriend, Venus Romero, who heard about the attack on her boyfriend and called Reyes to set up a trap of her own. Romero, along with three others, including two MS-13 members, took Reyes to a park where they tortured and interrogated her. One filmed as Venus and the others cut off Reyes's tattoo and took turns stabbing her to death. The video was later shared with MS-13 leaders in El Salvador in the hopes, according to prosecutors, they would get promoted.

5.

One of the women involved in Damaris Reyes's murder was Cindy Blanco, the friend of Alma's from high school who'd traveled with her to North Carolina. Blanco would later plead guilty in the case. She and Alma had lost touch when Alma went into her own downward spiral, which was only partially related to the gang.

In fact, Alma's reentry into the MS-13 in the DMV never officially happened. There was no reunification or beating-in ceremony. No one verified her story via international conference calls. Alma found that on the East Coast, she could redefine herself, almost daily. She could be part of the gang when it suited her and distance herself when it meant trouble.

At the time, Alma was still living with her older sister, Magdalena, and her mood swings were tearing her family apart. Magdalena was sympathetic. Alma had been abused. But Alma was violent, volatile and unruly. Her hours were unpredictable, and her disruptions to the family rhythm were constant.

Alma went to high school, and she bused tables at a local restaurant, but she poured most of her time into her social life. Alma told me she and her friends would smoke marijuana on the edge of the school grounds, then run when they saw the school's security guard driving his golf cart in their direction. He would give chase, but they would scamper up the hill and lose him. *Eskipear,* she called it. "Skipping."

Alma's biggest distraction was Paula. Paula was in another school, and Alma would meet her there, so the two could skip school together. Alma didn't open up about her more intimate moments with Paula, but it was clear that love was a new drug to her, and she would do almost anything to get more. So would Paula.

Paula's school contacted Paula's father about her absences. Sensing Alma was to blame, he'd call Alma's sister, Magdalena. But there was little Magdalena could do to control Alma, so Paula's father started calling the police. A pattern emerged: telephones rattled from the school to Paula's father to the police, who would come knocking on Magdalena's door. On one occasion, the police showed up at Magdalena's with Alma's book bag. They'd found it at a 7-Eleven. It had a knife in it. Nearly a decade had passed since Alma's stepgrandfather had raped her, and she still carried a knife with her wherever she went. Magdalena could no longer help her. Alma had to leave.

Magdalena got her sister a room in a nearby apartment and paid the first month's rent, but within a few weeks, during a multiday binge with Paula, Alma crossed the line that would ultimately send her back to El Salvador. The day began with Alma and Paula cutting class. The school notified Paula's father, and eventually the police were looking for the two girls again.

When I asked Alma about that day, she smiled. "It was stupid," she said.

In order to create a plausible excuse, Alma and Paula decided to tie up Paula and film a fake ransom video. The video reached the police, who launched a full-scale search in what was now a kidnapping investigation.

The police searched Alma's new apartment, but Alma hid Paula in the closet, and they didn't find her. Later, after officials figured out what had happened, Alma hid at Magdalena's. But the police went there, and Alma, who was drunk at the time, panicked and jumped from the third story window, fracturing her ankle.

The charade was over, but the problems were just beginning.

6.

Cristian also dabbled on the edges of gang life, but his involvement was involuntary. It began during his first week in Huntington High School. He marveled at the building's size and it's new brick facade, but he had no idea where to go. A sea of students, teachers and custodians shuffled through the hallways. Some of his classmates moved quickly to their classrooms, while others sauntered. Still others lingered outside and never stepped foot into the school. If it were up to Cristian, he would have never gone to school in the first place.

He couldn't understand what his teachers or other students were saying. He knew he was supposed to be in class, but he didn't know which class. A teacher noticed Cristian's reticence and decided to connect him with another classmate. It was, by all appearances, a good faith effort. The other student was someone the teacher realized shared his nationality, his language, and could orient him in his new surroundings. His name was José Novoa Ulloa. Like Cristian, Novoa was a recent arrival. Unlike Cristian, Novoa was a member of the MS-13.

"José," the teacher said. "Help this student find his classes."

From the moment that Novoa met Cristian, he latched on. They were going to be friends, he said, *homies*. Cristian did feel an affinity. He and José opted for the *vos* over the *tú* form favored by his Puerto Rican classmates. But José scared Cristian.

"I'm from San Miguel," Novoa belted out not long after they'd met, "and I'm from the mara."

The announcement startled Cristian.

"Vos sos chavala?" Novoa asked, referring to the 18th Street gang.

"No soy nada," Cristian responded.

It was the beginning of a three-year nightmare, which would culminate in an ICE interrogation room. Novoa would tail Cristian around the school, sit next to him in class and find him in the lunchroom. He would give him playful pats on the head. He would wait for him after school and invite him to smoke marijuana.

Novoa was a member of the Huntington Criminales Locos Salvatruchas (HCLS). He was high nearly all the time, and he made mistakes, getting arrested for selling marijuana and for assault. But Novoa seemed to bask in the notoriety. His nickname was Little Psycho. On Facebook, he posted renditions of gang symbols, photos of Nike Cortez shoes, pictures of the Joker, a popular gang moniker, and thinly veiled threats against snitches.

When challenged on the street, he stood up. In September 2016, for example, he and some of his friends from the HCLS clique spied a group of would-be rivals at a Huntington sports bar. The two sides clashed, then the HCLS chased one of the men and jumped him, beating him savagely and stabbing him in the back. The man's lung collapsed, but he survived.

Life inside the high school could be equally chaotic, albeit less violent. During the period that Cristian arrived, Huntington absorbed dozens of new students, most of them UACs. Like Cristian, the vast majority did not speak any English. They were also far behind academically, reading and writing in their own language at a grade school level.

Integration was difficult. The schools had limited resources and near constant issues with staffing. They did little to accommodate the needs of their new UAC students. But the issues went beyond school services. Long Island—Suffolk County in particular—had a history of discrimination. Latinos were regularly berated in public places. People threw bottles (or worse) at Latino day laborers as they waited to do the type of jobs their White counterparts shunned.

In 2008, seven high school students beat and stabbed to death an Ecuadorean immigrant in Patchogue. The suspects reportedly got drunk before declaring they were going to "jump a Mexican." Their classmates told journalists afterward that "beaner-hopping" was practically a rite of passage in the area and during the trial most of the accused admitted to several similar racially-motivated assaults.

Following an outcry after the death of the Ecuadorean, the Department of Justice (DOJ) and the Suffolk County Police Department (SCPD) initiated an inquiry. They discovered that the police regularly failed to investigate hate crimes against Latinos, discouraged Latino victims from filing criminal reports and ignored these crimes when they did fall on their desks. To cite one example, SCPD manuals did not require written reports following what was termed "youth disturbances." For police, beaner-hopping was a youth disturbance.

In 2014, the DOJ and SCPD entered an agreement to implement a "bias-free policing" program, which included training, updating police manuals and hiring more Spanish-speaking officers. Progress, however, was slow. When I first visited the county in 2017, civil society groups said the police were stopping Latino drivers with such frequency that locals had adopted the phrase already popular in Black communities: *driving while Latino.*

In July and August 2014, at the height of UAC immigration, a local chapter of the Ku Klux Klan dropped pamphlets along the streets of Hampton Bays in the dead of night. Some of the pamphlets called for troops at the border to "STOP the flood of illegal aliens," presaging national policies to come. Others promoted the area's "unique European (White) culture."

"WE WANT YOUR JOBS. WE WANT YOUR HOMES. WE WANT YOUR COUNTRY," read a header just below a depiction of a mustached, sombrero-wearing man on one pamphlet.

As the gang violence spiked in the years that followed, the government's reaction, predictably, was to bolster security. In 2018, on the anniversary of the MS-13 murder of the two girls, New York State Governor Andrew Cuomo, a Democrat, assigned state troopers to ten school districts, including Huntington's. The head of the district was flabbergasted, penning a letter to the governor: "At no point did any state official or otherwise reach out and ask what we need or don't need. At no point did anyone request a visit or invite a conversation of any sort. At no point have we received even fragments of information about the proposal."

However, the gap between soft and hard approaches was growing. Sini's own shift from thoughtful, Democratic police commissioner to hard-line district attorney was by then complete. In his new office, he quickly created a special gang unit that focused on the MS-13. At a press conference announcing the new unit, he stood next to a poster of a group of boys in silhouette and the words: "Wanted: Gang Members."

Sini's political capital had never been higher. The DOJ praised him for his work while he was police commissioner in creating a "bias-free" police force. "The steps he has taken to bring SCPD into compliance with the Agreement not only help ensure constitutional policing," the DOJ wrote in a 2018 progress report on the program, "but also lay the groundwork to bolster SCPD's community partnerships and enhance its ability to fight crime."

Cristian had fallen into Sini's and the US government's widening net, while at the same time being hounded by the gang, specifically by Novoa, for not joining. Novoa would send him Facebook messages at all hours of the night asking for money. He would pop by his house during the day, asking him if he wanted to smoke marijuana. Cristian was regularly skipping school, but not to go on benders like Alma. He was starting to get little jobs with the help of his brother.

Cristian hated school, and school officials did not like him. The situation was so bad that even the other Salvadorans made fun of him. When a teacher asked Cristian a question, he would sometimes try to answer, but then his classmates would tell him he was *stupid* and that he should just *shut up*.

So he did. He got some big *fuck-off* headphones and drowned out the world with music. His favorite was Arcángel, who was born in New York, raised in Puerto Rico and of Dominican descent. Arcangel's songs mixed criminal fantasy with heartfelt confusion about love, sex and professional jealousy. Like Cristian, he was from nowhere and everywhere; he had no clear path to fame and yet the world—and all the half-naked women he wanted—were at his fingertips.

In November 2014, Cristian got an in-school suspension for being "constantly disruptive in class." In January 2015, he got suspended again for raising "his middle finger up to a staff member." A week later, he left school grounds without permission. Two weeks later, a teacher said he told her "fuck you" and "bullshit" during class and skipped the last three periods of school.

He hadn't joined the gang, but to school officials, it had begun to look that way.

7.

From the beginning, Cristian said he had problems with one of the School Resource Officers. SROs are sworn police officers who monitor one or more schools at the request of the schools. Cristian says the SRO, who was Latino, frequently taunted him, calling him (and others) "shit immigrant" and challenging him to fight off school grounds. Cristian didn't want to fight anyone. In fact, looking back on it, he said the whole thing could be traced to a single, stupid incident that would ultimately catapult him back to Central America.

It was February 12, 2015. Cristian had been in the US for thirteen months, and in Huntington High School for about six. He was walking through the lunchroom, a juice box in his hand, when he says the SRO playfully hit him in the arm. Cristian flinched and the juice spilled. ICE would later report that Cristian began "posturing toward and continuously staring at said officer." The SRO took him to the principal's office. Cristian was fuming.

"If it's like this in the US," he told his mother later that day, referring to the discrimination he felt, "I wish they'd just killed me in El Salvador."

Cristian and his mother went to the principal to complain. The principal called in the SRO during the meeting who Rosa told me was furious about the rebuke. Meanwhile, the SRO wrote down his observations of Cristian's behavior, style of dress, and the company he kept. He would pass this information to his colleagues in the Suffolk County Police, who would pass it on to ICE.

There was no memorandum of understanding between the school and police regarding how this information was to be used, and in a *ProPublica* story about a similar case at Huntington High, the principal told an immigration lawyer the school did not share information with ICE. But in the end, even if Sini or the principal didn't want to admit it, this was an extension of 287(g)—immigration enforcement was now in the school.

A few weeks after the lunchroom incident, Cristian got his first three-day, out-of-school suspension for "disruptive behavior." About a week after that, he got in trouble for wearing his hat, taking pictures and listening to music in class. A couple days later, he got a two-day suspension. After five disruptions, the teacher had called security, and Cristian allegedly called her a "whore" and a "cocksucker" in Spanish.

By that spring, Cristian had a reputation for being aloof, defiant, uninterested. As he had done in El Salvador, he started skipping school and looking for work. With the help of his brother, he eventually got some part-time manual labor jobs, mostly landscaping and painting. One of his bosses would later send a short letter to government authorities vouching for Cristian's attitude and performance.

But at school, his problems continued. He was hit by a car leaving the grounds one day and spent weeks recovering in the hospital. His absence only deepened suspicion. He eventually recuperated but never fully returned to school. Instead, he opted to take classes toward the GED. He got tattoos, lots of them, the first of which read Antonio, an homage to his father. He bought stupid things, teenage things, like a phone case with the Joker on the back.

Family events and work dominated his life. At one point, a family friend invited him to go to an exhibition soccer match. The El Salvador national team was playing. As a present, she bought him a baseball jersey. On the front were the words El Salvador and the number 503, the international country code, which had been at least partially co-opted by the gang for its own purposes. Novoa, for instance, paid homage to the number on his Facebook page. Before the game, his mom and the family friend took a picture of him wearing the baseball jersey, and Cristian posted it to Facebook.

After he was picked up that September afternoon, ICE confronted Cristian with evidence like the photo of him in the baseball jersey, the phone case with the Joker on the back, and, most damning of all, testimonies from the SRO. In its report, ICE, citing "school officials," would say Cristian "associates with other known MS-13 gang members at Huntington High School such as José Novoa-Ulloa." And citing the SRO, ICE would say Cristian "always wears blue clothing and during the aforementioned incident [with the SRO in the lunchroom], the subject was wearing a blue shirt and blue shoelaces in his white sneakers."

According to the ICE report, Cristian had been photographed "while both middle fingers were up" wearing that blue El Salvador baseball jersey, with the numbers 503 emblazoned on the front. "Mercado Ramírez has been classified as an MS-13 gang member," the report concluded.

Forty-four states and the District of Columbia had developed different definitions for gangs. Nassau County used a list of twelve criteria to determine gang membership, which includes self-admission, tattoos, style of dress, gang graffiti on personal possessions and if the person "associates with known gang members." Would-be gang members had only to meet three of the twelve criteria, and "not necessarily on the same day." Suffolk had developed similar criteria.

But Cristian's case seemed to confirm only one thing: that those definitions and criteria hadn't worked in practice. A few months after I met him, a judge ruled that Cristian was not a gang member. But by then he was eighteen, no longer a minor so his Special Immigrant Juvenile Status had ended. He would have to go back to El Salvador.

Even worse, thanks to ICE's accusations, the gangs awaited his arrival. The 18th Street—including his cousins—wanted to kill him because they thought he had joined the MS-13. The MS-13 wanted to kill him because they thought he had falsely claimed to be a marero.

14

THE MONSTER

1.

THE LAST TIME NORMAN CAME TO THE UNITED States, he was trying to escape from the gang that had made him who he was. He couldn't see his own connection to that gang, didn't want to see it. He often differentiated himself from others in the gang, who he called "monsters." And he tried to bury his blood-stained past.

But his criminal record—the murders, extortions, assaults and drug dealing—chased him wherever he went. And his history was etched across his body—Sureños and a naked woman on one arm, his clique across another; a hand with the index and pinky spread into devil's horns below his Adam's apple; his wife's name, as well as symbols of his three girls, and the name of his sister sprinkled in between. The beast and the barrio inked on his skin.

He bought makeup and covered his tattoos as he made his

way through Honduras, then Guatemala. In Mexico, he got a fake identification. He was Gabriel Sánchez, his temporary work permit said, from Mexico. To cross the border, he would have to pay extra because he was in a gang and was therefore higher risk. While he waited, he could not be seen by other criminal groups. "Don't go out," the coyote warned.

In the meantime, his family, his blood family, caught up with him. His wife and three of his kids were also making the journey, and they reconnected at the border. The visit was brief; he didn't even have time to hug his son, who by then had become his center of gravity. His wife and children then crossed the bridge at McCallen and handed themselves to US customs, requesting asylum. Norman didn't have that option because of his mara past. After his siblings in the United States sent him the extra money the coyote demanded, he and a Salvadoran girl crossed the river with the aid of a flotation device.

The coyote then brought the two of them to a house near the border where they waited until they could make the next push. Norman went to Walgreens where he got a long-sleeved shirt and some more makeup. Then he practiced his English. The coyote had told him that he needed to say two words: *Yes, sir.*

Are you an American citizen? he said to himself. *Yes, sir. Are you an American citizen? Yes, sir.* The whole thing seemed so simple. Two words, and you were a new person—not a monster.

The Salvadoran girl practiced as well, but she was afraid, near shaking as they drove toward the checkpoint in Sarita. The border patrol motioned for them to stop, then the officer began.

"Are you an American citizen?"

"Yes, sir," Norman answered without pause.

Then the officer turned to the girl.

"Are you an American citizen?"

"High-ahn," she responded, trying to say "I am."

"Are you an American citizen?"

"High-ahn," she said again, confused, shaking now.

"Are you an American citizen?" he asked for a third time.

The girl burst out crying.

The officer ordered them out of the car and began speaking quickly in English to Norman, who couldn't understand.

"What's your name?" the officer finally asked him in Spanish.

"Gabriel Sánchez."

Incredulous, the officer took him to a little room and told him to take off his shirt. There he could see Norman's life story, could track the journey of the beast on one arm and the barrio on the other, culminating with the hand splayed like devil's horns.

"Tú eres pandillero," the officer finally said, referring to his gang membership.

Norman protested, but it was over. He was not Gabriel, the man with a work permit from Mexico. He was Norman, the monster from El Salvador.

2.

When I first saw him after he'd been deported, Cristian was spending his days in his room, perusing his phone. He had no friends, no school. He wasn't working or looking for a job. He was not a member of a church nor did he have any other support group. His uncle had picked him up at the Salvadoran airport and whisked him to a neighboring country.[17] He said he couldn't go back to El Congo. His neighborhood was controlled by the Huber Vatos Locos, a clique for the 18th Street. The MS-13 controlled downtown, and the 18th Street controlled the northern part of the city.

The MS-13 collected at least one dollar a day from the hundreds of vendors that spilled into the main thoroughfare. They also collected from restaurants and businesses, like the small medical store owned by a family friend of Cristian's who met

---

17 For security reasons, I am not giving the name of the place where Cristian moved.

me at a restaurant in their old neighborhood. She said her family had "negotiated," so they only paid $15 per month to the mara. Other businesses, she said, paid closer to $100. The 18th Street was the same: they "collected renta from everyone," she said, even the poor family-run restaurant where we were talking, a ramshackle structure that had no working toilet.

The gang-driven divisions impacted where people worked, went to school, shopped, organized events, socialized and prayed. The woman who met me was coming from a family worship at her grandmother's home. They couldn't go to their normal church services downtown because the men and growing boys in her extended family would draw the wrong kind of attention. Some of those boys opted to avoid the local schools altogether, choosing instead to attend schools in nearby Santa Ana or even San Salvador, which was an hour or more bus ride from El Congo.

The precautions locals took would have seemed ridiculous in other places. The dead were laid to rest far from their kin, and burials happened swiftly and in relative secrecy. Residents settled for rotten fruit or more expensive underwear even if they could get a better deal somewhere else. An afternoon rendezvous for ice cream happened at a mall in an international fast food chain, rather than at a homegrown vendor in a disputed territory.

To live in El Congo—and towns like it in El Salvador—required this near constant mapping of the city, a keen understanding of where and when one could socialize, and an ear to the ground to avoid any surprises. The woman said that when she was eighteen, for example, she was told she should not color her hair red or blond, since that was an indicator that she was dating someone from the rival gang. She had no idea if this was true or simply hysteria, but she followed the directive.

"You adapt," she said.

Still, it impacted her. She had few female friends. They were too shallow, she complained, by which she meant they drifted toward the gang. The same was true of Cristian's extended family. Both his brothers' former girlfriends were now partnered with 18th Street members, rearing their children—Cristian's niece and nephew—inside the 18th Street family. Cristian's family still owned a house in his old neighborhood, but his cousins, the ones who'd joined the 18th Street, lived there now and sent him threatening messages to remind him what would happen if he or anyone in his family returned to claim it.

In Cristian's new home in the neighboring country, he had family, but they were not his nuclear family, not the family that breathed life into him. He talked to his mother every day and his brother almost every day, but when his cellular data was running low, he simply stared at the TV for hours. Leaving the house was tricky because of his tattoos. The one on his neck—which read "family"—was the worst. It was an homage to his real family, but everyone seemed to think it was a reference to a gang.

He'd decided to get it removed. His uncle would bring him to the city every few weeks, and a specialist would shoot a laser at his skin, while he lay curled in a fetal position wearing protective goggles. He said it hurt more than getting the tattoo itself, and it took much longer—at least three sessions to get rid of one tattoo. Each session cost $100, he said, plus lost wages for his uncle and the costs of food and gasoline.

Cristian's presence had already provoked a bit of a stir in town. The police had come by the house with a prosecutor. They ordered Cristian to raise his shirt so they could look at his body art. Afterward, he never left the house without his uncle. And when he did, he would stay close to him. There were drug trafficking organizations and vigilantes in town. They lived by the local adage, *marero visto, marero muerto*—roughly translated, "gang-member seen, gang-member dead."

3.

When I first met Alma, she was living in El Salvador with her parents in the house where she grew up, about one hundred yards from the man who raped her. Her rapid spiral back to her home began after she and Paula's kidnapping ruse. Paula's father broke off the relationship, and Alma went to his house and set his car on fire. (The neighbor's car burned as well.)

After convincing the courts to give her a second chance and getting released, she got drunk with a man who told her he was "going to make a woman out of her." She pulled out the knife she always carried and stabbed him. A judge deported her soon afterward despite her and her family's pleas to allow her to move back into Magdalena's house.

During my second visit with her in El Salvador, Alma and I walked past her rapist's home. It sat on a hill just above the one USAID had built for Alma's family after the earthquakes in 2001. Alma's grandmother and her husband, the rapist, sat on the porch and just watched, motionless as we strolled in front of the cornfield where the crime occurred. The family effectively fractured after the news of Alma's rape spread. Her grandmother defended her husband. Alma's father defended Alma.

Alma's father was a slight man in his midsixties who still milked his cows, sold cheese at the market and tended to the sparse fields of corn and beans in the lush hills around them. Other relatives lived nearby. An uncle passed us while Alma and I walked through the fields. It was 11:00 a.m. He was drunk and looking for more alcohol. "He has problems with the bottle," Alma said before breaking into a mischievous smile.

Alma also continued to struggle with substance abuse. She told me she rarely went to town, because she knew she would get drunk, belligerent and dangerous. It had been six months, she proudly told me, and she'd only gotten drunk three times. She wanted to forget her gang, her rape; but without drugs and alcohol, the memories lingered right in front of her, one hundred yards up the hill. When I asked Alma's father about the rape, he winced and then slowly explained that it was hard for him to talk to his mother and that he had stopped speaking to his stepfather altogether. Alma's mother, he said, still didn't know.

I understood. Alma's mother seemed to be living in her own type of purgatory. She greeted me meekly and puttered around the house, cooking and wiping already clean counters. She was diminutive with thin facial features. She served us a late morning lunch of soup with a big piece of chicken, and a healthy dose of rice and beans, especially for Alma, who didn't eat chicken—it brought back memories of the US detention center, where she said they fed chicken to them nearly every day.

Alma's attraction to women was another dividing line in the family. Alma dressed "like a lesbian," she told me—long pants, high-top sneakers; she had shaved the side of her head. She also spent a lot of time with a woman in her late thirties, who Alma had known from her earlier time in the MS-13 because two of the woman's sons were mara. Alma's parents had to face rumors and snickering at their Catholic Church about her relationships with women. In fact, Alma's father was ready to leave the congregation because of the whispers, but the priest was surprisingly supportive. "You have to accept her as she is," the priest told him. He stayed in the Church.

Alma, however, did not seem like she would stay with her family much longer. Like Cristian, there was little for her to do in the area. There was no school or job training programs. When she applied for a job, she was told she didn't have experience or a high school diploma—requisites, they told her, for holding even the most basic post. When I asked her why she didn't want to work on the farm, she gave me a hard look. "For five dollars a day?" she snorted.

Security was also an issue. The gang members she ran with when she was a kid were dead, in prison or had left the area. Others who remembered her were keeping a low profile. Her "brother-in-law," the gang leader called El Tigre, was living in another city. Vigilante groups, led by a neighbor on the other side of the hill, had emerged since Alma fled to the United States. They patrolled in the evenings, imposing a de facto curfew at 8:00 p.m. Violators risked a flogging or worse. It was El Salvador's version of marero visto, marero muerto.

A couple years prior, suspected vigilantes had found and killed the sons of the woman with whom Alma had a relationship. When I visited with them, the woman showed me the photographs of her sons on her wall. They'd been killed in 2015, within a few months of each other by "death squads," she told me, the euphemism used to describe the vigilantes and police who snuff suspected gang members. The second son had died with three others in a "massacre" as they slept in an MS-13 destroyer in a nearby hamlet. Authorities called her to identify her son. "Their body parts were everywhere," she said of the crime scene.

Alma's emotions ranged from guilt, to bravado, to fear, to frustration. People knew who she was, remembered her even, and Alma continued to play with this power. She said she had gone to some of her victims and apologized. It was contrition, to be sure, but on her terms. And she did not apologize to her godmother, who she'd extorted for thousands of dollars before the same godmother saved her life by arranging for her escape to the US.

Alma was also afraid, which was probably why she remained with her parents. Her father was clearly her buffer. He spoke to the vigilantes and deflected the rumors about her possible continued gang affiliation. It was perhaps her last safe refuge, but it felt more like a jail. She said her only entertainment was purchasing pirated movies for $1.50 in town and watching them over and over.

It would not last, I feared. As we strolled along the edges of her USAID-built home, she confessed she had already reached out to her "brother-in-law," El Tigre—the same one who'd beaten her into the gang at her request more than a decade before—and had told him she was back.

Is he going to accept you, if you to start running with them again? I asked.

"Yes."

Are you going to rejoin the gang?

She smiled.

4.

I last saw gang-truce mediator Raúl Mijango in a courtroom in San Salvador. He was a broken man by then. He had diabetes, and he'd lost 60 percent of his vision. His kidneys were failing. He had thyroid issues and ulcers. He was wearing a white T-shirt, white shorts and knockoff plastic Crocs. His wrists and ankles were shackled. As we spoke, he slumped in a plastic chair shaped like a shallow bowl and connected to several rows of similar seats. They were all empty. No one had come to court that day.

Mijango was being tried with eighteen gang members for extorting the Arrocera San Francisco, the food production and distribution company he'd tried to help during the gang truce. Like Alex Sanchez in Los Angeles, Mijango had discovered the risk of gang mediation. Unlike Sanchez, Mijango believed he would pay the most serious price.

"I hope to get out of this alive," he told me during the recess in the trial.

It didn't look good. We had just listened as several police testified. Two of them talked about following Dany Boy Romero as he met with gang members in malls and other indiscrete locations to supposedly conspire about the Arrocera. As the police testified, Romero and other gang leaders watched on closed-circuit TV from a small room in prison. The courtroom had a TV too, so we could watch them while they watched the case.

Mijango's story was a tragedy. He had brokered with gang leaders to lower the extortion rate for the same company that later filed the criminal complaint against him. His counterpart, Bishop Fabio Colindres, and his boss, General David Munguía Payés, were not mentioned in the indictment. Colindres had returned to his normal duties at the Church; Munguía Payés had gone from security minister to defense minister.

"I'm the skinniest dog on this ship," Mijango told me glumly. "I feel defrauded," he added. "Here, there is a lot of hypocrisy."

Few reflected this hypocrisy more than Mijango's former comrades in the FMLN, the guerrilla group that had become the ruling party. As rebels in the 1980s, the FMLN decried the government's human rights violations. Now, in power, they presided over them. Police faced charges of extrajudicial executions and some would eventually get sentenced for these crimes. Military personnel who were meant to provide an extra layer of security around prisons were accused of torture. Throughout, the US stood by the government, helping to train and deploy police in this new, and as of yet, undefined war.

It was also hard not to see Mijango's case as a form of political persecution. The one-time guerrilla Mijango had betrayed the party's Marxist-Leninist hard-liners by leaving the FMLN some twenty years earlier, then aligning himself with Munguía Payés. The truce had further ignited their ire, since many believed it was a ploy by Munguía Payés to position himself for a run at the presidency against the FMLN.

The Arrocera San Francisco case gave the FMLN the perfect chance to get their revenge. Due to financial stress, the owners of the company had sold to a government-backed consortium that included the brother of a major FMLN political aide. That consortium was the one that filed the charges against Mijango in the extortion case.

"I've always said that I love this country," Mijango told me. "I'm just not sure this country loves me."

He was right. A few weeks later, Mijango was found guilty and sentenced to thirteen years in prison.

The truce, and the legal battles that emerged from it, had become a symbol of the eternal war. By some calculations, the short gang armistice had saved 5,500 lives. By others, it had simply delayed or hidden these murders. There was no consensus, only recriminations and prosecutions. To be sure, Salvadoran authorities mounted another case against Mijango and eighteen others for crimes allegedly committed during the truce, specifically that the accused, many of whom were former prison officials and police, had facilitated unlawful benefits to prisoners, including cash payments and televisions, as well as unauthorized prison transfers and raucous parties with liquor and prostitutes.

Among those charged in the other case was Luis Aguilar, the longtime policeman and intelligence official who had worked behind the scenes passing reports to Mijango's team at la mesa as part of the violence interruption scheme. I talked to Luis several times as the case was getting ready to go to trial. He told me he was not worried, that they had nothing on him, but he was petrified.

"In the academy, they told me that I need to respect life and now they want to fuck me? For what…?" he trailed off.

For nearly three decades, he'd been embroiled in police infighting, facing down accusations from one side or the other. Once, he'd been accused of cozying up to police officers who were leaving the force to join a right-wing political movement. Later, he was rumored to be too close with pro-FMLN factions within the police. At one point, someone even accused him of working with the gangs after a prison guard found his telephone number etched into a jailhouse wall. But nothing compared to this case.

"I never saw this [truce] as bad," he said to me, almost practicing his defense. "My job is to prevent crime."

He was still employed by the police, but he'd been largely sidelined. He spent most of his time working on a US government–funded intelligence-based policing program of the type he'd helped pioneer back in Lourdes. The program had expanded to fourteen precincts across the country. Luis had no qualms. He offered on-the-ground advice and trainings. And for his loyalty, he had earned US backing—the embassy had inquired about the judicial case against him, rattling cages at the highest levels.

"My conscience is clean," he told me the day before the verdict.

Still, like Mijango, Luis's clock was ticking. That same day he talked to me, he said goodbye to his colleagues, handed in his badges and his computer, and gave his family his last will and testament in case he was killed in jail.

The next day, he was found not guilty. He returned to his job, but his life, post-truce, was not the same. He'd been relegated to "special duties" and lost some of his health benefits. He moved slower now, with less vigor. His family too had been shaken. Collectively they felt vulnerable, as if their lives could be turned upside-down again at the any moment.

"You never recover," he told me after the favorable verdict in his case.

5.

The judge in Norman's case was not known for his leniency. In fact, he had denied asylum claims in over 90 percent of the cases he'd seen in the previous four years, far above the 57 percent average for an immigration judge in the US. What's more, Norman's case could not have elicited much sympathy. He was a victim, to be sure, but he was also clearly a victimizer.

The judge had to be aware of the changing political environment in the United States as well. President Trump had made the MS-13 his principal foil. He not only wanted the gang out of the country, he wanted to hurt them, once suggesting in a speech to Long Island police they could send a message to suspected gang members by "not lowering their heads" when they placed them into patrol cars.

Yet the judge was not there to assess Norman's crimes; nor the gang's crimes; nor to assess the political environment in which his decision was to be made. He was, in fact, obliged to ignore any incendiary political statements coming from the Trump administration or President Trump himself.

The judge had to use international law, specifically the Convention Against Torture (CAT), a rare legal statute that prioritized institutional violence over an individual's criminal past, a concept that is anathema to the US legal system. The judge took his job seriously—even if it imposed the type of moral ambiguity that we are taught to loathe in the United States and certainly contradicted Trump's own musings about police abuse—teasing out the violence Norman suffered at the hands of the Salvadoran police and prison guards, and the threat the gang posed to him and his family. It disturbed him.

"This case is haunted," the judge had said before calling for a break amidst the roach infestation in the courtroom that July 2017 day.

Indeed, there was a monster sitting in front of him. It lived. It breathed. It was a palpable reminder of the vicious cycles of systemic violence. Decades of hard-line policing. Self-serving US foreign policies, and the support of predatory local elites and a savage military apparatus. The creation of a neo-colonial state, and the double standards that open doors to capital and close them for labor. Inadequate schools and social services. Mass incarceration where rape is tolerated. Mass deportation from a country that increasingly criminalizes migrants and refugees alike.

The monster was Norman, yes; but the monster was also the system that created Norman and the MS-13.

After the break, the judge returned to the court and settled into his seat, flanked by the interpreter. Norman sat next to his legal representative. The government lawyer looked on from an adjacent table.

The judge began speaking in a low monotone, citing Norman's detention near the sugarcane field, where the police beat him and where one of them threatened to shoot him. He also talked about the abuse in prison, where guards urinated on Norman.

"The court would find that he has been harmed," the judge said, referring to these incidents.

The judge then turned to his decision.

"The court would further make a finding that it is likely that he will be harmed upon return for two reasons: one, because of his extensive tattoos; and secondly, because he is known to be a leader of the gang," he said.

Norman had, in essence, met the judge's threshold in one respect: he would be easily identifiable.

The judge continued: "And I don't think the respondent realistically would have a place where he could find safety in that country, and therefore I think that the respondent has in fact shown that it is more likely than not he would be subjected to physical, *physical* abuse should he return."

Norman had crossed the second threshold: that he faced a more than 50 percent chance of being tortured or killed in El Salvador.

Finally, the judge contemplated Norman's character.

"As heinous as his actions in the past may have been, that is irrelevant," he said. "The court finds that he has met his burden going forward for deferral of removal."

The judge exchanged some words with the government's lawyer, then addressed Norman directly.

"Alright sir, I've granted your case that you're eligible for, as I said, with this interpreted to you. The government has reserved the right to appeal. Your lawyer will explain what that means to you. Do you understand the decision of the court? If you don't, your lawyer will explain to you."

Norman looked at the judge, incredulous, choked up.

"Okay, *este, gracias*."

Still unsure, he turned to the interpreter who told him he'd won. He then turned to his legal representative who explained the ruling. Still trembling and now weeping, Norman hugged him.

The Justice Department did appeal the judge's decision, but the appeal was struck down, and on June 17, 2018, Norman was released. An official escorted him from the building and gave him a ride to where his family awaited. They'd gotten a cake: it was the day after Father's Day, and he'd recently celebrated his forty-third birthday. He grabbed his son and cradled him, then looked around. Tears welled in his eyes as he saw his kids and wife gathered in one place.

6.

Less than a year after he was deported, Cristian and three others arrived in Piedras Negras, Mexico, just across the border from Eagle Pass, Texas. His family had been clamoring for their skinny, awkward chele to return to Long Island. They'd moved from their previous home where ICE had detained Cristian and gained some distance from the Salvadoran community where the MS-13 remained a troubling presence.

Cristian's nemesis, José Novoa Ulloa—the one who'd been his appointed school guide and who'd tried to recruit him to the mara—was in federal custody, charged with attempted murder for the stabbing incident near the sports bar in Huntington. But he hadn't left Cristian alone. He sent him Facebook messages and once called him via the social media platform to ask why he and his brothers had gotten him in trouble with the law. While Cristian seemed less worried about these threats than he once was, he was baffled as to why Novoa was still in the US at all, and he was not.

"It's hard to understand the system," he told me flatly, during one of our many telephone conversations.

The Long Island scene had calmed considerably since the soccer field murders in April 2017. There was one registered MS-13–related homicide in 2018, compared to two dozen in the two years prior. The gang and authorities seemed to be following their pattern: a spike in violence, followed by a crackdown, followed by a lull, followed by another spike. Other areas in the DMV, New England, Texas and California were going through a similar lull, but no one expected the battle against the MS-13 to end anytime soon.

Still, the US was better than El Salvador, which remained mired in violence and crime. One of those traveling with Cristian to the US was the person who had spoken to me in El Congo. The group had come through Guatemala and Mexico on the equivalent of a luxury cruise: two-story buses with assigned seats, air-conditioning, internet and pillows. When Mexican authorities boarded to check for undocumented migrants, they ignored the passengers like Cristian who had paid them off.

The group spent two weeks in a house in Piedras Negras, before crossing the Rio Grande on a small boat under a moonless night. On the US side, another guide took them as far as Pearsall, just outside of San Antonio. There the guide dropped them along the highway, so they could skirt around an immigration checkpoint. They walked about fifteen minutes through the desert and found the meeting point where yet another guide was slated to bundle them into yet another car to get them to San Antonio where Cristian's brother was waiting to take them to Long Island.

That's when Cristian saw a little blinking red light in the air above him. It was a drone. Three minutes later, a helicopter swooped in and started to track the group with a spotlight as they scrambled aimlessly across the desert.

At first, authorities took Cristian and the others to a detention center where they would have normally been housed while immigration sorted through their cases. But as part of the Trump administration's more hard-line approach, they charged Cristian with a felony. The judge gave him the option of applying for asylum, but he would have to go through the process while in federal prison, not a detention center. Terrified, Cristian signed a waiver, so they could deport him.

Still, as the paperwork went through, he had to wait in federal prison. As he bounced in the van, legs and arms shackled, he imagined the worst—beatings, abuse, rape. When he arrived, he put on an orange prison jumpsuit and answered a series of questions before guards brought him to a large dormitory. There, close to one hundred prisoners were housed, and a few members of a prison gang immediately sized him up: *¿Qué barrio?*

Cristian shivered.

He bided his time, avoiding the gang's stares, and closely following their rules—making his bed when he woke up, wiping the toilet rims after he peed and bringing his plate to the kitchen following meals. After three days, the judge released him for "time served."

The next night, back at the detention center, guards cuffed him by the wrists and ankles and bused him to a military base. At 4:00 a.m., he and about two hundred others, who were also bound by their wrists and ankles, boarded a plane headed to El Salvador. As the aircraft crossed from the US into foreign air space, the guards went up and down the aisle and freed them from their shackles.

7.

While the government's appeal of Norman's case was making its way through the system, Norman remained in the detention center where he'd begun imagining all the ways he would be killed in El Salvador. In the holding cells gang members would employ a fake suicide technique, hanging someone, then say they'd woken up to find his lifeless body pressed against the bars. They also used the sneak attack—usually while you waited in line for food at the mess hall or for a toothbrush at the commissary—stabbing you with any bladed object they could find or forge. And then there was the slow death, in which they steadily severed fingers, limbs and other body parts until you bled out, passed out or simply died of shock. Norman had seen it all in his time in prison and could imagine each in excruciating detail.

Even after the US government freed him and he'd had his emotional reunion with his family, the mental torture continued. CAT provided a deferral from removal, not asylum. Norman had to report to a government agent every few months. Deportation always loomed if the attorney general decided he should go back on the next airplane. What's more, if the judge reviewed the case again and determined the situation had changed in El Salvador, the judge could also send Norman back. Meanwhile, his family's asylum process was wending through the system. Everything was on shaky ground.

Norman moved in with his family in their small apartment in a predominantly Latino neighborhood. He started going to church again. Someone in the congregation got him a job in construction.

At first, his struggles were like his neighbors'. He worked nonstop, mowing lawns in between his construction shifts, and rustled up $1,600 for a down payment on a used Dodge Caravan. A week later, the minivan puttered to a stop, the lights on the dash flashing. Norman had the car towed to the lot and spoke to a salesman, who told him he'd take care of it. Nothing happened. Norman returned to complain. Still, nothing happened. He returned again, and the salesman told him there was nothing he could do. Norman pressed, and the salesman cursed at him and said he could no longer help him. He was out $1,600.

Still, he had a job. He continued to work, to pray. His sister—his Ruquita who'd tried unsuccessfully to redirect him so many times—lived nearby, so he visited with her regularly. And they went to the same church. She remained his pillar, but he also helped her through her own problems, especially with her son, who struggled with substance abuse and mental health issues.

His daughter, the one who had remained in El Salvador, had also made her way to the United States, applied for asylum and begun settling into life in their new home. Even Norman's first child, now in his twenties—the son he'd abandoned prior to getting together with Carla—reached out to him, wanting to reconnect.

Norman went to work at 7:00 a.m., and his wife got the kids to school. For the first time, he was the one pouring Corn Flakes and milk into a bowl for his son and showing him Johny Johny music videos on his phone. At night, as a family, they sometimes watched classic movies together, like *The Count of Monte Cristo*. It was hectic. But things seemed to be settling down, until they weren't.

It started in front of their apartment. Norman was leaving their home when he noticed a driver in a car lowering his tinted windows and staring intently at him. Norman looked away and hurried to his vehicle, a used pickup he'd purchased after the minivan debacle. Then, a few weeks later, he was pumping gasoline when a car full of young Latino men pulled into the station. As he squeezed the metal handle tighter, hoping the gas might somehow enter his pickup faster, one of the men in the car got out and walked his way, looking right at him and passing slowly enough for Norman to see a tattoo of an eagle on his arm. He couldn't be 100 percent sure, but he felt like the mara were getting close.

Afraid, Norman gathered his family and their things and fled again, this time to another US city where his brother lived. There, they started fresh. They put the kids in school, and Norman got work in construction again. He focused on learning new things: how to lay tiles, build bathrooms, put in plumbing and fasten siding to houses. He stopped looking at every car that passed or trying to recognize every remotely familiar face. But his wife was unhappy. The cold. The small city. The lack of family. The lack of Latinos. He couldn't ignore her clamors. She had stuck with him for more than a decade while he was in prison, rearing their children, keeping the family whole.

They moved back, settling into a new apartment in their old neighborhood. He grew his hair out, and his eyes began scanning the terrain like a secret service agent again. Nothing immediately happened, and he started to question whether he'd seen anything in the first place. Was he just paranoid? His wife seemed to think so, and so did he, sometimes. "I will always feel like someone is following me," he told me the last time we met.

A few months later, a woman appeared in front of his apartment. He noticed because when he arrived home from work, she took out her phone and made a call. The next day, she did the same thing. On the third day, there was someone with her: a young man who wore a thick hoodie that hung over his face. It was strange because it was nearly one hundred degrees that day. For a second, Norman thought he was seeing things again, until his daughter asked him if he'd seen the woman across the street.

Over the next forty-eight hours, the family gathered their things and moved again. When Norman returned one last time to collect some small items still in the apartment, he noticed there were now three people across the street, hovering next to a black pickup truck. He scrambled, tossing what he could into his truck and jamming it into gear. In his rush to leave, he ran the car into a small pole lodged into the cement, then sped away to where his family awaited him.

★★★★★

ACKNOWLEDGMENTS

BOOKS LIKE THIS GET DONE BECAUSE PEOPLE OPEN their doors to researchers like me over long periods of time and they talk about their lives. In this regard, I would first like to thank Norman and his family. I interviewed Norman close to half a dozen times over a two-year period. He and parts of his family, most notably his sister, received my sometimes difficult questions with grace and patience.

Alex Sanchez also endured my pestering for an equally long period of time. I spoke to him on the phone, at his office, at an event and over dinner. I communicated with him on Facebook and via text. Ernesto Deras received me nearly the same number of times, opened up his work life and his office for me to see firsthand how he and Communities in Schools do gang prevention, then answered my follow-up questions on Facebook.

Alma and her family in El Salvador and the United States received me in their homes. She also communicated with me on

WhatsApp. Cristian and his family did the same. Cristian and his extended family also met me after he was deported. They are still in contact with me, trying to figure out ways to get Cristian back to the United States.

There were dozens of police, prosecutors, intelligence officers and other law enforcement throughout the region who helped me understand how they tackle the gang issue. Foremost were Frank Flores in Los Angeles and Luis Aguilar in El Salvador, both of whom spoke to me on numerous occasions about their lives, their experiences and their cases.

As noted in the methodology, numerous attorneys assisted me in many ways. Some of them have to remain anonymous, since their clients requested anonymity in the book. Others, such as Dawn Guidone, who introduced me to Cristian, did not request anonymity. I am indebted to all of them.

This book got its start in 2010, when Jeremy McDermott and I founded InSight Crime, a think tank on organized crime in the Americas that we still run together. Jeremy, as well as InSight Crime, supported me throughout. I leaned on them often, especially María Elena Ortegón, our indefatigable COO. Our graphics director, Elisa Roldán, did the timeline and the glossary; Juan José Restrepo did the maps. Natalia Moreno helped me with the fact-checking.

I also leaned on our longtime InSight Crime partner, American University's Center for Latin American and Latino Studies (CLALS). CLALS director Eric Hershberg has supported all my work with great enthusiasm, and the center's staff, especially Dennis Stinchcomb, has never failed to answer my queries or fix my accounting errors.

It was with CLALS that I acted as coprincipal on a three-year regional research project on the MS-13. During that project and thereafter, I got crucial help from Héctor Silva Ávalos and Juan José Martínez d'Aubuisson. Juan, in particular, consistently provided me with deep insight into the gang, given his tremendous research on the topic. A special thanks to him.

Throughout this project, I also relied on César Castro Fagoaga, who acted as my coresearcher, editor, travel companion and fact-checker. Castro connected me with everyone from victims in the El Mozote region to a lawyer, Raúl Leiva, who helped me track down court cases in El Salvador.

I should mention Carlos García, a prolific researcher of the MS-13, who will undoubtedly publish his own book on the gang soon. Carlos connected me to numerous people, including Ernesto and Alex in Los Angeles.

A special shout-out to Mark Adams—a friend of my sister's from high school and a considerably more accomplished writer—who put his agent, Daniel Greenberg, in touch with me after Greenberg queried him about writers who work on the gang issue. I owe Mark for making the connection and Daniel for believing in this project from the first conversation.

At HarperCollins, I was lucky to get John Glynn, a thoughtful and diligent editor (and accomplished writer) who kept my chapters tight and me focused on the central story lines. He also pushed me to apply for the Lukas Prize, which I did, thankfully. The prize helped me do the last trips and pull together the final, missing parts of the project, for which I thank the committee who selected me for such a prestigious award. Several HarperCollins copy editors, among them Tracy Wilson and Bonnie Lo, also corrected final drafts, and numerous other editors gave input to John. Thank you all.

Just as a project like this requires people to open their lives to you and tell you their stories, it also requires a family to support you through the ups and downs of writing. My sister, Becky, took time to read and comment on a draft of the book. My #QBH brother, Salvador Vidal-Ortiz, helped steer my thinking on everything from cultural bias to police abuse. Most of all, my spouse, Doctor Juliana Martínez, did what she always does:

asked the difficult questions, pushed me to make the difficult decisions, checked my privilege and challenged my theses. And when I stumbled, she caught me and propped me upright again.

METHODOLOGY AND NOTES

I HAVE COVERED THE MS-13 FOR A DECADE. AS THE codirector of the think tank InSight Crime, part of my purview is organized crime in Central America, where I have been traveling and working since the early 1990s, including dozens of trips to El Salvador. For this book, I also traveled to Los Angeles on numerous occasions, as well as to other parts of the United States, including Long Island. Part of my access came via colleagues—journalists and academics. Part came via authorities, who have gang members in custody and know which ones might be willing to speak to outsiders. And part came via gang-prevention specialists.

Some of the most vital access to the characters depicted in this book came via lawyers who were representing gang members and others seeking asylum or deferral from deportation under the Convention Against Torture (CAT). It's important to note that in some of these cases, I acted as an expert witness, providing affidavits on the country conditions in El Salvador. In these affidavits, I was careful to restrict my testimony to these conditions and their possible impact on these applicants. Thereafter, I sought and got permission to use their stories or parts of their stories for this book. I spent months going back and forth with them in person, on the phone or via other digital platforms.

At the request of a few of the subjects or their lawyers or both, I have changed most of the names and identifying features of their stories. The MS-13 has strict rules about speaking to outsiders and breaking those rules can lead to severe punishment. Similarly, I did not want to put them at risk of official retaliation from the Salvadoran or the US governments.

To corroborate stories, I spoke to other gang members, authorities, family members, lawyers, gang-prevention specialists and anyone else who could give me their version or interpretation of events. In addition, I used official, mostly judicial documents but also raw intelligence reports and other government reports, many of which are official, public accounts. Although they are far from perfect, criminal indictments and testimonies under oath are arguably the closest version of the truth we have in these cases. I used these to build out the story and corroborate my subjects' accounts. Some stories are better corroborated than others, and I try to indicate in the text when that is the case. I also state when there are conflicting versions.

Part of this book was also the result of a three-year regional project on the MS-13 that I codirected at American University in Washington, DC, with Professor Edward Maguire.[18] It permitted me to corroborate tendencies and patterns of gang and counter-gang activity. I worked with investigative journalist Héctor Silva Ávalos and anthropologist Juan José Martínez d'Aubuisson on the project, both of whom provided invaluable assistance in trying to get a handle on this gang and its story. Héctor has written a book, *Infiltrados* (2014), on the police that I

---

18 The project was funded by the National Institute of Justice, an arm of the US Department of Justice.

consulted early and often, and Juan has written two books—one, *El Niño de Hollywood* (2018), with his brother Óscar—on gangs that are must-reads for anyone who is interested in this topic. We did both qualitative and quantitative research, providing a region-wide look at the gang, which we published at InSight Crime in the spring of 2018 (Dudley and Silva Ávalos, 2018b).

In all instances, I try to be as transparent as I can in the notes for each chapter below. I urge anyone who would like to understand the process of reporting this book, or seeks more information, sources or a slightly deeper discussion about these topics, to look at the notes and, of course, the bibliography.

NOTES ON CHAPTERS

Introduction—Judging Norman

Norman and his family are the spine of this book. I spoke to him a half-dozen times, first in the detention center and later once he was released. I took written notes during those first meetings in the detention center, since I could not bring in a recorder. I also communicated with him via text.

I corroborated his stories with his sister and his wife, as well as via judicial documents that were part of his Convention Against Torture case and the cases against him in El Salvador. I went to several courthouses in El Salvador and accessed his judicial records, which I could not remove from the courthouse, so, for accuracy, I read the pertinent sections into a tape recorder, then had them transcribed.

This introduction is wrapped around Norman's testimony to the immigration judge, a partial recording of which I obtained independently. Immigration proceedings are not transcribed and provided to the public. I also spoke numerous times to Norman's legal representative and others regarding asylum law, strategies, the use of the Convention Against Torture and many other matters.

There are a lot of numbers regarding immigration in the introduction. Most of the numbers and analysis of the Salvadorans in the United States came from the Migration Policy Institute (Menjívar, 2018; Terrazas, 2010), which provides the most evenhanded understanding of migration policy in the United States. A more recent Pew Research Center look at the numbers reiterates the general tendencies of Salvadoran migration patterns and numbers of Salvadorans who live in the United States (Noe-Bustamante, et al., 2019). Remittances data came from the World Bank (Ratha, 2016).

To put the MS-13 in perspective, I drew from a *New York Times* explainer (Chinoy, et al., 2018), which drew from US Customs and Border Protection to say 228 MS-13 were captured in 2017. The same article sources the US Department of Justice to say the MS-13 is five times smaller than rival gangs, including the 18th Street. This information is also available from the FBI's annual review of gangs.

The Anti-Defamation League analyzed domestic extremism (Anti-Defamation League, 2019). The information for the Virginia Commonwealth study came from the director of that project, Michael Paarlberg, who participated in a panel with me for a Duke University–sponsored conference, then furnished me with numbers for those years. And a *Huffington Post*/YouGov survey showed that a majority of Trump voters had an outsize fear of the MS-13 (Liebelson, 2018).

For his part, Donald Trump mentioned the MS-13 on numerous occasions in speeches and in Tweets. The White House transcription of a speech in Long Island provides the source material for his depiction of the gang as "animals" (Trump, 2017). The White House does not provide transcriptions for the political speeches he gives at rallies, which provide source material for his outbursts about how the MS-13 is "occupying" towns (Trump, 2018, Montana), and how they had "invaded" the United States (Trump, 2018, Ohio). Trump's famous reference to Haiti, El Salvador and African nations as "shithole countries" came from the *Washington Post* (Dawsey, 2018).

Democrats have their own history with gangs like the MS-13 and deportation. Clinton declared a "war on gangs" in his 1997 state of the union (Clinton, 1997). Obama deported even more people than Trump did, if you compare their first three years in office (Hauslohner, 2019).

Chapter 1—The Beginning

This chapter was done with extensive interviews with Alex Sanchez and his brother, Oscar. Alex and I sat down on a half a dozen occasions, most of those times in Los Angeles. Oscar and I spoke at least four times, including via text messages when I was fact-checking. Alex's accounts to me coincide with stories he has told other journalists and people like Tom Hayden, who developed a close relationship with Alex during the years he was transitioning from the MS-13 to Homies Unidos (2004: 199–256).

Hayden's book *Street Wars* was also a key part of this and other chapters that touch on Alex, as well as the MS-13 and their evolution in Los Angeles. Hayden's book is a revelation and worth reading to get a history of gang intervention strategies in California during a thirty-year period he covers. Hayden, who died in 2016, was a tireless advocate for alternative strategies to tackle the gang issue. And he and Oscar became the center of Alex's support team after Alex was detained and later arrested.

The beginnings and core of the MS-13 in Los Angeles are chronicled best by anthropologist Tom Ward in his *Gangsters Without Borders* (2013). In it, Ward develops composite characters that encompass the essence of the gang's chaotic yet effective means of helping wayward youth in Los Angeles find their community. Carlos García, a researcher and writer, also helped steer me through this period and connected me to different former gang members, including with Alex Sanchez.

The study of barrio gangs in Los Angeles was led by Joan Moore and James Diego Vigil. Vigil's *Barrio Gangs* (1988) and Moore's *Going Down to the Barrio* (1991) were touchstones for me. They both wrote several other books and articles that served as my foundation for understanding the Mexican-American gangs in Los Angeles, as well as the debate concerning the longevity of these gangs. Moore, for example, explored "resistance theory" (Moore, 1991: 42) and studied this idea of "institutionalized" Latino gangs (Moore, 1978: 72; Moore, 1991: 6).

Vigil's "multiple marginality" came from an edited volume (2016), while Moore's detailed account of the White Fence came from *Homeboys* (1978: 63–69). Moore also looked at the impact of drugs on these gangs, especially heroin, which she called "a major turning point" (1991: 32). Some of the other details, such as the reference to "tomato gangs," came from William Dunn's *The Gangs of Los Angeles* (2007: 28–37).

My understanding of US history and its relationship with Latin America came mostly from my time at Cornell, where I had Walter LaFeber as a professor and Tom Holloway as an advisor. LaFeber was a realist more than a cynic, chronicling the exploits of the US in raw terms. Other writers, such as George Black (1988), also greatly influenced my thinking, but it is LaFeber (1993) who steered my thinking the most. For broader and equally critical perspectives of US history, I turned to Peter Andreas's *Smuggler Na-*

tion (2013) and Jill Lepore's *These Truths*, which provided the source material for the Calhoun quote (2018: 244).

Several books informed my understanding of Mexican and Chicano history in Los Angeles and the West Coast, but the one the most closely hewed to my topic was Tom Diaz's *No Boundaries* (2009), which I highly recommend, since it traces many of the same gang themes that I do but with more of a focus on the evolution of law enforcement's efforts to quell gangs. Diaz also frames the debate in historic terms, tracing it further back than I do and going into much more detail about Manifest Destiny and the Mexican-American War (2009: 48–49).

In addition, Diaz has a deep treatment of the development Chicano gangs up and through the Sleepy Lagoon case (2009: 57–86). The Justice Policy Institute's 2007 (Greene) overview of the evolution of enforcement is also very useful in this regard. I also consulted more than once Edward Escobar's *Race, Police, and the Making of a Political Identity* (1999), which delved deeper into the Sleepy Lagoon and Zoot Suit Riots. Escobar provided numbers of arrests (1999: 237), an analysis of the relationship between this historic event and "identity politics" (1999: 17), and the important observation of how White society used gangs as their "metaphor" through which they saw Latino communities (1999: 10).

On the Sleepy Lagoon case, I also consulted primary source documents from the period provided by the Online Archive of California, which has made available archives from several University of California libraries and provided source material for quotes from newspapers at the time (McWilliams, 1943), the appellate court decision (Second District Court of Appeals of California, 1944) and the Orson Welles letter (1944).

For a strong but concise dose of Mexican-American history, read Paul Ramos's recent article on the Alamo in *Guernica* (2019). The *New York Times* has also had some solid work on the topic of the history and legacy of racism against Latinos, including a 2006 article from Nina Bernstein and an op-ed by historians William D. Carrigan and Clive Webb (2015). Carrigan and Webb also wrote a book about lynchings of Mexican-Americans, which is cited in the op-ed.

Chapter 2—Norman's Wars

There are many history books that chronicle the Salvadoran civil war and US-Salvadoran relations, some more radical than others. I drew from my usual—LaFeber and Black—as well as Tommie Sue Montgomery's *Revo-*

lution in El Salvador (1982). Black's *Good Neighbor* provided the quote from Walker as well as an accounting of his exploits (1988: 6–7), and LaFeber the summation of US motivations for its foreign policy (1993: 39).

There was also a mountain of US media coverage of the war and its aftermath. El Salvador was where some of the best US journalists in a generation cut their teeth: Alma Guillermoprieto (1982) and Raymond Bonner (1982), who wrote the first accounts of the massacre at El Mozote, to name two. There are numerous others in between, from which I drew small but important bits of information. The number of forced recruits, for example, came from a 1989 *New York Times* article by Lindsey Gruson.

Mark Danner wrote the seminal account of the Mozote massacre for *The New Yorker* (1993) that later became a book, or what he aptly called a "central parable of the Cold War" (1994: 10). I drew from Danner for understanding of the training and the buildup to the massacre (1994: 35–50), Amaya's account of the massacre (1994: 62–84), and the US involvement and response to it, including Enders's comments (1994: 208–224) and the Reagan administration's determination to certify El Salvador for its human rights record (1994: 90) in spite of the atrocities. It should be noted that the Enders quote that I used came from Crossette's *New York Times* account (1982) of his testimony and differs slightly from Enders's written testimony provided in Danner's book.

There are also firsthand accounts of the war, mostly from ex-guerrillas. *Las mil y una historias de Radio Venceremos* (López Vigil, 1992) is the most famous, but I also drew from *Del ejército nacional al ejército guerrillero* (Mena Sandoval, 1993). And then there was the Truth Commission report (Betancur, 1993), which covered everything from the beginnings of the war to the massacre at El Mozote to the murder of Archbishop Romero to a forensic accounting of child victims and US-made military weapons in the massacre. This is the closest thing to an official account of the atrocities that we have. César Castro Fagoaga—who worked with me throughout this process and helped me do a thorough fact-check and cultural-check—took me to La Joya. There I could get my own account of the war in Morazán, albeit many years later, because César introduced me to numerous people.

The resident historian of Romero's murder is Carlos Dada, the founder of *El Faro*, the incredible online news and investigative source that is home to some of the best journalists in all Latin America. Their team includes Óscar and Carlos Martínez, José Luis Sanz and, up until recently, Roberto Valencia, all of whom have become the single most important source on gangs in El Salvador and beyond. For his part, Dada wrote in *El Faro* (2010) the most complete account of Romero's assassination by tracking down one of the assassins and interviewing him at length. Other bits and pieces came from news articles and accounts of the death, including one in Joan Didion's somber *Salvador* (1994), as well as that in the Truth Commission report (Betancur, 1993).

Liberation Theology is an entire division of religious studies, so it was hard to dip in my toe. In this, Phillip Berryman's *Liberation Theology* (1987) gave me my foundation. David Tombs's *Latin American Liberation Theology* (2002) provided me with a deeper look at the theological aspects of the movement. Tombs—who is my brother-in-law—also spent a lot of time deciphering Archbishop Romero's own theological underpinnings, and we have spoken over the years about this and other topics. Tommie Sue Montgomery (1982: 109) gave the count of the number of priests who were killed or were exiled.

For his part, Mijango wrote a number of books, including a fictional account of an ex-guerrilla, from which I took the quote about Liberation Theology and dogmatic rebel leaders (2009: 15–17). Romero's March 23 sermon is widely quoted in books and reproductions online, including the one that I used to quote it (Romero, 1980).

Chapter 3—The Making of a Street Gang

This chapter relies heavily on Alex's account. The two basic elements of it concerning the gang—the evolution of the gang as predatory rather than an entrepreneurial gang and the development of destroyers—are corroborated by numerous gang, media and academic sources that I have interviewed over the years. As part of our report on the MS-13 at InSight Crime for the National Institute of Justice, we also went through dozens of criminal indictments against the MS-13, which clearly established this pattern (Dudley and Silva Ávalos, 2018a).

Alex's story about the Fedora is corroborated by Diego Vigil's chapter in *A Rainbow of Gangs* called "'Where Is My Father?': Arturo's Story" (2004: 146–158). In that chapter, the story of his character hews along the same lines of Alex's story regarding the Fedora Locos and the dispute with the mara. Vigil's account does differ from Alex's in one important respect: he says the MS-13 were the ones selling the drugs.

Vigil does not go into great detail on this, but if it is of interest—and it certainly is an ongoing debate—Joan Moore's monograph (1990) may offer a primer, at least as this discussion stood in the late 1980s. Malcolm Klein, et al. (1991) provide an analysis of the crime statistics from the mid-1980s in the journal *Criminology*—a study, by the way, funded by the US Department of Justice—that bolsters the arguments of those seeking to illustrate that drug violence and gang violence are not necessarily synonymous.

The presence of the Crazy Riders and other gangs in the area was corroborated using news accounts, including a *Los Angeles* magazine report on MacArthur Park titled a "A Glock in the Park" (2013), which notes that gang's formation in the mid-1980s in the area.

The broadest and, in some ways, most difficult topic to broach in this chapter was the evolution of the LA Police Department. The LAPD is the subject of thousands of media reports, journalistic and academic books, documentaries and movies. One of the best contemporary books on this topic is Jill Leovy's *Ghettoside* (2015), which I do not cite but which influenced my thinking on this and many other topics.

However, I was interested in chronicling how the police had militarized over the years. In this regard, the most important source for me was Joe Domanick's *To Protect and Serve.* The book recounts the rise of Bill Parker (1994: 85–94; 107–111) and Daryl Gates (1994: 12–17; 243–246), including discussing at length the fallout from Gates's famous quote about African-Americans' "veins" (1994: 299), as well as numerous other racially charged incidents over the years.

Domanick also talked about the use of television to bolster the LAPD's image (1994: 133) and summed up how the LAPD culture shunned those who they considered "traitors" (1994: 234). And he paid close attention to details such as the number of minorities hired into the LAPD (1994: 292) and the number of Blacks choked to death by the police (1994: 264), statistics cited in this chapter.

Others, such as Escobar's *Race, Police, and the Making of a Political Identity* (1999) and Diaz's *No Boundaries* (2009), were also fundamental in understanding the evolution of the LAPD and, in Diaz's case, law enforcement in general. While I was investigating the Rampart scandal, I also came across an article in *The New Yorker* by Peter Boyer (2001) and a corresponding television documentary, "LAPD Blues" by *Frontline* (2001), that covered many of the same topics, in addition to their deep dive into the Rampart case and *Frontline*'s interview with Gates (Young, 2001).

To corroborate much of these accounts, I turned to the *Los Angeles Times*, an invaluable resource throughout this process. The details of Gates's use of a battering ram, for example, came from a *Times* article (Editorial Board, 1985), although it was also recounted in Domanick (1994: 307); or the account of the American Civil Liberties Union (ACLU) report about how many LAPD live outside of their jurisdiction of enforcement (Newton, 1994). The poll concerning the police's and Gates's performance came from the *Times* (Freed, 1988), as well as the letter to the editor Gates wrote (1991).

To corroborate the material concerning the origins of the fight with the 18th Street, I turned to Ward (2013: 147–150), Sanz and Martínez's account in *El Faro* (2012a), and to Óscar and Juan José Martínez's recent *El Niño de Hollywood* (2018). I know, from speaking to Juan, that the Martínez brothers debate these and other points about the gang endlessly, usually under the fog of rum and cigarettes.

I also reviewed numerous primary source documents. The producer for the *Frontline* report, Rick Young, who is a good friend, gave me access to his reporting files, which included numerous reports on police conduct and interviews. In addition, I accessed Justice Department reports that were readily available online, the "Christopher Commission" report (Christopher, 1991), the LAPD inquiry into the Rampart scandal (Parks, 2000), and the Police Foundation's report (Pate, 1991) on the policing in the six largest cities in the US, among them Los Angeles.

For statistics, I relied on primary sources as much as possible. California has some good online databases, such as Open Justice, a California state database where I obtained arrest statistics of Hispanics over the years, and the state auditor has put out some strong reports, such as one that explores the question of gang databases (2015). For more nuanced analysis of statistics, I had to rely on secondary sources, such as the JAMA (Hutson, 1995) article cited. Separating gang-related homicides from other homicides is admittedly difficult,[19] and the researchers' reliance on police data may trouble some people, but it is the best we currently have.

I was not nearly as forgiving as it related to the troubles around defining gangs and the repercussions that mislabeling people can have in the short and long term. This debate emerges in full force in academic journals, such as the monograph from which I drew Moore's conceptualization of the gangs vis-à-vis organized crime (1990: 165).

It is also apparent in investigative journalistic accounts, such as recent coverage of this topic in the Center for Investigative Reporting at Berkeley, California (Winston, 2016). Among the most important journal articles, I would mention Ana Muniz's account of the first gang injunction (2014) in the Cadillac-Corning area, Joshua Wright's exploration of the constitutional implications (2005) and Daniel Alarcón's *New York Times Magazine* article (2015).

---

19 I have researched and written about this subject at length in InSight Crime (Dudley, 2017).

Chapter 4—The Ghost of William Walker

To put this chapter together, I spoke with Ernesto Deras on several occasions, both in his office and as he drove around the city. I also communicated with him via Facebook. Ernesto has told parts of his story to various media outlets, and I carefully checked to make sure his stories were consistent. They were.

The war and final offensive received substantial coverage from the US media. The Guazapa volcano was a source of near endless fascination because of the inability of the army to dislodge the guerrillas, something chronicled by the Associated Press (Grant Mine, 1990).

Data about how much the US was assisting El Salvador throughout the war was harder to piece together. Assistance packages are bundled in complex ways that often differ depending on the fiscal year provided. For my part, I relied on Danner's account of the El Mozote massacre (1993), since I know the *New Yorker* has some of the best fact-checkers in the business. I also checked estimates from news accounts from the time period (Crossette, 1982).

There are years of research and debate on neoliberal economic policies. The data is mixed. I relied on the World Bank for information regarding inequality and poverty rates in El Salvador over the last twenty years (2019), which have improved. But growth has been closer to half the regional average (World Bank, 2019), and social spending in 2017 was 9.5 percent of the budget, compared to 24.5 percent in the region (OECD/IDB, 2017). Meanwhile, the urban growth, data for which came from the United Nations—DESA/Population Division (2018), continued.

The exploits of the Belloso Battalion were taken from a United States Bureau of Citizenship and Immigration Services report (2000), which also cited the *Boston Globe* story (Fainaru, 1996). The Yellow Book was produced by the National Security Archive and the Center for Human Rights (Doyle, 2014b).

The murder of the Jesuits, their housekeeper and their housekeeper's daughter was chronicled in detail by the Truth Commission (Betancur, 1993). The US diplomatic cables and memorandums from both before and after the massacre came from the National Security Archive's Freedom of Information Act (FOIA) requests (Doyle, 2014a).

These cables included: Walker's first reaction to the massacre (1989a); the CIA's ambiguous assessment that it could have been "rightist extremists" and their accounting of d'Aubuisson's press conference prior to the killings (CIA, 1989b); Walker's assessment of Cristiani as a "decent human being" (Walker, 1989b); and the embassy's report on the attacks against their own vehicles (CIA, 1989a).

Chapter 5—Los Señores

People filmed the LA riots from numerous angles. Smithsonian Channel produced "The Lost Tapes: LA Riots" (Jennings, 2017), which compiled the footage for my account of the attack on Fidel Lopez, as well as footage of the Reginald Denny beating. "The Lost Tapes" also had an interview with Judge Karlin in which she explained her reasons for giving the Korean store owner probation instead of jail time after the owner shot the teenager from behind. This shooting sparked *Los Angeles Times* columnist Al Martinez (1992) to remark how gunning down someone Black led to less jail time than firing a weapon at a dog.

The *Los Angeles Times* also gave a timeline of events (Banks, 2012), which included placing Chief Daryl Gates's whereabouts and comments that April day and the events at the Parker Center, where the protests began. And the *Los Angeles Times* described the famous raid on Dalton Avenue and 39th Street (Mitchell, 2001).

I researched the Mexican Mafia and its relationship with the MS-13 for months as part of our InSight Crime research project on the MS-13 (Dudley and Silva Ávalos, 2018b). The footage of the January 1992 meeting between Ojeda and the Sureños gangs in El Salvador park came from the *Orange County Register* (Salazar, 2011). The account of the August meeting came from the *Los Angeles Times* (Wilgoren, 1992). The account of the Elysian Park meeting came, in part, from a member of the MS-13 who did not want to reveal himself for security reasons. Much of this account is corroborated in Hayden's book (2004: 211–212). The Rene "Boxer" Enriquez quote came from a video that is widely circulated on YouTube but for which I could not find the origin.

There are two other contemporary scholars who also greatly influenced my thinking on gangs, prisons and power. One is Benjamin Lessing, who has explored in depth Brazilian prison gangs and their rise and spread through the Southern Cone (2018); the other is Anthony Fontes, whose brilliant and tortured book of Guatemala gangs explores the deep, often unspoken relationship between oppressive regimes and crime (2018).

Rape inside prisons is a difficult subject, and statistics tend to vary greatly. As the *Guardian* reported (Filipovic, 2012), the United States Bureau of Justice Statistics (BJS)—prodded, in part, by the *New York Review of Books* (Kaiser and Stannow, 2011)—estimated there were as many as 216,000 victims of rape and sexual assault in the penitentiary system in 2008. Results of later surveys by the BJS (Beck, 2010) estimated there were closer to 88,000 victims of rape and sexual assault in the same time period.

The analysis of the gang-related homicides of Hispanics came from the JAMA article (Hutson, 1995). Ernesto also provided me with an account of his first meetings with Blinky and Big D, as well as his experience with the gang truces in the Valley.

Chapter 6—The Deported

This chapter is mostly based on extensive conversations with Norman and his sister, Laura. Norman's timeline and record were memorialized during his efforts to fight deportation in 2017, documents that I accessed during my research. The case for which he was convicted was detailed in El Salvador court records, which I accessed with help from a Salvadoran lawyer. As noted earlier, in some instances I could not photocopy the material, so I taped myself reading it out loud, then had it transcribed, which is how I quote the case extensively at the end of the chapter.

Deportation of gang members started as a trickle in the early 1990s and became a flood by the end of the decade and through the first two decades of this century. The information on criminal deportations—comparing, for example, the number of criminal deportees in Nicaragua versus the Northern Triangle—came directly from the "Yearbook of Immigration Statistics" (DHS, 2019), which is available for every year beginning in 1996.

There are, unfortunately, no statistics that I could find that disaggregate those who were connected to gang-related crimes in these large numbers of deportees. Nonetheless, others, most notably Óscar Martínez and Juan José Martínez d'Aubuisson (2018), have chronicled this phenomenon in depth, in particular how it related to the development of the MS-13.

There is also not a lot of academic work on this subject in these countries, but at least one connects deportation of criminals to higher levels of violence (Ambrosius and Leblang, 2018). And a 2007 United Nations/World Bank report on Jamaica reported that a small number of violent criminals is enough to change the criminal dynamic of any nation. "In such small countries, it does not take a large number of offenders to have a large impact, particularly if they assume a leadership role in criminal gangs on their return or provide perverse role models for youth," the report concluded (UNODC and World Bank, 2007).

The *Los Angeles Times* wrote numerous articles about the INS-CRASH efforts to deport gang members, including one that describes the origins of the city ordinance that prohibits that effort (Rutten, 2009) and another in which the LAPD touts how it had "decimated" the MS-13 (Braun, 1989). A Youth Justice Coalition report (2012) provided the numbers of how many youth were in the California gang database and how many of those were Hispanic and Black. The California State Auditor noted how the database had forty-two people who were added to the database when they were infants (2015).

Chapter 7—"We go to war."

This chapter came from extensive conversations with Alex Sanchez, Frank Flores and two others who worked on the case against Sanchez but who did not want to go on the record. I also drew heavily from the case file, including the indictment (US v. Jose Alfaro, 2009) from the Central District of California, the wiretapped phone conversations of Alex and the gang members in El Salvador, Flores's analysis of the phone calls, Boyle's counter-analysis of the phone calls, and the transcripts of the bond proceedings.

A hat-tip also goes to Edward Humes for his coverage of the Sanchez case at the time (2011) in *California Lawyer,* and to *WitnessLA*, which provided critical, ongoing coverage of the trial as well as links to other sources. Celeste Fremon of *WitnessLA*, for example, was in the courtroom to chronicle Alex's demeanor as he was led from the courtroom after his bail hearing (2009), which I cite at the end of the chapter.

Tom Hayden also recounted Alex's odyssey in vivid detail in his book *Street Wars,* especially Alex's persistent struggles with the CRASH unit officers, and his efforts to beat back the attempts to deport him from the US (2004: 232–256). I talked to Alex about this time period as well, but I used Hayden's book to corroborate much of Alex's account, such as the meetings in the Immanuel Presbyterian Church in Wilshire in which the police stood waiting at the back, ready to arrest him and others.

The efforts to vilify Sanchez were also chronicled in part by Anne-Marie O'Connor in the *Los Angeles Times* (2000a). O'Connor also covered when Homies Unidos filed a lawsuit against the city (2000c), and she covered the revelation that the FBI was pressuring the INS to help the LAPD incarcerate and deport the 18th Street (O'Connor, 2000b). Tom Diaz has a deeper account of the beginnings (2009: 116–117) and evolution of this program, as well as how it steadily went national. And Hayden gives good account of how this INS strategy overlapped with CRASH's efforts in Rampart and surrounding areas (2004: 225–227).

Diaz did the most thorough accounting of Nelson Comandari's life (2009: 200–208), helping steer my own queries with the one current and the one former Salvadoran policemen who spoke to me about the Comandari family. Both the policemen and press accounts identified Comandari's uncle as a "powerful drug trafficker" (*El Tiempo*, 1992). There were judicial documents as well, including an indictment against Comandari out of the Southern District of New York (2004), as well as a California Appellate Court case in which he is identified as only "N.C." (2007). I also spoke directly to gang members about Comandari, including Alex Sanchez.

The statistics for homicides in California during this time period came from California Office of the Attorney General's own online database (2019). The killing of Parks's granddaughter was covered by the *Los Angeles Times* (Newton, 2000).

The United States government's use of informants is chronicled in a 2011 article by Justin Scheck and John R. Emshwiller in the *Wall Street Journal* (2011). In it, they refer to Jorge Pineda, alias Dopey, one of the most legendary informants in MS-13's illustrious informant history, and the two others I refer to in this chapter. Their article lays bare the perverted nature of the relationship, and the FBI's seemingly wanton approach towards informants.

Chapter 8—"We ruled."

This chapter is based mostly on two conversations I had with Alma in El Salvador. To corroborate her account, I spoke to her sister Magdalena, her partner in El Salvador and her father. I also got help from her lawyer, who provided me with sworn affidavits from Alma, Magdalena and a third sibling, as well as other court documents. They all corroborate Alma's story about the rape by her stepgrandfather.

The *Washington Post* chronicled the rise of the MS-13 (Tucker, 2003) in the DMV, as well as the gang-related violence in the area, specifically the stabbing case (Jackman, 2000) and the shooting in front of the convenience store (Glod, 2001). The *Post* also described Mount Pleasant, the first landing area for the Salvadoran migrants in the DMV, as "the most ethnically diverse" area of people who "hardly live together" (Farhi, 1990). It was the *Christian Science Monitor* that said it was frequently described in press accounts as a "rundown Hispanic neighborhood" (Feldmann, 1991).

There have been few investigations into the MS-13's treatment of women, and even fewer still that deal with the subject in its proper context: as an extension of the way Salvadoran society treats women writ large. Among the most thorough that I read were Tom Ward's discussion of the topic in his book *Gangsters Without Borders* (2013: 112–140), which describes the difference between sexing in and being beaten into the gang, as well as the deep mistrust of the female gang members (e.g., *trust no bitch*). Juan José

Martínez d'Aubuisson also wrote a detailed account of how this plays out in El Salvador in *Revista Factum* (2016) that is equally useful and disturbing.

The case I chronicle concerning the brutal murder of several women came directly from a Salvadoran appellate court decision against members of the Iberia clique (El Salvador v. Armando Reyes Soriano Molina, et al., 2007). By then, the gang had most likely stopped admitting women, in part because of the Brenda Paz case. To reconstruct the Paz case, there are dozens of articles, but I mostly relied on Sam Logan's *This is for the Mara Salvatrucha* (2009). Logan's book is an incredible foundation for understanding the gang's rise in the US in the early 2000s.

Chapter 9—Escape from Zacatraz

As noted, I spoke to Norman on numerous occasions. I also spoke to his wife and sister. His legal representative gave me the timeline of prison stints and events, since he needed it to argue his case for Convention Against Torture. I also accessed case files at courthouses in two states in El Salvador, as well as the few that are online, which chronicled family efforts to get Norman transferred, and efforts to isolate Norman (and other mara) in Mariona. The case files also go through accusations and sentences for Norman (and other accused).

As part of a project on prisons in the region, Juan José Martínez d'Aubuisson and I did a long report on the El Salvador prison system and an intra-gang fight among the MS-13, from which I drew a lot for the section on Bruno's control of the prison system and the MS-13's steady takeover (Dudley and Martínez d'Aubuisson, 2017). We split up the reporting. I talked to mostly the US and Salvadoran authorities about the fight between the leadership of the MS-13 and Walter Antonio Carrillo Alfaro, alias El Chory. Juan focused on reconstructing the history of the prison system, especially during the time of Bruno. I later did more reporting on the murder of El Chory for this book.

There is no significant work on sexual assault and rape in El Salvador. The estimates for sexual torture for political prisoners during the war came from an article in Chatham House (Goodley, 2019). The Gilligan citations about rape in US prisons and how rape is employed to control the inmate population came from his masterful book *Violence* (1996: 168–175).

I gathered and cited information concerning Norman's and the MS-13's drug dealing inside the prison from an appellate court decision (El Salvador v. Erick Geovanny Quintanilla Tovar, 2003). The numbers concerning the uptick in extortions from 2003 and 2009 came from a National Public

Security Academy report, which Juan José Martínez d'Aubuisson and I cite in our story on the MS-13 and prisons in El Salvador (2017).

Chapter 10—The Gang Truce

I met Luis Aguilar in 2010, but I only approached him about being part of this book after he was charged with the crimes following the truce. We spoke about a half-dozen times to reconstruct his life and participation in the truce. I also interviewed Raúl Mijango twice, one time for a project for the Center for Latin American and Latino Studies at American University (Dudley, 2013) and one time for this project in the courthouse. Part of that interview appeared in InSight Crime (Dudley, 2018a).

I should also mention a profile of Mijango written by Carlos Martínez d'Aubuisson (2018), which provided the details regarding Mijango's AK-47, as well as corroborating material regarding Mijango's tangled life; and another profile in *La Prensa Gráfica* (2016), which chronicled his ambush of Munguía Payes and the unlikely friendship between them in the years that followed.

In addition, I interviewed two others who had direct participation in the truce. They both preferred to remain anonymous, but they corroborated much of the account provided in this chapter, including the way the gang used the intelligence passed to them to keep a lid on the violence. One of those cases I cite—the one concerning the murder of five students—was covered at the time by the Associated Press (2012). The other story of how the two 18th Street factions resolved their conflict relied on accounts from inside the gang truce negotiating team.

From the gang side, I spoke to several members, including Norman, although he was very reticent about this topic. Officials filed several indictments later that covered parts of the truce, among them an operation they termed Jaque (El Salvador v. Edwin Ernesto Cedillos Rodríguez, et al., 2016).

Finally, I spoke to Bishop Colindres and Father Antonio Rodríguez while researching the gang truce for American University. I extracted the quote that Rodríguez read from the press release issued by the gangs from prison (MS-13 and Barrio 18, 2010).

Nicholas Phillips wrote the definitive article on Dany Boy Romero in InSight Crime (2017). The BBC covered the 2009 "strike" in eleven prisons (Lemus, 2009) and the 2010 transport strike (Lemus, 2010). A good, concise, well-sourced description of why gang truces fail was published by Muggah, et al. (2013) in InSight Crime.

The descriptions of the attacks between gang members in which Norman participated came from a combination of his interviews with me and court documents. I am not identifying which case file, since that would compromise his identity.

Chapter 11—God and the Beast

This chapter was based mostly on numerous visits to Los Angeles during the investigation of this book. Both Ernesto and Alex allowed me to visit their offices on several occasions, and Ernesto invited me to go with him as he worked with his clients for Communities in Schools. I also spoke to others at Homies Unidos and Communities in Schools, including Blinky Rodriguez and one of Ernesto's colleagues, a former MS-13 member named Wilfredo Vides, alias Skippy. Vides was the one who was arrested in July 2019, as part of a RICO case against fourteen members of the gang in Los Angeles.

In general, the topic of gang- and violence-intervention strategies deserves and has numerous fantastic people writing about it. I would highlight two recent works for further reading that explores strategies in the US and beyond: Thomas Abt's *Bleeding Out* (2019) and Rachel Kleinfeld's *A Savage Order* (2018). Others, such as Rachel Locke at the University of California San Diego, have done deep work on this topic in the US and Latin America. Locke headed up a team that investigated the possibility of implementing focused deterrence in El Salvador for the USAID (Locke, et al., 2018).

I have spoken with all three of the above-mentioned scholars and worked once with Kleinfeld on a USAID-funded assessment of Honduras. Along the way, I have also had extensive conversations about this topic with current and former government officials, including Miguel Reabold and Ben Rempell, while they were at USAID; Enrique Roig when he was at USAID and later when he moved to Creative Associates; and Enrique Betancourt at Chemonics.

There is notable research cited in this chapter. Arguably our deepest understanding of current gang dynamics came with a survey led by Florida International University's José Miguel Cruz, one of the premier MS-13 researchers in the world, and his fantastic team of Florida- and El Salvador–based investigators and surveyors (Cruz, et al., 2017).

Robert Brenneman's *Homies and Hermanos* (2011) is one of the few sociological deep dives into why religion is such a central escape hatch. I should note that I wrote about this topic, including Deras's conversion, in a *New York Times* op-ed (2018b).

Much of the judicial cases came from US Department of Justice documents. To unravel Alex's case, for instance, I relied on court documents but also some testimony of current and ex gang members who were active during the time that Lacinos killed Smokey, then Zombie killed Lacinos. I also spoke to agents on the case, in addition to Frank, as well as authorities in El Salvador.

The information on Dreamer came mostly from the two federal indictments against him in California (US v. Elvis Edgardo Molina, et al., 2013) and New Jersey (US v. José Juan Rodríguez Juárez, et al., 2013), as well as conversations with law enforcement and private investigators. His case was first reported at length in InSight Crime by Carlos García (2016b), a gang specialist who has done some of the best work on the MS-13 that I have ever seen (and had the privilege to edit). García also wrote about Lil' One in InSight Crime (2016a), which I drew from, as well as an indictment of the MS-13 leader (US v. José Rodríguez-Landa, et al., 2013).

I followed up on García's work with some of my own reporting on Larry Jesus Navarete, alias Nica (Dudley and Silva Ávalos, 2018a). Operating from a California jail, Navarete created a network that distributed small consignments of methamphetamines in the Southwestern United States. This network included Nelson Alexander Flores, alias Mula (US v. Martin Neftali Aguilar-Rivera, et al., 2018), who operated from Tijuana and eventually became a member of the Mexican Mafia, before being arrested in Mexico and sent to the US to face trial (Dudley, 2018c).

Chapter 12—The New War

I drew from the indictment to describe the Arrocera case (El Salvador v. Mario Alberto Mijango Menjivar, et al., 2014). I also spoke to Mijango (Dudley, 2018a) at the courthouse, while the trial was in a break, as well as two others who worked with him on the la mesa, about the Arrocera case. As the multiple cases against Mijango proceeded, I spoke with his lawyer.

The descriptions of the gang's "lines" of command came from the Jaque indictment (El Salvador v. Edwin Ernesto Cedillos Rodríguez, et al., 2016). The reorganization of the MS-13 outside of the prison during this time period, as well as who became leaders, also came from the Jaque indictment.

The Chory fight with Piwa was described in Jaque, and, as noted above, Juan José Martínez d'Aubuisson and I wrote a treatise on this subject for InSight Crime (2017), which included numerous corroborating interviews with gang members and authorities. Piwa's efforts to corral resources for the gang was in Jaque.

El Faro obtained video from the meeting between the gangs and ARENA (Labrador and Ascencio, 2016), as well as audio from a separate meeting between the gangs and the then–security minister of the FMLN government (Martínez d'Aubuisson and Valencia, 2016). *El Faro* and *Revista Factum* got the video from a meeting between the gangs and the FMLN (Martínez d'Aubuisson and Martínez, 2016).

Meanwhile, James Cockayne's chapter on Boss Tweed and Tammany Hall (2016: 59–79) gave me a more theoretical, historical and comparative perspective (as well as one of the book's motifs) on how politicians have long brokered "across the gap between the state and the street" (2016: 79).

The MS-13's dealings with Norman following the Peligro debacle came from my conversations with him, as well as sworn statements he made to the immigration court in the United States. The descriptions of murders he allegedly committed or participated in came from his case files and other indictments that I am not identifying so as not to compromise his identity. Norman also talked to me—as well as gave written and oral testimony to the immigration court—about his half brother's efforts to assassinate him.

The quote from Douglas Farah came from one of his many articles on this topic (2012). Farah is a friend and a colleague, but we differ on our understanding of how much the gang is involved in international drug trafficking, among other topics.

The accounting of a gang informant's testimony against Mijango came from *El Faro* (Martínez, Martínez and Lemus, 2017), which also broke the story on the San Blas massacre (Valencia, et al., 2016). *El Faro*, specifically the meticulous Spanish reporter Roberto Valencia, who has also written an amazing book about the gangs (2018), analyzed the murders by police of suspected gang members (2016). The number of police killed during 2015, meanwhile, came from InSight Crime's coverage (Daugherty, 2016).

Chapter 13—Nothing to Hide

To develop this chapter, I spoke with Cristian on numerous occasions in person—first in a United States detention center and later in his home of exile abroad—as well as on the phone, which included long text exchanges via encrypted platforms.

I also spoke to his mother, Rosa, his brother, his lawyer in Long Island and the paralegal. His lawyer provided me with the documents of the case, including ICE's evaluation of his case, school records, sworn affidavits, forensic reports and materials from the murders of his father and his grandmother.

These documents are sometimes incomplete, at best. The autopsy report of his father, for instance, makes no mention of motive or the possible perpetrators, but it does confirm that two fatal bullets passed through Antonio Domingo's head at kilometer 51 on the Pan-American highway leading to Santa Ana.

The program to find and deport suspected members of the MS-13 began long before Operation Matador. Beginning in 2005, under the banner of something called Operation Community Shield, the Department of Homeland Security (DHS), which oversees ICE, had turned its attention and limited resources toward potentially violent undocumented migrants.

By 2012, DHS was saying it had arrested 25,629 street gang "members" and "associates" of gangs nationwide (2012); of these, DHS said that 3,910 were "members" or "associates" of the MS-13. By 2018, DHS (2018a) claimed the number of MS-13 "leaders," "members" or "associates" arrested as part of the initiative had topped 8,200, which included results of Matador. In November 2018, the DHS gave Operation Matador an award for "excellence" (2018b).

To recount the arrival and proliferation of the MS-13 in Long Island and their battles with Salvadorans With Pride (SWP), I relied on Sarah Garland's terrific *Gangs in Garden City* (2009), which chronicles the lives of members of the SWP and the MS-13, including the leader of the MS-13 who tried to start an organization to help ex-gang members but refused to denounce the gang (and was eventually deported). Carlos García also wrote a great account of the emergence of the MS-13 in New York for InSight Crime (2018).

John Moreno Gonzales of *Newsday*, who I cite, wrote about how the SWP was perceived (2000). I drew from a half-dozen US indictments to draw out the names and cases of MS-13 attacks on the SWP during that time period. I also went through recent indictments, including the one that I cite concerning the soccer field massacre in 2017 (US v. Edwin Amaya-Sanchez, et al., 2016).

I spoke to numerous Suffolk County authorities and the lead federal prosecutor on the MS-13 regarding the uptick in murders to gain their perspective on the who, how and why of the MS-13 surge. I also cite an indictment to illustrate the chaotic, haphazard nature of the gang along the East Coast (US v. Edwin Mancia Flores, 2017).

Sini gave his estimates on the number of UAC, as well as his accounting of the 287(g) agreement, to the Senate Homeland Security and Governmental Affairs Committee (2017). DeMarco spoke on Fox News (2017). Sini was evaluated for his efforts to establish a "bias-free" police force by the US Department of Justice (2018). Sini's office did not respond to numerous requests to be interviewed on the record for this book.

To be fair, there is little consensus over 287(g). But it is worth noting that, as chief of the LAPD, Daryl Gates implemented Special Order 40, which forbade the police from interacting with suspects about their immigration status (Smith, 2017). And that a 2011 US Department of Justice investigation (2011) into Maricopa County Sheriff's Office under Joe Arpaio found that Arpaio's office "has implemented its immigration enforcement program in a way that has created a 'wall of distrust' between MCSO officers and Maricopa County's Latino residents—a wall of distrust that has significantly compromised MCSO's ability to provide police protection to Maricopa County's Latino residents."

The Huntington district superintendent's response to Cuomo's proposal to militarize his schools came from a local news outlet (McAtee, 2017), which provided a link to the press release on the district's Facebook page.

I drew heavily on Hannah Dreier's great ProPublica story on other Huntington High students who were picked up by ICE in Operation Matador (2018). Dreier talked to the SRO, as well as the principal. She also cited the immigration lawyer of the Honduran who was deported after the sweep, who tape-recorded the principal saying, "We don't send anything to Immigration and Customs."

There are other reports that I consulted that cover Operation Matador, most notably "Swept Up in the Sweep" (Arastu, 2018), which details the SRO's role and complaints about how they became the de facto immigration authorities inside schools. And the ACLU filed a lawsuit in August 2017 (Lorenza Gomez, et al. v. Jefferson Sessions, et al.), which details numerous cases.

In its introduction, the ACLU alleges that: "Under the guise of a 'crackdown' on transnational street gangs, federal immigration authorities and the federal agency responsible for the care and custody of unaccompanied immigrant children have undertaken a concerted effort to arrest, detain, and transport children far from their families and attorneys, and to deny them immigration benefits and services to which they are entitled under US law, based on flimsy, unreliable and unsubstantiated allegations of gang affiliation."

Chapter 14—The Monster

As noted, I spoke to Norman on numerous occasions. He also submitted written statements regarding parts of his story as part of his efforts to receive deferral from deportation, to which I had access. I spoke with his legal representative after Norman got a deferral and saw him during that time period.

I traveled to see Cristian and Alma two times each. There I spoke to them and others cited in the text. I went to El Congo twice, once with one of Cristian's uncles, who drove me around, and once to see the family friend whom I cite. I also obtained police intelligence reports about the area, which included a map delineating which gang controlled what part of the town. After Cristian tried and failed to get into the United States again, I spoke to him, his brother and his mother.

I spoke to Raúl Mijango for the last time for this book in the courtroom during a break in the trial. His lawyer was present. Part of this interview appeared in InSight Crime (Dudley, 2018a). And I talked to Luis several times before and after his trial ended.

The statistics for Norman's judge came from an online tracking tool called Transactional Records Access Clearinghouse (TRAC), a Syracuse University–based initiative that tracks several aspects of the US government, including immigration (2018). I purposely did not provide the exact page so as not to reveal who Norman's judge was.

I did, as noted, obtain a partial recording of the proceedings in which Norman testified and the judge gave him a deferral under CAT. And I visited Norman and his family a little more than a year after he was released.

BIBLIOGRAPHY

Abt, Thomas. *Bleeding Out: The Devastating Consequences of Urban Violence—and a Bold New Plan for Peace in the Streets*. New York: Basic Books. 2019.

Abt, Thomas, and Christopher Winship. "What Works in Reducing Community Violence: A Meta-Review and Field Study for the Northern Triangle." USAID. 2016.

Alarcón, Daniel. "How Do You Define a Gang Member?" *New York Times Magazine*. 2015. Retrieved from: https://www.nytimes.com/2015/05/31/magazine/how-do-you-define-a-gang-member.html

Ambrosius, Christian, and David A. Leblang. "Exporting Murder: US Deportations & the Spread of Violence." Social Science Research Network. 2018. Retrieved from: https://ssrn.com/abstract=3213383 or http://dx.doi.org/10.2139/ssrn.3213383

Andreas, Peter. *Smuggler Nation: How Illicit Trade Made America*. New York: Oxford. 2013.

Anti-Defamation League. "Murder and Extremism in the United States in

2018." 2019. Retrieved from: https://www.adl.org/murder-and-extremism-2018#the-murders

Arastu, Nermeen, et al. "Swept Up in the Sweep: The Impact of Gang Allegations on Immigrant New Yorkers." New York Immigration Coalition, City University of New York School of Law's Immigrant and Non-Citizen Rights Clinic. 2018. Retrieved from: https://www.law.cuny.edu/wp-content/uploads/page-assets/academics/clinics/immigration/SweptUp_Report_Final-1.pdf

Associated Press. "Asesinato de estudiantes sacude tregua salvadoreña." 2012. Retrieved from: https://www.telemetro.com/internacionales/2012/09/09/asesinato-estudiantes-sacude-tregua-salvadorena/1941001.html

Banks, Sandy. "From Oppressor to Partner." *Los Angeles Times*. 2012. Retrieved from: https://www.latimes.com/archives/la-xpm-2012-apr-22-la-me-riot-cops-20120422-story.html

Beck, Allen J., et al. "Sexual Victimization in Prisons and Jails Reported by Inmates, 2008–09." Bureau of Justice Statistics (BJS). 2010. Retrieved from: http://www.bjs.gov/index.cfm?ty=pbdetail&iid=2202

Bernstein, Nina. "100 Years in the Back Door, Out the Front." *New York Times*. 2006. Retrieved from: https://www.nytimes.com/2006/05/21/weekinreview/21bernstein.html

Berryman, Phillip. *Liberation Theology: The Essential Facts About the Revolutionary Movement in Latin America and Beyond*. Bloomington: Meyer Stone Books. 1987.

Betancur, Belisario, chairman. "From Madness to Hope: The 12-Year War in El Salvador. The Report of the Commission on the Truth for El Salvador." United Nations Security Council. 1993. Retrieved from: https://www.usip.org/sites/default/files/file/ElSalvador-Report.pdf

Black, George. *The Good Neighbor: How the United States Wrote the History of Central America and the Caribbean*. New York: Pantheon Books. 1988.

Bonner, Raymond. "Massacre of Hundreds Reported in Salvadoran Village." *New York Times*. 1982.

Boyer, Peter J. "Bad Cops." *The New Yorker.* 2001.

Braun, Stephen. "US-LA Task Force Deports 175 with Ties to Drug, Gang Activity." *Los Angeles Times.* 1989. Retrieved from: https://www.latimes.com/archives/la-xpm-1989-04-12-me-1770-story.html

Brenneman, Robert. *Homies and Hermanos: God and Gangs in Central America.* Oxford: Oxford University Press. 2011.

Bruneau, Thomas, Lucía Dammert, and Elizabeth Skinner, eds. *Maras: Gang Violence and Security in Central America.* Austin: University of Texas Press. 2011.

California Court of Appeal. "People v. Morales." Second Appellate District. 2007.

California Office of the Attorney General. "Open Justice." 2019. Retrieved from: https://openjustice.doj.ca.gov/crime-statistics/crimes-clearances

California State Auditor. "The CalGang Criminal Intelligence System: As the Result of Its Weak Oversight Structure, It Contains Questionable Information That May Violate Individuals' Privacy Rights." 2015. Retrieved from: https://www.voiceofsandiego.org/wp-content/uploads/2016/08/CalGangs-audit.pdf

Carrigan, William D., and Clive Webb. "When Americans Lynched Mexicans." *New York Times.* 2015. Retrieved from: https://www.nytimes.com/2015/02/20/opinion/when-americans-lynched-mexicans.html

Central Intelligence Agency. "2-891116 CIA—Situation Report as of 1430 Hours Local Time." 1989a. Retrieved from: https://nsarchive2.gwu.edu/NSAEBB/NSAEBB492/docs/2-891116%20CIA%20Situation%20Report%20As%20of%201430%20Hours%20Local%20Time.pdf

———. "4-891117 CIA—Killing of Dr Ignacio Ellacuria." 1989b. Retrieved from: https://nsarchive2.gwu.edu/NSAEBB/NSAEBB492/docs/4-891117%20CIA%20Killing%20of%20Dr%20Ignacio%20Ellacuria.pdf

Chinoy, Sahil, Jessia Ma, and Stuart A. Thompson. "MS-13 Is Far from the 'Infestation' Trump Describes." *New York Times.* 2018. Retrieved from:

https://www.nytimes.com/interactive/2018/06/27/opinion/trump-ms13-immigration.html

Christopher, Warren, et al. "Report of the Independent Commission on the Los Angeles Police Department." The City of Los Angeles. 1991.

Clinton, William. "1997 State of the Union Address." Speech, Washington, DC, February 4, 1997. Retrieved from: https://clintonwhitehouse2.archives.gov/WH/SOU97/

Cockayne, James. *Hidden Power: The Strategic Logic of Organised Crime*. Oxford: Oxford University Press. 2016.

Crossette, Barbara. "US Disputes Report of 926 Killed in El Salvador." *New York Times*. 1982. Retrieved from: https://www.nytimes.com/1982/02/02/world/us-disputes-report-of-926-killed-in-el-salvador.html

Cruz, José Miguel, Jonathan D. Rosen, Luis Enrique Amaya, and Yulia Vorobyeva. "The New Face of Street Gangs: The Gang Phenomenon in El Salvador." Florida International University. 2017. Retrieved from: https://lacc.fiu.edu/research/the-new-face-of-street-gangs_final-report_eng.pdf

Dada, Carlos. "How We Killed Archbishop Romero." *El Faro*. 2010. Retrieved from: https://elfaro.net/es/201003/noticias/1416/How-we-killed-Archbishop-Romero.htm

Dalton, Roque. "O.E.A." *Taberna y otros lugares*. 1969. Retrieved from: http://www.elortiba.org/old/pdf/Roque-Dalton-Taberna-y-otros-lugares.pdf

Danner, Mark. *The Massacre at El Mozote: A Parable of War*. New York: Vintage Books. 1994.

———. "The Truth of El Mozote." *The New Yorker*. 1993.

Daugherty, Arron. "Record Number of El Salvador Police Quit as Violence Takes Its Toll." *InSight Crime*. 2016. Retrieved from: https://www.insightcrime.org/news/brief/el-salvador-police-quitting-amid-threats-violence/

Dawsey, Josh. "Trump Derides Protections for Immigrants from 'Shithole' Countries." *Washington Post*. 2018. Retrieved from: https://www.

washingtonpost.com/politics/trump-attacks-protections-for-immigrants-from-shithole-countries-in-oval-office-meeting/2018/01/11/bfc0725c-f711-11e7-91af-31ac729add94_story.html

Diaz, Tom. *No Boundaries: Transnational Latino Gangs and American Law Enforcement*. Ann Arbor: University of Michigan Press. 2009.

Didion, Joan. *Salvador*. New York: Vintage International. 1994.

Domanick, Joe. *To Protect and To Serve: The LAPD's Century of War in the City of Dreams*. New York: Pocket Books. 1994.

Doyle, Kate, et al. "25th Anniversary of El Salvador Jesuit Murders." National Security Archive. 2014a. Retrieved from: https://nsarchive2.gwu.edu/NSAEBB/NSAEBB492/

———. "The Yellow Book: Secret Salvadoran Military Document from the Civil War Era Catalogued 'Enemies,' Many Killed or Disappeared." National Security Archive in collaboration with the Human Rights Data Analysis. 2014b. Retrieved from: https://nsarchive2.gwu.edu/NSAEBB/NSAEBB486/

Dreier, Hannah. "He Drew His School Mascot—and ICE Labeled Him a Gang Member." *ProPublica*. 2018. Retrieved from: https://features.propublica.org/ms-13-immigrant-students/huntington-school-deportations-ice-honduras/

Dudley, Steven. "El Salvador Catholic Church: Pawn or Player in Gang Truce?" *InSight Crime*. 2013. Retrieved from: https://www.insightcrime.org/news/analysis/el-salvador-catholic-church-pawn-or-player-in-gang-truce/

———. "El Salvador's Jailed Gang Mediator: 'I Feel Defrauded.'" *InSight Crime*. 2018a. Retrieved from: https://www.insightcrime.org/news/analysis/el-salvadors-jailed-gang-mediator-feel-defrauded/

———. "Homicides in Guatemala." *InSight Crime*. 2017. Retrieved from: https://www.insightcrime.org/investigations/homicides-in-guatemala/

———. "How to Leave MS-13 Alive." *New York Times*. 2018b. Retrieved from: https://www.nytimes.com/2018/04/26/opinion/ms-13-gang-religion.html

———. "Mexico Arrests MS13 Leader Busting Up Latest Gang Trafficking Ring." *InSight Crime*. 2018c. Retrieved from: https://www.insightcrime.org/news/analysis/mexico-arrests-ms13-leader-busting-up-latest-gang-trafficking-ring/

Dudley, Steven, and Héctor Silva Ávalos. "MS13 and International Drug Trafficking: Gang Project vs. Entrepreneurism." *InSight Crime*. 2018a. Retrieved from: https://www.insightcrime.org/investigations/ms13-drug-trafficking-project-entrepreneurism/

———. "MS13 in the Americas: How the World's Most Notorious Gang Defies Logic, Resists Destruction." *InSight Crime* and the Center for Latin American and Latino Studies at American University. 2018b. Retrieved from: https://www.insightcrime.org/wp-content/uploads/2018/02/MS13-in-the-Americas-InSight-Crime-English.pdf

Dudley, Steven, and Juan José Martínez d'Aubuisson. "El Salvador Prisons and the Battle for the MS13's Soul." *InSight Crime*. 2017. Retrieved from: https://www.insightcrime.org/investigations/el-salvador-prisons-battle-ms13-soul/

Dunn, William. *The Gangs of Los Angeles*. New York: iUniverse. 2007.

Editorial Board. "The New Battering Ram." *Los Angeles Times*. 1985. Retrieved from: https://www.latimes.com/archives/la-xpm-1985-02-13-me-4639-story.html

El Salvador v. Armando Reyes Soriano Molina, et al. 214-2-2007. 2007.

El Salvador v. Edwin Ernesto Cedillos Rodríguez, et al. 644-UEA-15. 2016.

El Salvador v. Erick Geovanny Quintanilla Tovar. *Tribunal Primero de Sentencia Santa Ana*. 0201-16-2003. 2003.

El Salvador v. Mario Alberto Mijango Menjivar, et al. 457-52-UEA-2014. 2014.

El Tiempo. "Quién está detrás del complot para matar a Pablo Escobar."

1992. Retrieved from: https://www.eltiempo.com/archivo/documento/MAM-59376

Escobar, Edward J. *Race, Police, and the Making of a Political Identity: Mexican Americans and the Los Angeles Police Department, 1900–1945*. Berkeley: University of California Press. 1999.

Fainaru, Steve. "A Country Awakes to the Reality of Its 'Disappeared' Children." *Boston Globe*. 1996. Retrieved from: http://poundpuplegacy.org/node/29658

Farah, Douglas. "The Transformation of El Salvador's Gangs into Political Actors." Center for Strategic and International Studies. 2012. Retrieved from: http://csis.org/files/publication/120621_Farah_ Gangs_HemFocus.pdf

Farhi, Paul. "Living on Edge in Mount Pleasant." *Washington Post*. 1990. Retrieved from: https://www.washingtonpost.com/archive/politics/1990/10/07/living-on-edge-in-mount-pleasant/a509019a-0b02-40f7-bf7c-e7195c26d1b5/

Feldmann, Linda. "Mt. Pleasant Residents Join Hands to Shake Riots' Stigma of Violence." *Christian Science Monitor*. 1991. Retrieved from: https://www.csmonitor.com/1991/0529/29081.html

Filipovic, Jill. "Is the US the Only Country Where More Men Are Raped Than Women?" *Guardian*. 2012. Retrieved from: https://www.theguardian.com/commentisfree/cifamerica/2012/feb/21/us-more-men-raped-than-women

Fontes, Anthony W. *Mortal Doubt: Transnational Gangs and Social Order in Guatemala City*. Berkeley: University of California Press. 2018.

Fox News. "Trump Administration Goes After MS-13: Vincent DeMarco Sounds Off." 2017. Retrieved from: https://video.foxnews.com/v/5428600285001#sp=show-clips

Freed, David. "The Times Poll: Performances of Gates, LAPD Get High Marks." *Los Angeles Times*. 1988. Retrieved from: https://www.latimes.com/archives/la-xpm-1988-03-28-mn-142-story.html

Fremon, Celeste. "The Arrest of Alex Sanchez: Part 3—The Bail Hearing." *WitnessLA*. 2009. Retrieved from: https://witnessla.com/alex-sanchez-part-3-the-bail-hearing/

García, Carlos. "The Birth of the MS13 in New York." *InSight Crime*. 2018. Retrieved from: https://www.insightcrime.org/news/analysis/birth-MS13-new-york/

———. "How the MS13 Got Its Foothold in Transnational Drug Trafficking." *InSight Crime*. 2016a. Retrieved from: https://www.insightcrime.org/investigations/how-the-ms13-got-its-foothold-in-transnational-drug-trafficking/

———. "How the MS13 Tried (and Failed) to Create a Single Gang in the US." *InSight Crime*. 2016b. Retrieved from: https://www.insightcrime.org/investigations/how-ms13-tried-failed-create-single-gang-us/

Garland, Sarah. *Gangs in Garden City*. New York: Nation Books. 2009.

Gates, Daryl. "Letter to the Editor: LAPD's Efforts to Stop Gangs." *Los Angeles Times*. 1991. Retrieved from: https://www.latimes.com/archives/la-xpm-1991-10-28-me-279-story.html

Gilligan, James. *Violence: Reflections on a National Epidemic*. New York: Putnam. 1996.

Goodley, Heloise. "Ignoring Male Victims of Sexual Violence in Conflict Is Short-Sighted and Wrong." Chatham House. 2019. Retrieved from: https://www.chathamhouse.org/expert/comment/ignoring-male-victims-sexual-violence-conflict-short-sighted-and-wrong

Grant Mine, Douglas. "Blood-Soaked Mountainside Calls On Salvadoran Guerrillas to Return." Associated Press, reprinted in the *Los Angeles Times*. 1990. Retrieved from: https://www.latimes.com/archives/la-xpm-1990-12-23-mn-9598-story.html

Greene, Judith, and Kevin Pranis. "Gang Wars: The Failure of Enforcement Tactics and the Need for Effective Public Safety Strategies." *Justice Policy Institute*. 2007. Retrieved from: http://www.justicepolicy.org/uploads/justicepolicy/documents/07-07_rep_gangwars_gc-ps-ac-jj.pdf

Gruson, Lindsey. "Salvador Army Fills Ranks by Force." *New York Times.* 1989. Retrieved from: https://www.nytimes.com/1989/04/21/world/salvador-army-fills-ranks-by-force.html

Guillermoprieto, Alma. "Salvadoran Peasants Describe Mass Killing; Woman Tells of Children's Death." *Washington Post.* 1982.

Hauslohner, Abigail. "The Trump Administration's Immigration Jails Are Packed, but Deportations Are Lower Than in Obama Era." *Washington Post.* 2019. Retrieved from: https://www.washingtonpost.com/immigration/the-trump-administrations-immigration-jails-are-packed-but-deportations-are-lower-than-in-obama-era/2019/11/17/27ad0e44-f057-11e9-89eb-ec56cd414732_story.html

Hayden, Tom. *Street Wars: Gangs and the Future of Violence.* New York: The New Press. 2004.

Homeland Security and Governmental Affairs. "Border Insecurity: The Rise of MS-13 and Other Transnational Criminal Organizations." US Senate Committee. 2017. Retrieved from: https://www.hsgac.senate.gov/hearings/border-insecurity-the-rise-of-ms-13-and-other-transnational-criminal-organizations

Humes, Edward. "The Wire." *California Lawyer.* 2011. Retrieved from: https://www.dailyjournal.com/articles/254711-the-wire

Hutson, H. Range, Deirdre Anglin, Demetrios N. Kyriacou, Joel Hart, and Kelvin Spears. "The Epidemic of Gang-Related Homicides in Los Angeles County from 1979 through 1994." *Journal of American Medical Association* (JAMA) Vol. 274, No. 13 (1995): 1,031–1,036.

Illegal Immigration Reform & Immigrant Responsibility Act. H.R. 3610; Pub. L. 104-208; 110 Stat. 3009-546. 104th Congress; September 30, 1996.

Jackman, Tom. "Va. Gang Member Admits Complicity in Fatal Stabbing." *Washington Post.* 2000. Retrieved from: https://www.washingtonpost.com/archive/local/2000/11/23/va-gang-member-admits-complicity-in-fatal-stabbing/ee4c3297-cc74-4cf2-8b5a-4abafff103ef/

Jennings, Tom. "The Lost Tapes: LA Riots." Smithsonian Channel. 2017.

Kaiser, David, and Lovisa Stannow. "Prison Rape and Government." *New York Review of Books*. 2011. Retrieved from: https://www.nybooks.com/articles/2011/03/24/prison-rape-and-government/?pagination=false

Keen, Sam. *Faces of the Enemy: Reflections of the Hostile Imagination*. San Francisco: Harper & Row. 1988.

Klein, Malcolm, Cheryl L. Maxson, and Lea C. Cunningham. "'Crack,' Street Gangs and Violence." *Criminology* Vol. 29, Issue 4 (1991): 623–650.

Kleinfeld, Rachel. *A Savage Order: How the World's Deadliest Countries Can Forge a Path to Security*. New York: Pantheon. 2018.

La Prensa Gráfica. "Las guerras de Mijango." 2016. Retrieved from: https://www.laprensagrafica.com/revistas/Las-guerras-de-Mijango-20160221-0045.html

Labrador, Gabriel, and Carla Ascencio. "Arena prometió a las pandillas una nueva tregua si ganaba la presidencia." *El Faro*. 2016. Retrieved from: https://www.elfaro.net/es/201603/video/18213/Arena-prometi%C3%B3-a-las-pandillas-una-nueva-tregua-si-ganaba-la-presidencia.htm

LaFeber, Walter. *Inevitable Revolutions: The United States in Central America*. New York: WW Norton & Company. 1993.

Lemus, Eric. "El Salvador: reos de brazos caídos." BBC. 2009. Retrieved from: http://news.bbc.co.uk/hi/spanish/latin_america/newsid_7895000/7895939.stm

———. "El Salvador semiparalizado por reclamo de pandillas." BBC. 2010. Retrieved from: https://www.bbc.com/mundo/america_latina/2010/09/100906_salvador_funes_maras_negociacion_pea

Leovy, Jill. *Ghettoside: A True Story of Murder in America*. New York: Random House. 2015.

Lepore, Jill. *These Truths: A History of the United States*. New York: WW Norton & Company. 2018.

Lessing, Benjamin. *Making Peace in Drug Wars*. Cambridge: Cambridge University Press. 2018.

Liebelson, Dana, and Ariel Edwards-Levy. "Most Trump Voters Say MS-13 Is a Threat to the Entire US." *Huffington Post.* 2018. Retrieved from: https://www.huffpost.com/entry/most-trump-voters-say-ms-13-is-a-threat-to-the-entire-us_n_5b490310e4b022fdcc594c5d

Locke, Rachel, Luis Enrique Amaya, and Adrienne Klein. "El Salvador Feasibility Study—Final Report." 2018. Retrieved from: https://pdf.usaid.gov/pdf_docs/PA00TR24.pdf

Logan, Sam. *This is for the Mara Salvatrucha.* New York: Hyperion. 2009.

López Vigil, José Ignacio. *Las mil y una historias de Radio Venceremos.* San Salvador: UCA Editores. 1992.

Lorenza Gomez, et al. v. Jefferson Sessions, et al. 3:17-cv-03615-VC. 2017. Retrieved from: https://www.aclunc.org/docs/20170811-first_amended_petition.pdf

Martinez, Al. "The Ghost That Won't Go Away." *Los Angeles Times.* 1992.

Martínez, Carlos. "Arístides Valencia: 'Nosotros les ayudamos a sacar los DUI o lo que sea necesario.'" *El Faro.* 2016. Retrieved from: https://www.elfaro.net/es/206005/salanegra/18554/Ar%C3%ADstides-Valencia-%E2%80%9CNosotros-les-ayudamos-a-sacar-los-DUI-o-lo-que-sea-necesario%E2%80%9D.htm

———. "Mijango viste de blanco." *El Faro.* 2018. Retrieved from: https://www.elfaro.net/es/201805/salanegra/21859/Mijango-viste-de-blanco.htm?st-full_text=all&tpl=11

Martínez, Carlos, and José Luis Sanz. "I. El origen del odio." *El Faro.* 2012a. Retrieved from: https://salanegra.elfaro.net/es/201208/cronicas/9301/I-El-origen-del-odio.htm

———. "II. La letra 13." *El Faro.* 2012b. Retrieved from: https://salanegra.elfaro.net/es/201208/cronicas/9302/II-La-letra-13.htm

Martínez, Óscar, and Juan José Martínez d'Aubuisson. *El Niño de Hollywood.* Mexico: Penguin. 2018.

Martínez, Óscar, Carlos Martínez, and Efren Lemus. "Relato de un fraude electoral, narrado por un pandillero." *El Faro*. 2017. Retrieved from: https://elfaro.net/es/201708/salanegra/20737/Relato-de-un-fraude-electoral-narrado-por-un-pandillero.htm

Martínez d'Aubuisson, Juan José. "Así viven y mueren las mujeres pandilleras en El Salvador." *Revista Factum*. 2016. Retrieved from: https://www.revistafactum.com/asi-viven-y-mueren-las-mujeres-pandilleras-en-el-salvador/

Martínez d'Aubuisson, Juan José, and Carlos Martínez. "Videos Show FMLN Leaders Offering El Salvador Gangs $10 Mn in Micro-Credit." *InSight Crime*. 2016. Retrieved from: https://www.insightcrime.org/news/analysis/videos-show-fmln-leaders-offering-el-salvador-gangs-10-mn-in-micro-credit/

McAtee, Paige. "Huntington HS Was Uninformed of State's Gang Prevention Plan, Superintendent Says." *Patch*. 2017. Retrieved from: https://patch.com/new-york/huntington/huntington-h-s-was-uninformed-states-gang-prevention-plan-superintendent-says

McWilliams, Carey. "Press Release." Sleepy Lagoon Defense Committee. 1943. Retrieved from: https://oac.cdlib.org/view?docId=hb809nb8rh&chunk.id=&brand=oac4&doc.view=entire_text

Mena Sandoval, Francisco Emilio. *Del ejército nacional al ejército guerrillero*. San Salvador: Edición Arcoiris. 1993.

Menjívar, Cecilia, and Andrea Gómez Cervantes. "El Salvador: Civil War, Natural Disasters, and Gang Violence Drive Migration." Migration Policy Institute. 2018. Retrieved from: https://www.migrationpolicy.org/article/el-salvador-civil-war-natural-disasters-and-gang-violence-drive-migration

Mijango, Mario Alberto. *Con El Santo de Espaldas*. San Salvador: Red Imprenta. 2009.

Mitchell, John L. "The Raid That Still Haunts LA." *Los Angeles Times*. 2001. Retrieved from: https://www.latimes.com/archives/la-xpm-2001-mar-14-mn-37553-story.html

Montgomery, Tommie Sue. *Revolution in El Salvador: Origins and Evolution*. Boulder: Westview. 1982.

Moore, Joan. "Gangs, Drugs and Violence." In *Drugs and Violence: Causes, Correlates and Consequences.* Mario de la Rosa, Elizabeth Lambert, and Bernard Gropper, eds. Rockville: National Institute on Drug Abuse Research. 1990.

———. *Going Down to the Barrio: Homeboys and Homegirls in Change.* Philadelphia: Temple University Press. 1991.

———. *Homeboys: Gangs, Drugs, and Prison in the Barrios of Los Angeles.* Philadelphia: Temple University Press. 1978.

Moreno Gonzales, John. "One Group, Two Personas: Police See a Gang, Members Say They're Non-Violent." *Newsday.* 2000.

MS-13 and Barrio 18. "Comunicado de las Mara MS-13 y la Pandilla 18." 2010. Retrieved from: http://hombrescontralaviolencia.blogspot.com/2010/09/comunicado-de-las-mara-ms13-y-la.html

Muggah, Robert, Ami Carpenter, and Topher McDougal. "The Inconvenient Truth About Gang Truces in the Americas." *InSight Crime.* 2013. Retrieved from: https://www.insightcrime.org/news/analysis/the-inconvenient-truth-about-gang-truces-in-the-americas/

Muniz, Ana. "Maintaining Racial Boundaries: Criminalization, Neighborhood Context, and the Origins of Gang Injunctions." *Social Problems* Vol. 61, No. 2 (2014): 216–236.

Newton, Jim. "ACLU Says 83% of Police Live Outside L.A." *Los Angeles Times.* 1994. Retrieved from: https://www.latimes.com/archives/la-xpm-1994-03-29-me-39666-story.html

———. "Man Held in Killing of Parks' Granddaughter." *Los Angeles Times.* 2000. Retrieved from: https://www.latimes.com/archives/la-xpm-2000-jun-09-mn-39168-story.html

Noe-Bustamante, Luis, Antonio Flores, and Sono Shah. "Facts on Hispanics of Salvadoran Origin in the United States, 2017." *Pew Research Center.* 2019. Retrieved from: https://www.pewresearch.org/hispanic/fact-sheet/u-s-hispanics-facts-on-salvadoran-origin-latinos/

O'Connor, Anne-Marie. "Activist Says Officer Sought His Deportation." *Los Angeles Times.* 2000a. Retrieved from: https://www.latimes.com/archives/la-xpm-2000-feb-17-mn-65395-story.html

———. "FBI Pressured INS to Aid L.A. Police Anti-Gang Effort." *Los Angeles Times.* 2000b. Retrieved from: https://www.latimes.com/archives/la-xpm-2000-feb-29-mn-3691-story.html

———. "Suit Alleges Harassment of L.A. Gang Peace Group." *Los Angeles Times.* 2000c. Retrieved from: https://www.latimes.com/archives/la-xpm-2000-jun-03-me-36892-story.html

OECD/IDB. "Country Fact Sheet—El Salvador." 2017. Retrieved from: https://www.oecd.org/gov/lac-el-salvador.pdf

Parks, Bernard. "Board of Inquiry into the Rampart Area Corruption Incident." Los Angeles Police Department. 2000. Retrieved from: http://assets.lapdonline.org/assets/pdf/boi_pub.pdf

Pate, Anthony, and Edwin E. Hamilton. "The Big Six: Policing America's Largest Cities." The Police Foundation. 1991. Retrieved from: https://www.policefoundation.org/publication/the-big-six-policing-americas-largest-cities/

Phillips, Nicholas. "The Allegory of El Salvador's 'Dany Boy': MS13 Gang Leader, Activist, or Both?" *InSight Crime.* 2017. Retrieved from: https://www.insightcrime.org/investigations/allegory-el-salvador-dany-boy-romero-ms13-gang-leader-activist-or-both/

Ramos, Paul. "The Alamo Is a Rupture." *Guernica.* 2019. Retrieved from: https://www.guernicamag.com/the-alamo-is-a-rupture-texas-mexico-imperialism-history/

Ratha, Dilip, Sonia Plaza, and Ervin Dervisevic. "Migration and Remittances Factbook 2016: Third Edition." World Bank Group. 2016. Retrieved from: https://www.knomad.org/sites/default/files/2017-03/9781464803192_0.pdf

Romero, Oscar. "Sermon: The Church in the Service of Personal, Community and Transcendent Liberation, March 23, 1980." Retrieved from:

http://www.romerotrust.org.uk/sites/default/files/homilies/in_service_of_transcendent_liberation.pdf

Rutten, Tim. "The Enduring Wisdom of Special Order 40." *Los Angeles Times*. 2009. Retrieved from: https://www.latimes.com/archives/la-xpm-2009-dec-23-la-oe-rutten23-2009dec23-story.html

Salazar, Denisse, and Salvador Hernandez. "Video: O.C.'s Mexican Mafia: Control of Mean Streets." *Orange County Register*. 2011. Retrieved from: https://www.ocregister.com/2011/08/12/video-ocs-mexican-mafia-control-of-mean-streets/

Scheck, Justin, and John R. Emshwiller. "Rogue Informants Imperil Massive US Gang Bust." *Wall Street Journal*. 2011. Retrieved from: https://www.wsj.com/articles/SB10001424052702304906004576369980920377592

Second District Court of Appeals of California. "In the Sleepy Lagoon Case." 1944. Retrieved from: https://oac.cdlib.org/view?docId=hb6z09p578&brand=oac4&doc.view=entire_text

Silva Ávalos, Héctor. *Infiltrados: Crónica de la corrupción en la PNC (1992–2013)*. San Salvador: UCA Editores. 2014.

Simpson, David Mark. "A Glock in the Park: A Guide to the Gangs of the MacArthur Greens." *Los Angeles Magazine*. 2013. Retrieved from: https://www.lamag.com/citythinkblog/a-glock-in-the-park-a-guide-to-the-gangs-of-the-macarthur-greens/

Smith, Doug. "How LAPD's Law-and-Order Chief Revolutionized the Way Cops Treated Illegal Immigration." *Los Angeles Times*. 2017. Retrieved from: https://www.latimes.com/local/lanow/la-me-ln-special-order-40-retrospective-20170205-story.html

Street Terrorism Enforcement and Prevention Act [186.20–186.36]. Retrieved from: https://leginfo.legislature.ca.gov/faces/codes_displayText.xhtml?lawCode=PEN&division=&title=7.&part=1.&chapter=11.&article=

Terrazas, Aaron. "Salvadoran Immigrants in the United States." Migration Policy Institute. 2010. Retrieved from: https://www.migrationpolicy.org/article/salvadoran-immigrants-united-states

Thrasher, Frederick. *The Gang: A Study of 1,313 Gangs in Chicago*. Chicago: University of Chicago Press. 1927.

Tombs, David. "Archbishop Romero and Reconciliation in El Salvador." In *Latin America between Conflict and Reconciliation*. Martin Leiner and Susan Flämig, eds. Bristol: Vandenhoeck & Ruprecht. 2012.

———. *Latin American Liberation Theology*. Boston: Brill Academic Publishers, Inc. 2002.

Trac-Immigration. Trac. 2018. Retrieved from: https://trac.syr.edu/immigration/index.html

Trump, Donald. "Remarks by President Trump to Law Enforcement Officials on MS-13." Speech, Ronkonkoma, New York, July 28, 2017. White House transcript.

———. "Speech: Donald Trump Holds a Political Rally in Great Falls, Montana, July 5, 2018." Retrieved from: https://factba.se/trump

———. "Speech: Donald Trump Holds a Political Rally in Lebanon, Ohio, October 12, 2018." Retrieved from: https://factba.se/trump

Tucker, Neely. "Gangs Growing in Numbers, Bravado Across Area." *Washington Post*. 2003. Retrieved from: https://www.washingtonpost.com/archive/politics/2003/09/18/gangs-growing-in-numbers-bravado-across-area/3f53b706-f470-44e9-827a-d4646f46c40b/

United Nations—DESA/Population Division. 2018. Retrieved from: https://population.un.org/wup/Country-Profiles/

United Nations Office on Drugs and Crime (UNODC) and World Bank. "Crime, Violence, and Development: Trends, Costs, and Policy Options in the Caribbean." 2007. Retrieved from: https://www.unodc.org/pdf/research/Cr_and_Vio_Car_E.pdf

United States Bureau of Citizenship and Immigration Services, El Salvador: Belloso Battalion, 14 August 2000, SLV00005.ZSF. Retrieved from: https://www.refworld.org/docid/3dee01af4.html

US Department of Homeland Security (DHS). "Joint Operation Nets

24 Transnational Gang Members, 475 Total Arrests Under Operation Matador." 2018a. Retrieved from: https://www.ice.gov/news/releases/joint-operation-nets-24-transnational-gang-members-475-total-arrests-under-operation#wcm-survey-target-id

———. "The Secretary's Award for Excellence 2018—Operation Matador—U.S. Immigration and Customs Enforcement." 2018b. Retrieved from: https://www.dhs.gov/photo/secretary-s-award-excellence-2018-operation-matador-us-immigration-and-customs-enforcement

———. "637 Gang Members and Associates Arrested During Project Nefarious." 2012. Retrieved from: https://www.ice.gov/news/releases/637-gang-members-and-associates-arrested-during-project-nefarious

———. "Yearbook of Immigration Statistics." 2019. Retrieved from: https://www.dhs.gov/immigration-statistics/yearbook

US Department of Justice. "Sixth Report Assessing Settlement Agreement Compliance by Suffolk County Police Department." 2018. Retrieved from: https://www.justice.gov/crt/case-document/file/1054396/download

———. "United States' Investigation of the Maricopa County Sheriff's Office." 2011. Retrieved from: https://www.justice.gov/sites/default/files/crt/legacy/2011/12/15/mcso_findletter_12-15-11.pdf

US v. Edwin Amaya-Sanchez, et al. Eastern District of New York. CR-16-403. 2016.

US v. Edwin Mancia Flores. District of Massachusetts. CR-17-10284. 2017.

US v. Elvis Edgardo Molina, et al. Central District of California. CR13-0826. 2013.

US v. Jose Alfaro, et al. Central District of California. CR-09-00466. 2009.

US v. José Avelar, et al. Central District of California. CR-13-0817. 2013.

US v. José Juan Rodríguez Juárez, et al. District of New Jersey. RO-1210. 2013.

US v. José Rodríguez-Landa, et al. Central District of California. CR-13-0484. 2013.

US v. Martin Neftali Aguilar-Rivera, et al. Southern District of Ohio. 2:17-CR-164. 2018.

US v. Nelson Augustin Martinez Comandari. Southern District of New York. No. S1 04 CR-384. 2004.

Valencia, Roberto. *Carta desde Zacatraz*. Madrid: Libros del KO. 2018.

———. "Casi que Guardia Nacional Civil." *El Faro*. 2016. Retrieved from: https://elfaro.net/es/201610/salanegra/19277/Casi-que-Guardia-Nacional-Civil.htm

Valencia, Roberto, Óscar Martínez, and Daniel Valencia Caravantes. "Police Massacre at the San Blas Farm." *El Faro*. 2016. Retrieved from: https://salanegra.elfaro.net/es/201508/cronicas/17289/Police-Massacre-at-the-San-Blas-Farm.htm

Vigil, James Diego. *Barrio Gangs: Street Life and Identity in Southern California*. Austin: University of Texas Press. 1988.

———. "Multiple Marginality: A Comparative Framework for Understanding Gangs." In *Methods That Matter: Integrating Mixed Methods for More Effective Social Science Research*. M. Cameron Hay, ed. Oxford: Oxford University Press. 2016.

———. *A Rainbow of Gangs*. Austin: University of Texas Press. 2004.

Walker, William. "1-891116 EMB—Jesuit Rector of UCA Shot Dead Seven Others Killed." US Department of State Diplomatic Cable. 1989a. Retrieved from: https://nsarchive2.gwu.edu/NSAEBB/NSAEBB492/docs/1-891116%20EMB%20Jesuit%20Rector%20of%20UCA%20Shot%20Dead%20Seven%20Others%20Killed.pdf

———. "6-8911119 EMB—Ellacuria Assassination." US Department of State Diplomatic Cable. 1989b. Retrieved from: https://nsarchive2.gwu.edu/NSAEBB/NSAEBB492/docs/6-891119%20EMB%20Ellacuria%20Assassination.pdf

Ward, Tom. *Gangsters Without Borders: An Ethnography of a Salvadoran Street Gang*. New York: Oxford University Press. 2013.

Welles, Orson. "Letter to Parole Board." 1944. Retrieved from: https://oac.cdlib.org/view?docId=hb3m3nb5sz&chunk.id=&brand=oac4&doc.view=entire_text

Wilgoren, Jodi. "Latino Gang Members Sign Truce Pact: Treaty: The Men, Meeting in a Santa Ana Park, Agree to Lay Down Their Weapons." *Los Angeles Times*. 1992. Retrieved from: https://www.latimes.com/archives/la-xpm-1992-08-30-me-8461-story.html

Winston, Ali. "You May Be in California's Gang Database and Not Even Know It." *Reveal*—The Center for Investigative Reporting. 2016. Retrieved from: https://www.revealnews.org/article/you-may-be-in-californias-gang-database-and-not-even-know-it/

Wolf, Sonja. "Street Gangs of El Salvador." In *Maras: Gang Violence and Security in Central America*. Tom C. Bruneau, Lucia Dammert, and Elizabeth Skinner, eds. Austin: University of Texas Press. 2011.

World Bank. "The World Bank in El Salvador." 2019. Retrieved from: https://www.worldbank.org/en/country/elsalvador/overview#1

Wright, Joshua D. "The Constitutional Failure of Gang Databases." *Stanford Journal of Civil Rights & Civil Liberties* 2 (2005): 115–365.

Young, Rick. "LAPD Blues." *Frontline*. 2001. Retrieved from: https://www.pbs.org/wgbh/pages/frontline/shows/lapd/bare.html

———. "To Protect and To Serve—LAPD Culture." *Frontline*. 2001. Retrieved from: https://www.pbs.org/wgbh/pages/frontline/shows/lapd/race/protectserve.html

Youth Justice Coalition (YJC). "Tracked and Trapped: Youth of Color, Gang Databases and Gang Injunctions." 2012. Retrieved from: https://youthjusticela.org/wp-content/uploads/2012/12/TrackedandTrapped.pdf

GLOSSARY OF MAJOR GANG TERMS USED IN THIS BOOK

EL BARRIO – Literally, "neighborhood"; gang; also spelled *varrio*.

LA BESTIA – Literally, "beast" or "the devil"; something evil or a reference to the criminal life.

BRINCAR – Literally, "to jump"; to initiate into a gang.

BRINCO – The act of being initiated into a gang.

CALMADO – Retired or semiretired gang member.

CHAVALA – Girl; punk, coward; a rival gang member.

CHEQUEO – Second-stage recruit in a "probation" period when given increasingly more difficult and compromising tasks; not yet a member.

CHOLO – A male gang member or gang wannabe; often a reference to Mexican American gang members or their style.

CLICA – Literally, "clique"; gang's smallest unit of organization.

CORTE – Literally, "court"; internal gang trial or justice system.

DESTROYER – Crash pad, hideout, party house, meeting place, torture chamber, weapons depot.

FEDERATION – The leadership of the gang outside of the prison in El Salvador.

GATILLEROS – Assassins.

HANGEAR – To hang out.

HOMEBOY – Clique or gang companion (masculine); often a term of endearment.

HOMIE – Fellow gang member; fully initiated.

HUILA – Secret message passed in prison; also spelled *wuila*.

JAINA – Girlfriend; woman.

LÍNEA – Committee designed to deal with major issues in El Salvador.

LOCA/O – Crazy girl or boy; gang member.

MARA - A small group of friends; a gang or someone who belongs to the Mara Salvatrucha.

MARERO – Gang member, usually in reference to someone from the MS-13 (18th Street uses the term *pandillero*).

MIRIN– Meeting.

NARCO – Drug trafficker.

ONDA – Mood, attitude, groove.

PARO – Gang initiate, often doing errands or small jobs; not yet a member.

POSTE – Gang initiate, often doing errands or small jobs; not yet a member.

POSTEAR – Keeping watch; surveilling or spying.

PROGRAM – A part of the gang that groups together a number of cliques.

RANFLA - Lowrider; the national gang leadership in El Salvador.

RANFLERO – Gang leader.

RENTA – Extortion payment.

SALVATRUCHA – Savvy Salvadoran; reference to those who fought against William Walker's forces in the 1800s.

SHOT CALLER – Maximum leader.

SUREÑOS – Umbrella organization for gangs working under the Mexican Mafia prison gang.

TAKA – Pseudonym; often only name fellow gang members know.

TRAQUETERO – Local drug peddler; also spelled *traketero*.

TRUCHA – Savvy, watchful.

VATO – Man, guy; dude.

INDEX